Ulster Presbyterians and the Scots Irish Diaspora,
1750–1764

Christianities in the Trans-Atlantic World, 1500–1800

General Editors:

Professor Crawford Gribben, Queen's University Belfast, UK
Dr Scott Spurlock, University of Glasgow, UK

Editorial Board: Professor John Coffey (Leicester University)
Professor Jeff Jue (Westminster Theological Seminary)
Professor Susan Hardman Moore (University of Edinburgh)
Professor John Morrill (University of Cambridge)
Professor David Mullan (Cape Breton University)
Professor Richard Muller (Calvin Theological Seminary)
Professor Jane Ohlmeyer (Trinity College Dublin)
Professor Margo Todd (University of Pennsylvania)
Professor Arthur Williamson (University of California, Sacramento)

Building upon the recent recovery of interest in religion in the early modern trans-Atlantic world, this series offers fresh, lively and inter-disciplinary perspectives on the broad view of its subject. Books in the series will work strategically and systematically to address major but under-studied or overly simplified themes in the religious and cultural history of the early modern trans-Atlantic.

Forthcoming titles:

Benjamin Bankhurst
ULSTER PRESBYTERIANS AND THE SCOTS IRISH DIASPORA, 1750–1764

Crawford Gribben and Scott Spurlock (*editors*)
PURITANISM IN THE TRANS-ATLANTIC WORLD 1600–1800

Mark Sweetnam
MISSION AND EMPIRE IN THE EARLY MODERN PUBLIC SPHERE

Ulster Presbyterians and the Scots Irish Diaspora, 1750–1764

Benjamin Bankhurst
Fellow King's College London and Research Assistant at Queen Mary, University of London

palgrave
macmillan

First published 2013 by
PALGRAVE MACMILLAN

Palgrave Macmillan in the UK is an imprint of Macmillan Publishers Limited, registered in England, company number 785998, of Houndmills, Basingstoke, Hampshire RG21 6XS.

Palgrave Macmillan in the US is a division of St Martin's Press LLC, 175 Fifth Avenue, New York, NY 10010.

Palgrave Macmillan is the global academic imprint of the above companies and has companies and representatives throughout the world.

Palgrave® and Macmillan® are registered trademarks in the United States, the United Kingdom, Europe and other countries.

ISBN 978–1–137–32819–9

This book is printed on paper suitable for recycling and made from fully managed and sustained forest sources. Logging, pulping and manufacturing processes are expected to conform to the environmental regulations of the country of origin.

A catalogue record for this book is available from the British Library.

A catalog record for this book is available from the Library of Congress.

Typeset by MPS Limited, Chennai, India.

For Arthur and Lois Bankhurst

Contents

Figures

Appendices

Acknowledgements

My research has led me to archives in three countries on both sides of the Atlantic Ocean and I have been aided by numerous knowledgeable and helpful people along the way. I would like to thank the staff of the many archives that I have visited over the course of my research, including the Public Record Office of Northern Ireland, the National Library of Scotland, the British Library, the National Archives at Kew and Queen's University, Belfast. I would like to thank the archivists and staff of the Historical Society of Pennsylvania, University of Pennsylvania Archives and the Presbyterian Historical Society in Philadelphia. I owe a special debt of gratitude to Jennifer Dickson at the Presbyterian Historical Society of Ireland for her help and patience with me as I scoured the stacks of church session books in the Strong Room.

Funding for this dissertation was made possible by an Overseas Research Student Award from the Vice Chancellors and Principles of the Universities of the United Kingdom. I received further financial support for research in Ireland and Scotland in the forms of a Royal Historical Society Research Support Grant, a King's College London School of Humanities Research Grant and British Association for Irish Studies, Postgraduate Research Bursary. My first year at King's was partially funded by a grant from the Clan MacBean Foundation. My time as an E. Rhodes and Leona Carpenter dissertation fellow at the McNeil Center for Early American Studies in Philadelphia was particularly formative, inspiring and productive.

Many people influenced the direction of this project and supported me both during my research and in the often-difficult process of writing. Crawford Gribben and Scott Spurlock have been supportive, energetic and generous series editors. The editors of the manuscript – Holly Tyler, Jenny McCall and Peter Andrews – and the staff at Palgrave Macmillan have been wonderful throughout. Holly, Jenny and Peter have made the daunting task of publishing my first monograph an enjoyable and engaging process. I have learned much from conversations and correspondence with Patrick Griffin, Peter Silver, Daniel K. Richter, Michael Brown, Eoin Magennis, Patrick Walsh, Tim Hitchcock, Andrew Holmes, Martyn Powell and Padhraig Higgins. Melvin Yazawa and Anne Goldgar have always been available at a moment's notice to offer advice and support when it was needed. Of course, this book would not have been possible without Ian McBride who oversaw the completion of the PhD thesis upon which it is based. Ian has been a generous and attentive friend and supervisor. His thoughtful insights and unwavering encouragement have sustained this project from the beginning.

I am indebted to my friends and colleagues for all of the help that they have given me over the last seven years. Ian Barrett, Jeffrey Bibbee, Macdara Dwyer, Bronwen Everill, Pieter François, Ultán Gillen, Benjamin Heller, Rachel Johnson, Gillian Kennedy, Emily Manktelow, Philip Mead, Tim Reinke-Williams, Kyle Roberts, Jonathan Saha, Carolanne Selway and Allison Stagg have all inspired and supported me along the way. Maurice and Karen Bowe have welcomed me into their family and have made England a home away from home. In particular, I would like to thank my wife Catherine for all of her help and encouragement. She has tolerated my clutter strewn over four tiny flats and has been a patient listener and editor throughout. Finally, this project would not have been possible without the love and support of my parents, Lois and Arthur Bankhurst. This book is dedicated to them.

Abbreviations

BNL	*Belfast News-Letter*
DC	*Dublin Courier*
FDJ	*Faulkner's Dublin Journal*
HSP	Historical Society of Pennsylvania
MPCA	*Minutes of the Presbyterian Church in America, 1706–1788,* ed. Guy S. Klett (Philadelphia, 1976)
NA (PRO)	The National Archives, Kew (formerly the Public Record Office)
PHS (Phila.)	Presbyterian Historical Society (Philadelphia)
PHSI	Presbyterian Historical Society of Ireland
PMHB	*Pennsylvania Magazine of History and Biography*
PRONI	Public Record Office of Northern Ireland
RGSU	*Records of the General Synod of Ulster from 1691 to 1820,* 3 vols (Belfast, 1890–9)
WMQ	*William and Mary Quarterly*

Introduction: John Moore's Crossing, 1760

In the spring of 1760, John Moore and his sister heeded the call of family members across the ocean to join them in enjoying the opportunities available in the British North American colonies. That May the two set out for the port of Larne from their family home in Carrickfergus, County Antrim. On 24 May they set sail for New York in the company of thirty-five other passengers aboard the *Cape Breton*, a vessel named in honour of the recent British victory over the French at the Canadian fortress of Louisbourg. The British may have won that battle but the conflict during which it had occurred was certainly not over. This fact was made terrifyingly clear to Moore and the other passengers when on their fifth day at sea the crew spotted what they took to be a French privateer. Moore recalled the crew and passengers' panic at the sight of the vessel, and their relief that it did not pursue them. Later Moore, looking out from the deck of the *Cape Breton* at the expanse of the Atlantic Ocean, perceived that God moved on the water. He recorded his impressions of the seascape in his journal: 'what a surprisingly pleasing scene the watery world affords to anyone that will seriously contemplate upon it in a calm, and in a storm what a pleasing dread does it cast over the mind and cause it to look up to the great creator of all things'.[1] He looked with contempt upon professional sailors, whose conversations were filled 'with oaths and obscenity'. Moore was astonished that sailors who 'see the works of the Lord and his wonders in the great deep, should in general (with respect to Christianity) be such abandoned stupid mortals'.[2] Moore, like many of his kinfolk in Presbyterian areas of Ulster, understood the world in providential terms and filtered his experiences through the lens of his Christian belief. Natural occurrences and human events – including the war then still raging in America – were all expressions of divine will. Woe be it to those who did not recognize

1

God's presence in all things or otherwise consciously disregarded those signs and demonstrations of his will on earth.

On 23 July the ship anchored in New York Harbour. Immediately after landing, the Moores made their way to Albany in order to join their uncle who was employed as a contracted supplier with the British Army. On the way, John jotted down some casual observations regarding his new environment. At night, for instance, he was surprised by the sight of insects that appeared 'like a large spark of fire not continually but alternatively, as they fly in a certain manner'.[3] The brother and sister arrived at their destination on 1 August and John set about finding work. His search sent him on a journey to Fort Ticonderoga, where, on the new roads of western New York, Moore recorded his first impressions of the American woods:

> What a solemn, wild romantic scene, does the lakes and shores, all covered with trees, display! to me not used with woods, it appears like another world; to see all just as it came from the hands of the creator, without the least foot step of man, and no inhabitants but the wolves and bears. How lifeless and gloomy, does everything look, without the Lord of creation; Man.[4]

Moore's impressions on this occasion reflected European conceptions of America beyond the boundaries of colonial settlement. 'Unsettled' America was a frightening and uncompromising place. Its mystery and presumed vastness haunted the European imagination.[5] But the wilds of America were also a place of opportunity, as demonstrated by the constant stream of European migrants who, like Moore, made a direct line for the frontier upon arriving in the new world. After its subjugation to the 'Lord of creation' the land would provide a bounty well worth the dangers of relocation. Throughout the eighteenth century thousands of Irish Presbyterian immigrants poured into the 'wastes' of the American interior in the hope that they might bend the land to their will and, in so doing, make a better life for themselves.

But, as James Merrill points out, 'wilderness is a state of mind, not a state of nature'.[6] The lands sought by European immigrants, as Moore himself would soon come to realize, were not 'lifeless' or empty. Nor did all land west of Atlantic settlement constitute one vast forest. The interior, of course, was home to many thousands of American Indians inhabiting large towns sustained by yields from agriculture as well as hunting and extensive continental trade.[7] Euro-American visions of a frightening and empty wilderness served an important function in furthering colonial expansion by providing justification for the clearing and seizure of land, and the expulsion of those who had, in the mind of the settler, left it uncultivated. Land seizure had obvious consequences. The renewal of hostilities between France and Britain in the Ohio Valley in 1754 led to widespread Indian raids on western settlements, many of them with high Irish-born populations, in the Pennsylvania and New York backcountry. For decades tensions over Euro-American land grabs and the gradual encroachment of white settlements on Indian lands had bred resentment among the Native Peoples of Pennsylvania. This resentment was particularly strong among the Lenape or Delaware peoples who in 1737 suffered the loss of hundreds of square miles of their land as a result of the infamous Walking Purchase.[8] In part, the brutal raids of the 1750s and early 1760s were a reaction to European encroachment on Indian land and settlers' disregard for native conceptions of land usage and ownership. Over the course of the Seven Years War the Indian raider became an extension of the hostile American landscape in the eyes of both the British and Irish press. For those reading about the American Indian wars in Ulster's only newspaper the *Belfast News-Letter* it appeared as if the woods themselves had risen in rebellion against European encroachment. Grisly narratives turned out in the paper week-after-week between 1754 and 1758, for example, depicted the wilderness devouring settlers taken into captivity among the native peoples of the Ohio valley.

Presbyterian areas of Ireland were broadly ignorant of many of the factors that led to attacks on British settlements in America. Ulster Presbyterians were, however, very aware of the effects of the war itself, especially the devastation it brought to frontier civilian communities with large Irish populations. Their newspapers were inundated with stories of murder, mutilation and torture in the woods of America. For many Irish Presbyterians in the 1750s and early 1760s America was therefore a place of contradictions. It was both a land of bounty and, simultaneously, a place of gruesome violence.[9] Kinfolk networks between the northern Irish province of Ulster and Britain's middle Atlantic colonies intensified both the allure of western migration and popular sympathy for the victims of frontier conflict. This emotional investment bred Ulster Presbyterian attachment to the British Atlantic Empire. During the imperial crisis leading to American independence, however, Irish Presbyterian enthusiasm for empire transformed into sympathy for their American kin and underpinned limited support for the colonists' political grievances.

John Moore's experience of transatlantic migration was shared by hundreds of thousands of his countrymen and women over the course of the eighteenth century. Over 250,000 men and women left Ireland in the century before 1815.[10] A significant proportion of the overall total of eighteenth-century migrants sailed for America in the period between 1760 and 1775. Perhaps as many as 55,000 Irish Protestants, or 2.3 per cent of the total Irish population, arrived in the colonies during these years.[11] This percentage was undoubtedly much higher among the total Presbyterian population. Continual migration from Ireland across the century altered the ethnic complexion of America. By the time of the first federal census of 1790, a sizeable minority of Americans were either Irish-born or descended from Irish migrants. The census revealed that between 6 per cent and 15 per cent of white heads of households in the new republic were of Scots Irish (Ulster Protestant) ancestry. Taken together, the ethnic group constituted a little over 10 per cent of the US population, while 21 per cent of Pennsylvanians, 24 per cent of South Carolinians and 27 per cent of Georgians could trace their ancestry to Ireland.[12] David Doyle states that 'late colonial America was proportionally more Irish than the United States in 1850 or 1900, if the Irish-born and their American offspring are any measure'.[13]

At this point it might be helpful to clarify terms used throughout this book to describe the different groups that made up the Irish Presbyterian Diaspora in the eighteenth century. Debates over what to call Irish immigrants to Colonial America have raged since the nineteenth century when the term 'Scotch-Irish' came into favour as a way to differentiate second- or third-generation Irish Americans from the Catholics then arriving en masse in eastern ports.[14] The ambiguity over the religious and ethnic background of Irish migrants to early America and the subsequent controversies over what to label them have led the group's most recent historian to dub them the 'people with no name'.[15] Following the lead of David Doyle, the term 'Scots Irish' (as opposed to the more common but controversial 'Scotch-Irish') is used here when making reference to people of Irish Presbyterian ancestry in North America.[16] I use 'Ulster/Irish Presbyterian' to refer to the Presbyterians of the north of Ireland (including those living in the Ulster counties that are now part of the Republic of Ireland) and the Dublin congregations under the bounds of the General Synod of Ulster. Finally, the term 'Scots Irish Diaspora' encompasses all Presbyterians of Irish extraction on both sides of the ocean. While accepting that eighteenth-century Irish migration to North America was in fact quite diverse and included large numbers of Catholics and Protestants from other denominations, this book focuses exclusively on the Presbyterian experience.[17]

Historians of the Scots Irish Diaspora typically structure their work within a linear narrative of migration. These studies begin either in late seventeenth-century Ulster or fifteenth-century Scotland and end on the frontiers of Revolutionary or Early Republican America. Once the focus shifts to America, it is difficult for scholars to disrupt the narrative and turn again to the lingering effects of migration on Irish society and culture. Patrick Griffin's *The People with No Name* is the most comprehensive treatment of the topic undertaken in this generation. In it, Griffin examines the Scots Irish within the paradigm of Atlantic historiography. *The People with No Name*'s significance lies not in the fact that it updated a familiar narrative for a new generation of Atlantic historians. Rather Griffin asks new and interesting questions about how Scots Irish ethnic identity functioned in the American environment. For Griffin, Irish migrants' identity 'resembled less an ideology, vision, or static set of traits than a dynamic process through which individuals struggled to come to terms with and acted upon the world around them'.[18] The cultural heritage of Irish Presbyterian immigrants in America, particularly their religious traditions and practices, as well as their group mobility, provided them with a tool box that they used to make sense of their new home. Griffin's main aim in the *The People with No Name* is to demonstrate the dynamics of cultural identity formation in early America.[19] As such Ireland fades from view in the second half of his narrative, until disappearing altogether by the early 1740s. This study seeks to build upon Griffin's work by examining how migration and war on the American frontier affected Ulster Presbyterian opinion, imperial imagination and ethnic empathy for their colonial brethren. Identity formation in Ulster, as on the American frontier, was a process spurred by social change. At mid-century, war in the colonies and the legacy of mass migration converged to stimulate Irish Presbyterian awareness of, and enthusiasm for, British imperial expansion. This, in turn, led to a new way of imagining their community and its place within the larger world.

The evolution of Irish Protestant popular imperialism in the eighteenth century sits uneasily alongside the contemporaneous emergence of modern Irish nationalism in the closing years of the period. In the two decades after the Seven Years War these two developments formed alongside and in dialogue with each other. Until recently, scholarship on the latter subject has largely focused on the United Irishmen and the revolutionary decade of the 1790s. A new crop of historians has broken the spell of 1798, however, and turned their attention to mass politicization and national identity in the 1770s and 1780s. In his *Irish*

Opinion and the American Revolution, Vincent Morley demonstrates how the circumstances surrounding the American War of Independence – including the siphoning of British troops to pacify the rebellious colonies, the rise of the Volunteers in their absence, and the force of the American revolutionary example – conspired to reshape Irish politics.[20] Morley shows that the patriot agenda of the Volunteers combined with Catholic longing for British defeat in America to create a space in which both groups could imagine an inclusive Irish political interest.

Similarly, Padhraig Higgins turns to the volunteering movement as an engine of mass politicization and the formative force behind a new Irish national patriotism. His work, along with that of Martyn Powell, investigates how the politics of consumption both accompanied and influenced Irish patriotism in the 1770s.[21] Higgins notes that even at the height of the non-importation movement at the end of the decade Irish consumers relied upon English manufacturers, such as Josiah Wedgewood, to supply them with goods celebrating the Volunteers.[22] Like the North American colonies, Ireland remained bound to an imperial system of trade in which luxury manufactured goods were imported from the emerging industrial regions of Britain.

At its heart, the Irish patriot movement of the 1770s and 1780s was underpinned by the desire to preserve Irish liberties through the restoration of a balanced constitution. The term 'patriotism' in mid-to-late eighteenth-century Ireland had a very different meaning from our understanding of the word.[23] Many Protestants and increasing numbers of middling Catholics understood it to mean serving the national interest. It did not generally indicate a desire for a complete national independence. Patriots desired to see their kingdom afforded equal status as a partner in empire alongside Britain. This was to be achieved through the establishment of an independent legislature and the guarantee of free trade. Indeed, the patriot movement was not implicitly anti-imperial in nature. Rather, it called for a recalibration of imperial influence at the centre that would better represent Irish interests within the system as a whole. As one poet recalled after the concession of free trade in 1779, the tenacity of the volunteers had resulted in a new era of both wealth and freedom for Ireland, but had also increased the kingdom's 'Imperial sway' and standing alongside Britain within an Atlantic context.[24]

Both Higgins and Morley locate the growth of the Irish patriot movement in the 1770s within the context of the wider disintegration of the first British Empire. A decade earlier, however, Irish Protestants – like the colonists themselves – had been emotionally invested in the expansion of British dominance in North America. They had been programmed, in the trials of a war that had also engulfed their island, to think of the colonials as fellow Protestants and Britons.[25] National self-identification in Ireland and Britain evolved within the context of the larger imperial superstructure. Of course, Ireland and the colonies, at least nominally, governed themselves through their own legislatures, yet they were all united in a single extended polity under an imperial crown. Popular interest in the Seven Years War fostered a general awareness of the British Atlantic world in Ireland. Irish newspapers, for instance, fed the public a steady diet of gore and violence from the war on the colonial frontier. These same papers also frequently printed descriptions of British America, including the character of its people, details on the flora and fauna found in the various colonies, and the material resources of the New World. Within Ulster Presbyterian communities, familial and commercial attachments with the colonies were particularly strong owing to the expansion of the linen industry and forty years of mass emigration. The Atlantic outlook of Ulster Presbyterians added to the weight of the 'American example' in later decades.

The era of the Seven Years War has largely failed to garner much scholarly attention despite recent historical interest in the third quarter of the century. This may have something to with the fact that it is difficult to factor widespread Protestant enthusiasm for British imperial accomplishments at the zenith of the Atlantic empire into the master narratives of eighteenth-century Irish history. We are trained to think of the Irish as victims of British imperialism not as active agents in the maintenance and expansion of the Empire. This is partially owing to the diffusion and influence of post-colonial theory, in which Ireland is cast as a colony, culturally victimized by British rule. The image of an imperial Ireland also contradicts our romanticized view of the period, particularly the 1790s, as a point during which a national consensus emerged in opposition to London's influence on the island. Irish popular imperialism was clearly expressed in the 1750s and 60s, decades that tend to fall through the cracks of the fractured historiography of eighteenth-century Ireland. Largely, scholars split the century into halves and plump for either the 'Age of Swift' at the beginning of the century or the 'Age of Revolution' at its end. The middle decades tend to be of peripheral interest to each group and thus remain under-explored. The few years following Britain's *annus mirablis* – or year of victories – in 1759 not only saw the British Empire reach its eighteenth-century peak but also marked the high point of cross-denominational Irish Protestant enthusiasm for imperial expansion.

This book is primarily concerned with the development and expression of popular imperialism in Ireland at the height of the first British Empire. Specifically, it examines how the Atlantic Presbyterian networks born out of migration underpinned Ulster Presbyterian empathy for their colonial brethren during the Seven Years War in North America (1754–63). The first chapter lays out the scope of eighteenth-century Presbyterian emigration to America before focusing on the scope of the phenomenon at mid-century. It then examines how America was imagined in the Ulster Presbyterian imagination in consequence of the ever-present possibility of emigration. Following on, the next three chapters examine how America, war and empire were discussed in print. In particular, they rely on pamphlets and newspapers in order to demonstrate the centrality of these issues in public discourse in both Dublin and Belfast. The Seven Years War saw the European powers divided into two groups roughly along confessional lines. As such, British and Irish newspapers portrayed the conflict as a battle between an aggressive Catholic alliance and a geopolitically weak, but divinely favoured, collection of Protestant nations. Many Irish Protestants saw their Scots Irish brethren in America and Prussia as allies in an eschatological war for the fate of Christendom. This, in turn, broadened the Ulster Presbyterian world-view and their positive impressions of Britain's imperial mission in America.

Chapter 2 examines the development and character of Ulster's only newspaper at the time, the *Belfast News-Letter*, in order to demonstrate the role that the paper played in the diffusion of imperial news in the region. The centrality of the American theatre to the conflict stoked the public's curiosity regarding their kinfolk and fellow subjects on the other side of the ocean and thus their interest in the imperial project in general. In the third chapter, I briefly sketch the ebb and flow of the conflict, from its disastrous beginnings to the *annus mirablis*, 1759. During the beginning of the war Irish Protestants of all denominations fasted in order to appease an angry God for the sins of the nation. From 1759 onwards, however, they were unified in celebration at news of each British victory. Throughout the conflict the press made it clear that Protestants across the Empire were involved in the same activities. In so doing, they shrank the ocean by portraying the British Atlantic world as a unified Protestant polity.

The majority of Irish migrants to the colonies settled on the fringes of European settlement in the mid-Atlantic and southern colonies. Their communities therefore suffered heavily from Indian raids on the frontiers after 1754. Chapter 4 focuses on accounts of Indian violence in the Irish press, particularly in the pages of the *Belfast News-Letter*. Its careful analysis of the genre of American Indian atrocity narratives over the course of a decade represents the most in-depth analysis of this kind ever attempted on the paper before. Northern audiences were subjected to more stories of scalping, torture and abduction than those in any other province. This, I argue, is due to Presbyterian concern for those who had migrated in the years before the war. Periodically, the *News-Letter* made it clear that those men, women and children who were suffering in the American backcountry were Irish.

Chapter 5 focuses on American fundraising in Ireland from 1750 to 1764. By supporting these charities, Ulster Presbyterians demonstrated unambiguous sympathy for their American cousins in a period of conflict and uncertainty. In these years, two American Presbyterian campaigns visited Ulster seeking financial assistance. In particular, the success of the 1760 tour on behalf of Presbyterian ministers' widows and Pennsylvania frontier refugees demonstrated Irish concern for the well-being of their distant coreligionists and kinfolk. Ian McBride notes that Irish Presbyterians 'inhabited a transatlantic subculture stretching from Scotland to Ulster to the American colonies'.[26] This subculture was sustained by kinfolk networks between the three countries and was largely centred on the Scottish universities at Glasgow and Edinburgh in which many Irish and American ministers were trained.[27] Other historians have observed that familial and commercial links underpinned Irish Presbyterian sympathy for American colonists during the imperial crisis and subsequent war between 1765 and 1783.[28] Most often this sense of kinship is assumed rather than concretely demonstrated as it rarely manifested in anything more substantial than a printed letter or political petition. The degree to which northern Presbyterians demonstrated sympathy towards the misfortunes of their colonial brethren at earlier points in the century has yet to be examined. The Seven Years War forced Ulster Presbyterians to reassess their relationship with the British Empire. It also forced them to re-evaluate what it meant to be both British and Protestant in an expanding Atlantic world.

1

Atlantic Migration and North America in the Irish Presbyterian Imagination

Protestant migration was a highly visible and contentious phenomenon in Ireland throughout the eighteenth century, one that touched upon the lives of a large proportion of the population – especially in the Presbyterian hinterlands of the north. Communities felt the absence of those who had left. Congregations noticed empty pews in meeting-houses; landlords felt the sting of rents left unpaid by departed tenants; and onlookers living near ports witnessed the annual migration of families as they made their way to waiting ships. One such worried observer was Edmond Kaine, an agent on the Barrett Estate in County Monaghan, who claimed to have watched one hundred families travel through the town of Clones on their way to the ocean in March 1719.[1] Constant seasonal migration and the ever-present opportunity to emi-grate determined how ordinary Presbyterians imagined America and how they perceived British imperial expansion more broadly.

By the middle of the century, transatlantic migration had become an established part of life throughout the province. It was a life strategy open to Protestants of all backgrounds. Those who could not afford the cost of the voyage – £3 5s in the early 1770s – could sign a contract of indenture, whereupon the cost of the voyage was covered in exchange for a service contract.[2] These 'redemptioners' usually served a term of between two and four years' service in America before setting out on their own in search of cheap land in the west. In the 1720s one-in-five migrants crossed the ocean as indentured servants.[3] The majority of those who left Ireland in the wake of the potato crop failure and meagre harvest of 1739 paid their fare through indenture.[4] The possibility of migration for Presbyterians across the social spectrum ensured a broad audience for propaganda advertising the high quality of life across the Atlantic. James Leyburn notes that the inclination to migration was not simply the product of economic or religious circumstances: 'there was also the constant stimulus of widespread propaganda – broadsides, letters from the colonies, [and] pamphlets'.[5] This material – to which could be added the consistent printing of shipping advertisements in local newspapers – dogged prospective migrants throughout the year. The prospect of migration and an idealized image of America became embedded in the Ulster Presbyterian consciousness through the ever-present white noise of merchant propaganda. Such ephemera served as a constant reminder of the existence of the Atlantic empire and buoyed Ulster Presbyterians' sense of imperial belonging.[6]

Much of the passenger traffic between Ulster and America was the product of chain migration. Chain migration is a phenomenon whereby an anchor community of immigrants, once established, encourages the further migration of friends and family from the home country. Many emigrants maintained correspondence with their relatives in Ulster.[7] Authors of these letters often included favourable information about the colonies in the hope that they could entice friends and relatives to emigrate. These letters were often meant for a larger audience and not the recipient alone. Sometimes shipping agents or newspaper editors printed and distributed copies of emigrant letters, thereby further increasing their circulation and appeal. One such letter was published in the *Pennsylvania Gazette* in October 1737. The letter was originally sent from a migrant named James Murray who had sent it to a minister in County Tyrone named Baptist Boyd. The paper explained that Murray had sent the letter to 'his Countrymen, to encourage them to come over thither; which, that it might have the Effect on the People, was printed and dispers'd in Ireland'.[8] He told of the cheapness of land and its fertility, telling Boyd, 'The young Folke in Eireland are aw but a Pack of Couards, for I will tell ye in short, this is a bonny country.'[9] In 1789, John Denison wrote to his brother Samuel, then living in County Down, describing the province of Pennsylvania. Denison told his brother that he had built his new life upon Irish foundations by employing skills that he had learned in Ulster to earn his wages in America. He made 10s a day weaving linen before saving enough to buy land 150 miles north of Baltimore in Franklin township. John told Samuel that a man could buy an acre of land at good prices – in his area about the equivalent of 20s – with minimal taxes. John wished to see his brother again and told him 'if you ware hear and setled nigh to me I would not see you want untill you would have time to fix yourself'.[10] In the same year John Dunlop, a printer from County Tyrone then established in Philadelphia, wrote to his brother, Robert Rutherford, imploring him to send his son Billy to Pennsylvania before the Irish Parliament moved to restrict emigration. Dunlop told Rutherford that while he may not wish to come over himself, yet it might be the best option for his son: 'People with a family advanced in life find great difficulties in Emigration but the young men of ireland [sic] who wish in the world where a man meet as rich a reward for good conduct and industry as in America.'[11] These shared letters circulating around the Irish countryside were perhaps the most significant 'pull' factor enticing Presbyterians across the ocean.

The complex web of family relations that linked Ulster to America is illustrated in the preface of the journal kept by the South Carolina loyalist Alexander Chesney during the American Revolutionary War. While still a teenager, Chesney sailed with his mother, father and seven siblings from Larne to Charleston aboard the ship *Mary James* in 1772. Their voyage was not an easy one. Alexander's eight month-old sister Peggy succumbed to smallpox en route. The family's misery did not end upon their arrival in South Carolina. The outbreak of smallpox on the ship resulted in the quarantining of its passengers and crew on Sullivan Island at the edge of Charleston Harbour. They were kept in confinement for seven weeks before being permitted to set foot on the mainland. The first portion of Chesney's journal includes a detailed family genealogy. He began the section with his father's family. Chesney's aunt Martha left for America four years before his family made their voyage. She was 'married to Matthew Gillespy [sic] who went also to Carolina and [Martha] died there shortly after their arrival'. His father's other sister 'Sarah has been married to John Cook who died in Pennsylvania'; she then 'removed to Pacholet river South Carolina, where her children are married and settled'. Alexander's family on his mother's side also contained many migrants. Elizabeth Purdy, Chesney's mother, was the youngest of twelve children, at least four of whom had also sailed for the colonies. In his youth Chesney remembered his Uncle William, 'who lived in Glenraire [County Antrim] and went with his family to South Carolina'. Presumably, this uncle was among the many thousands who sailed for the colonies in the 1760s. Finally, his uncles 'Thomas and John went to Pensylvenia' where they both set-tled in the town of Carlisle.[12] When the Chesney family finally arrived in northwestern South Carolina, they found themselves welcomed by family members and other Irish settlers in what had become a thriving Presbyterian community.

Similarly, John Moore and his sister relied upon a continent-wide sup-port network of kinfolk when they found themselves in trouble within months of their arrival in New York in 1760. John had been enticed to leave Ireland by his uncle Robert Cobham who lived near Albany. When the relationship between the two men soured, John and his sister were able to move to Philadelphia where they received support from an aunt who lived in the city.[13] These were the extensive kinfolk networks that bound Ulster to the North American colonies. Such networks, along with the ever-present possibility of migration, transformed the ways in which Irish Presbyterians imagined the British Empire and their place within it. The formation of a Scottish and Irish Presbyterian Atlantic Diaspora was, at mid-century, a unifying process that integrated the north of Ireland into the British imperial polity. For these reasons, the scope and nature of eighteenth-century Irish Presbyterian migration warrants closer examination.

Ulster Presbyterian migration to America in the eighteenth century

Eighteenth-century mass migration from Ulster to the colonies began in earnest between 1717 and 1719. Before 1717, only a handful of dissenters made their way from Ulster to the colonies. In these years many of the cheap leases issued at the end of the Williamite Wars expired, leading many Ulster landlords to raise the cost of leases. These 'rack-renting' landlords hoped to capitalize on the increased demand for land that resulted from years of political stability and population growth.[14] While rents increased, yields from agriculture and industry decreased. From 1715 to 1720 was a period of drought and crop failure. The linen industry also suffered a decline. In 1717–18 the amount of linen exported from Derry to Britain fell from 2,400,000 yards to 2,200,000 yards.[15] In the years 1717 to 1719 between 4,500 and 7,000 people left Ulster ports for America. This was the beginning of a cycle of migration that would repeat itself throughout the century at periods when economic hardship, lease expiration and increase, and industrial recession converged. It differed from those that preceded it not only in size but also in destination.[16] Unlike the sparse migration that occurred between 1680 and 1716, where the principal destination of Ulster migrants had been New England, the bulkhead exodus of the late teens was directed at Philadelphia and other Delaware ports. Once established, Irish settlements in the middle and southern colonies became beacons luring many thousands of immigrants into the trans-Appalachian interior.

The next wave of settlers arrived in the late 1720s, particularly in the years after the 1729 Irish famine. About 15,000 Protestants left Ireland in these years, again preferring to settle in western Pennsylvania. The

1728–9 famine accelerated a migratory trend that had begun following the poor harvests of 1725–6 and resulted in the first of two great waves of Protestant emigration from the north to British North America.[17] The size of the 1728–9 migration was unlike anything witnessed in post-plantation Ireland. It terrified the Anglican gentry who feared that Presbyterian migration undermined the Protestant interest in the kingdom. Catholics did not seem to be migrating; leading many to conclude that plantation itself was in jeopardy.[18] Lord Primate Hugh Boulter wrote to the Archbishop of Canterbury describing the dire situation in the north: 'the scarcity of provisions certainly makes many quit us: there are now seven ships at *Belfast* that are carrying off about 1000 passengers thither [to America]'.[19] Even if the Irish government outlawed the passenger trade to stem the tide of people leaving, it would do no good. Boulter continued, '[I]f we knew how to stop them, as most of them can neither get victuals nor work at home, it would be cruel to do it.' Between 1717 and 1730 Presbyterian emigration became an issue of national concern. By the mid-1730s annual migration levelled-out and popular anxiety regarding the issue subsided. The issue re-emerged between 1765 and 1775, when the last, and greatest, series of Presbyterian migrations of the century struck the island.

Presbyterians left eighteenth-century Ireland in great numbers for many reasons. Political and religious discrimination, as well as perceived lack of economic opportunity, influenced the decision to migrate. In many respects, Irish Presbyterians were deprived of the full rights of citizenship that they believed were due to them as Protestant subjects who had risked their lives and livelihoods for the Williamite cause. In the early decades of the eighteenth century the Anglican Ascendancy gradually ate away at the limited toleration established by William III. In 1704 a sacramental test was introduced requiring anyone who wished to take public office to first take communion within the Church of Ireland. This effectively excluded all Catholics and Protestant dissenters from most positions of government authority and from holding military commissions. Presbyterian church sessions did not enjoy the support of the civil establishment and marriages administered by Presbyterian ministers were illegal until 1738. On top of this, Presbyterians were expected to pay tithes towards the support of the established Church of Ireland, a church to which they did not belong and whose clergy continually lobbied for the suppression of their religious liberties.[20] It was against this background of oppression that the majority of Presbyterian migrants understood or justified their decision to leave Ireland. Whether or not religious grievances stimulated migration to a greater extent than did economic hardship at different points in the century is the subject of much historical debate.[21] When asked, however, many Presbyterians blamed the Church of Ireland and the parliamentarians at College Green. One commentator claimed that Presbyterians referred to restrictive legislation including the Test Act as a 'kind of vassallage and slavery' and they could 'easily help themselves, by removing to some parts of his majesty's dominions in *America*, where no such hardships' were imposed.[22]

In February 1729, the Presbyterian ministers Francis Iredell and Robert Craghead wrote to each of the northern Presbyteries at the behest of the Lords Justices of Ireland asking them to outline their views on the nature and causes of Protestant migration. Thankfully, Tyrone's report to Iredell survives. The Presbyterian leadership treaded lightly regarding what to say and how to say it. They knew that Dublin Castle was well aware of the complex causes that contributed to Presbyterian migration and was generally unsympathetic to the civil plight of dissenters. The Tyrone memorial outlined the various economic and social reasons for the exodus, including high rents and encouragement from family already in America. For all of this, it is still a politically charged document that attacked the Ascendancy establishment for upholding discriminatory legislation against dissenters. Presbyterians realized that emigration had spooked the Ascendancy like no petition or pamphlet had done before. They therefore jumped at the chance to use it as a weapon in their quest to achieve a general toleration for all Protestants. The report blamed the Test Act for the exodus. Why were thousands of Presbyterians risking the Atlantic passage every year? The 'Answer is plain and Ready, That they are excluded by the Sacramental Test Act, from doing [the kingdom] anymore Service, than an Irish papist, its avowed Enemies.'[23] In 1733 the campaign to remove the Test Act was quashed. Yet religious intolerance faded as a primary feature of shipping advertisements in the north.[24] This indicates that while many migrants may have later justified their decision to migrate on religious grounds, other factors contributed to their initial choice to do so.[25] To be sure, Presbyterians continued to resent their second-class status in Irish society. This resentment continued to bubble-up in the odd shipping advertisement in the years to come. Other economic factors, however, became the primary complaint of migrants leaving the province in the 1750s and 60s.

Throughout the first half of the century, Church of Ireland officials attempted to disarm critics of the Test Act of 1704 by playing down the Presbyterian character of Protestant migration. The Archbishop of

Dublin, William King, claimed that migrants 'never thought of leaving this kingdom, till oppressed by excessive [rents?] & other temporal hardships; nor do only dissenters leave us, but proportionately of all sorts, except Papists'.[26] Church of Ireland observers were eager to point out that tithes were not as excessive as their opponents claimed and that the principal reasons for the migrations stemmed from economic hardship and increasing rents. These problems affected everyone in rural Ulster and not just the Presbyterians. Yet it was impossible to deny that Catholics did not migrate in the same numbers as their Protestant neighbours. This they found especially troubling. By the late 1720s, it became clear that government needed to intercede in order to save the plantation. In 1729 a bill was drafted to stem transatlantic migration. It was entitled 'An act to prevent persons from clandestinely transporting themselves to America to defraud creditors'. The aim of the Bill was wider than the name suggests as it aimed to discourage all Protestant migration, not just those fleeing debt.[27] The English Privy Council, however, failed to endorse coercive measures in 1730 because it was clear that emigration rates had declined from the levels seen the previous year.[28]

The Irish Parliament's inability to secure support from Westminster for a law prohibiting Protestant emigration left the issue in the hands of local landlords and magistrates. In April 1736 the Collector for the Port of Belfast, George Macartney, forbade nine ships bound for America from leaving the harbour. Macartney did so on the grounds that these ships were engaged in the illegal exportation of Irish woollen goods. His real intention, however, was to halt Protestant migration and to this effect he had the full support of landlords around the town of Belfast. Macartney's case was a rather flimsy one. Passengers required wool blankets and bedding for the transatlantic passage. These were taken out of the kingdom, thereby the passengers and shipmasters were in violation of the Woolens Act of 1699. The merchants of the town, many of whom stood to lose money if the vessels did not sail, were shocked. Eleven men drafted a petition attacking Macartney's decision. They noted that the passenger trade between Ireland and America had always been 'open and free' and that 'no reasonable necessaries of bedding or wearing apparel' had been denied previous passengers.[29] They were 'ignorant that the gentlemen of this kingdom were offended at such trade' and promised that they would not take on passengers who were criminals or servants fleeing their masters.[30]

In May an Irish ship captain named John Stewart wrote to William Penn, the founder and chief proprietor of Pennsylvania, then in London, describing the situation in the north.[31] In the weeks prior to Macartney's actions in Belfast, local landlords had attempted to make an example of agents involved in the passenger trade. Owners and masters of America-bound vessels were arrested together with the printers and distributors of handbills that advertised transatlantic voyages. They were charged with 'Encouraging his Majesty's subjects' to transport themselves 'from one plantation to another' and were then presented with a stark choice: accept a £1,000 bond 'to apear att Carickfergus assizes or be thrown into a Lowthsome Geol'.[32] Not surprisingly they chose the latter option and were all eventually acquitted of wrongdoing. The court's decision provoked strong reactions. One magistrate who disagreed with his colleagues rose in anger when the verdict was announced. He shouted at the defendants '& swore by G-d if anny came to Lisburn the town in wh he lived to puplise an advertizement he would Whipe him throw the Town'.[33] The 1,700 to 1,800 passengers waiting on the quays of Belfast suffered throughout the Macartney ordeal. Stewart's letter revealed that many could not pay for lodging or, indeed, the expense of the voyage in the first place. They certainly had not anticipated the expense of being waylaid in Belfast for an extra month. Many were to be indentured upon arrival in Pennsylvania or had some financial assistance from acquaintances already there. Some had pinned their hopes on survival in the new world on the 'yearly' accounts of the bounties of America that arrived in the province with the merchant fleet.[34] During the Carickfergus trial the prosecution struck out against these optimistic visions of a land of milk and honey touted by shipping agents across the province, claiming that they were 'Forgerys & Lyes'.[35]

A few years earlier Jonathan Swift made the same accusation in his *Intelligencer no. 19*. Swift claimed that the colonial legislatures employed agents to censor messages sent by dissatisfied migrants. Instead they manufactured celebratory accounts and sent them to Irish printers, who, in turn, distributed them throughout the countryside.[36] In reality, Presbyterian immigrants were sent to a dangerous frontier where their settlements served as an expendable defensive barrier against Indian incursion. The colonial landowners, Swift wrote,

> are in great want of Men to inhabit that Tract of Ground, which lies between them and the *wild Indians*, who are not reduced under their Dominion. We read of some barbarous People, whom the *Romans* placed in their Armies, for no other Service than to blunt their Enemies Swords, and afterwards to fill up Trenches with their dead Bodies. And thus our People, who transport themselves, are settled in those interjacent Tracts, as a Screen against the Insults of *Savages*.[37]

This jibe was not without foundation. James Logan, William Penn's Irish-born secretary for the province of Pennsylvania, encouraged Irish Protestant migration for just that purpose. In 1720 he wrote that the colony was 'apprehensive from the Northern Indians [Delawares and Iroquois]' and that he 'therefore thought it prudent to plant a settlement of such men as those who formerly had so bravely defended Londonderry and Inniskillen as a frontier in case of any disturbance'.[38]

Irish Government and landlord disquiet over Protestant migration lessened during the middle decades of the century. Annual migration continued throughout these years but did not reach the peaks seen in 1727–9. Two minor spikes in the numbers emigrating occurred in 1740–1 and 1754–5. These episodes, however, failed to rouse much official interest, as it was clear the Protestant communities of the north could handle these irregular demographic haemorrhages without destabilizing the plantation as a whole. This changed in the late 1760s and early 1770s when Ulster experienced the largest spike of Protestant migration of the century. In the five years between 1770 and 1775 as many 30,000 people left Ulster ports.[39] In 1772 Henry Joy claimed that 'the North of Ireland has in the last five or six years been drained of one-fourth of its trading cash, and the like proportion of the Manufacturing people'.[40] The topic of emigration loomed large as a topic of conversation in the period. Arthur Young, on his tour of the north in 1776, routinely asked his hosts about the nature of Protestant migration. Young was an English economist who was, like many gentleman of the day, interested in agricultural productivity and land improvement. On his tour of Ireland, he seemed particularly interested in what sort of people emigrated and how their departure affected the economy of the communities they left behind.[41] William Drennan wrote to his friend in Dublin Dr William Bruce informing him of the 'vast numbers' streaming onto ships in Newry. 'Some of the richer sort in this town and the country around are about to migrate,' Drennan informed Bruce.[42] He further claimed, 'If I had it in my power I would offer 500£ reward in the best written dissuasive against Emigration which ought to be immediately published and dispersed thro' the Country.'[43] As a student in Glasgow, Drennan had once confessed to his sister that he too contemplated emigration if unable to find employment in Ireland or Scotland.[44]

As in 1727–9, panic that Presbyterian migration might undermine the Protestant interest in the kingdom resulted in renewed calls for the government to restrict the numbers leaving. Many prominent landlords, including the earls of Hillsborough and Hertford, formed an association to help remove the causes of northern emigration and to petition

Parliament for greater restrictions on the passenger trade.[45] The board of trade had become increasingly nervous about the size of the migrations in the early 1770s. By the time the English government took notice of Irish migration in 1773, however, the wave had crested and passenger levels were decreasing. As was the case in the 1720s, London was only concerned with emigration when it posed an immediate threat to the security of the realm.[46] By the time they realized the scope of the problem it had abated, leading Parliament to forget the issue.

Ulster migration at mid-century and America in the Presbyterian imagination

By the middle of the 1750s the number of emigrants boarding America-bound ships in Ulster ports exceeded 1,000 per year.[47] By this point the migratory phenomena had become rather mundane and commonplace. Transatlantic migration was firmly established within the repertoire of life strategies open to Ulster Protestants and was now an accepted fact of life throughout the north. The 1750s did not witness the short-term spikes in Protestant migration that so worried government observers and landlords in the closing years of the 1720s and 1730s. To be sure, the decision to abandon one's homeland for a foreign, and often dangerous, country was still a daunting one. This was especially true when Indian war raged on the frontiers. Yet the allure of cheap land and religious toleration seemed to be worth the risk.

Mid-century migration was strong in south Ulster, where the possibility of emigration had become firmly established after thirty years of annual migration from the area. Evidence of the ubiquity of the temptation of America arises in surprising places. In April 1756, Margaret Macre brought the charge of rape against John Wales before the church session of the Seceder congregation in the Cahans region that straddled the counties of Monaghan, west Armagh and north Cavan. She testified that, prior to the incident, Wales had tried to seduce her on several occasions by professing his love for her. She claimed that he had even 'proposed selling his farm if she would go to America with him'.[48] Walsh was later cleared of the charge by the session. Whether true or fabricated, Macre's testimony revealed that American emigration factored into the popular imagination, if not possible life strategies, of Monaghan Presbyterians. Emigration as a romanticized form of escape was a theme in a series of poems published locally by a printer named John Brown in the 1780s. This cheap chapbook literature was widely popular. The poems themselves were sung to the tune of well-known songs. The first, 'The Phoenix of Ulster', describes the sorrow of a young man who had fallen in love with an unattainable young woman whom he had seen on Mill Street in Newry.[49] In a rejoinder entitled, 'An Answer to the Phoenix of Ulster', we find the young man had returned to see his love in Newry only to be rebuffed. In his misery, he boarded a vessel to leave Ireland, saying, 'Unto America I mean to sail over ... Into some desart I mean for to hie, / Where I will in sorrow lament grieve & cry'.[50] These references, though brief, hint at the looming presence of colonial migration in the northern imagination. Regular migration was a part of life throughout the province. As a result, an often romanticized image of America had burrowed its way into the popular consciousness.

Eight years after Macre's allegations were heard by the session, the majority of her congregation departed for America. In May 1764, approximately 300 Presbyterians, or about 100 families, led by their minister Thomas Clark, embarked from Newry to begin a new life in New York. This famous migration has come to be known in the north of Ireland as the 'Cahans exodus'. Those involved certainly saw it in biblical terms, casting themselves as the Israelites fleeing Egyptian bondage. Clark and his congregation had a troubled relationship with local government officials and the other Presbyterian congregations belonging to the General Synod of Ulster. In 1753 Clark was arrested for refusing to kiss the Bible before taking the Abjuration Oath of loyalty to the Crown. This led to his arrest on the grounds of disloyalty, a case eventually thrown out by a circuit judge in Monaghan. Clark's release, however, was not the end of official harassment of his congregation. William Craig, an elder within the congregation, was imprisoned for several months on the same charges.[51]

The economic downturn of the late 1750s finally convinced Clark of the necessity to emigrate. He forwarded the names of those interested in emigrating to the colonial officials, who set aside 40,000 acres of land at the head of Lake George for the use of Clark and his congregation. Upon arrival in New York, Clark's congregation divided into two groups. Several families decided to join pre-war migrants in the southern backcountry. They soon sailed for South Carolina. Upon their arrival they occupied land at Cedar Spring and Long Cane. Clark and the remaining portion of his congregation never made it to their land grant on Lake George, instead establishing themselves on 12,000 acres of land in Albany County (now Washington County), New York. Another mass-migration of an entire congregation occurred eight years later when Rev. William Martin led 467 families of his congregation from Ballymoney, County Antrim, to South Carolina.[52]

The largest group of migrants to depart Ulster for America in the years immediately before the war was enticed to do so by their landlord. This migration was small compared to many of those that came before and after it. It did, nevertheless, live on in the popular imagination, particularly as it introduced North Carolina as a possible destination for Ulster migrants.[53] Arthur Dobbs was a large property holder in County Antrim and was a well-respected figure in both domestic and imperial politics.[54] He became the deputy governor of Carrickfergus in 1728 and represented the town in the Irish Parliament between 1727 and 1730. In 1733 Robert Walpole appointed him engineer-in-chief and surveyor-general of Ireland. Prior to accepting these appointments, Dobbs had written a two-part treatise entitled an *Essay on the Improvement of Ireland,* in which he argued for free trade between Britain and Ireland. In the *Essay* he railed against Protestant migration to America. By 1745, however, he had apparently changed his mind on the issue.

Throughout his career Dobbs had been keenly interested in colonial affairs and in 1745 had purchased 4,000 acres of land in North Carolina. In 1751 he made his first tour of the colony and, through the help of Lord Halifax, was appointed governor the following year. Dobbs styled himself an imperial improver, working to bring prosperity to Ireland and North Carolina within the larger framework of the British Atlantic commonwealth. Dobbs's portrait was painted by William Hoare to commemorate the occasion. In 1755 James McArdell engraved Hoare's painting in London (see Fig. 1.1). The portrait and engraving depicted Dobbs as a studious imperial agent. Dobbs is pictured leaning on a table on which also sits a globe. He holds a map of North Carolina in his left hand, and a cartographer's compass in his right. In the background we see a ship sailing to a distant and faintly visible shore, perhaps Ireland. Here, Dobbs is a man of empire, a committed servant in the quest of improvement, British expansion and Atlantic commerce. This self-image trumped the narrow concerns he might have had as an Ascendency landlord regarding the 'Protestant interest' of Ireland. He was now obsessed with the global extension and development of the British Empire. Dobbs's focus on international affairs later affected hundreds of his Presbyterian tenants who, when the option was presented to them, became willing pawns in their landlord's imperial ambitions.

Shortly after receiving his commission as governor, Dobbs enlisted willing tenants from his Antrim estates to settle his holdings in North Carolina. He organized a small cluster of families on a preliminary expedition to America in April 1751. The 'several families' were adequately impressed with the land that they were offered, and Dobbs set to work

Figure 1.1   His Excellency Arthur Dobbs, Esq., engraved by James McArdell after a work by William Hoare (London, 1755[?]). Image courtesy of the Colonial Williamsburg Foundation.

preparing future voyages.[55] He next chartered *The Elisabeth,* which sailed from Belfast Lough in July 1753. It was followed by at least four other vessels over the next two years. A Belfast merchant, Samuel Smith, saw profits in Dobbs's colonial ventures and subsequently set up his own expedition to North Carolina. In 1755 he chartered a vessel bound for the Carolinas and the *Dobbs Galley* in the hopes that he could entice stragglers who had not taken part in the earlier expeditions to sail with him.

Despite the opening of the Carolinas to Irish migration, Pennsylvania continued to enjoy a privileged place among the thirteen colonies in the

Ulster Presbyterian imagination. Most immigrant ships from the 1720s onwards made landfall at ports along the Delaware River. Immigrants were channelled into the interior through large towns such as New-castle and, above all, the metropolis of British America, Philadelphia.[56] Pennsylvania's population and economy rapidly expanded in the first half of the eighteenth century. Kinfolk networks and the prospect of eco-nomic advancement fuelled further Irish immigration.[57] This stimulated widespread interest in Ulster for that colony in particular. For example, in 1777 Rev. William Caldwell of Armagh annotated cut-out sections of newspapers detailing the religious demographics of Pennsylvania and the total populations of the other British North American colonies on the inside cover of a manuscript on Trinitarian doctrine.[58]

Pennsylvania was known for the virtues of religious tolerance and peaceful ethnic cohabitation. The free practice of religion for all Christians, enshrined in William Penn's 1701 Charter of Privileges, was particularly alluring to Ulster Presbyterians, who resented their status as second-class subjects in Ireland. Joseph Pollock, Presbyterian elder in the non-subscribing congregation at Newry and leading figure in the Patriot Volunteer movement of the 1770s and 80s, praised Pennsylvania as a model of toleration that should be emulated in Ireland. Writing under the pseudonym of Owen Roe O'Nial, Pollock produced the most radical pamphlet published in Ireland during the 1770s. In it, he argued that the ancient divisions between planter and native, Protestant and Catholic could be overcome if a general toleration were established. He pointed to 'the great and amiable virtues of Pennsylvania' to prove his point:

> The state of Pennsylvania is equally various in its religion. The laws of this province are more liberal than the spirit of any other prov-inces. They give no preference to any sect. They tolerate all sects. All sects are therefore not only peaceable but content.[59]

Pollock's idealized image of Pennsylvania, then in the midst of its own struggle for independence, coloured his vision of what a sovereign and united Ireland could achieve if the British connection were severed and the Episcopal Church disestablished.

In the early nineteenth century a Dr Smith sent Irish patriot activ-ist William Drennan a piece of the concord tree of Shackamaxon under which William Penn signed his famous treaty with the Lenape (Delaware) Indians in 1682.[60] The treaty stipulated that land belonging to the Indians would be purchased at fair rates through the office of the colonial proprietor. The episode was subsequently mythologized, most famously in Benjamin West's 1772 painting *Penn's Treaty with the Indians*. Drennan was so humbled and inspired by the gift that he composed a poem on the subject. In it he claimed that Penn's actions were a beacon for all humanity who had forgotten the example set by his benevolence during the many wars of the eighteenth century. The tree, though fallen, remained a symbol of tolerance and a beacon of humanity's ability to achieve peace and prosperity through mutual respect. Drennan wrote of the famous tree that 'though every branch be now decayed / And all its scattered leaves be dry', yet hopefully 'The withered branch again shall grow / Till on the earth its shade extend / And this – the gift of foe to foe – / becomes the gift of friend to friend'.[61]

The grim reality of frontier war sat uneasily next to the idealized image of Penn's colony. By the end of the Seven Years War the 'Holy Experiment' of peaceable coexistence between euro-Americans and Indians had been abandoned. Settlers of Irish descent played a large part in undermining Penn's vision.[62] This was a reality, however, either unknown or ignored in Ulster where the bond of kinship led people to turn a blind eye towards atrocities committed by their own in America. This settler bias is clear in contemporary newspapers where the image of the victimized settler trumped that of the victimized Indian.

The *News-Letter* often printed news from Pennsylvania as it arrived in Belfast. It routinely published government speeches and legislative news from both New Jersey and Pennsylvania.[63] Sometimes the stories included in the paper reflected the biases born out of the Presbyterian commercial networks that stretched between Ulster and the Delaware ports. Drennan's future respect for American Quakerism was not found in Irish newspaper coverage of Pennsylvanian politics during the 1750s. The Friends dominated the assembly and refused, on religious grounds, to support measures to raise money for the defence of the colony. Many believed that the frontier counties, and their large Presbyterian populations, suffered as a consequence. The paper included an extract from 'an authentic letter' written in Philadelphia on 13 December 1754. It reported the presence of a force of 2,000 French troops, not including their Indian allies, within 200 miles of the city. 'I only wish', the letter began, 'that His Majesty and British Parliament knew our Danger, and that of the whole English Northern Continent.'[64] The author followed with the claim, 'Our assembly consists of 36 Members 30 whereof are Quakers, and nothing can be done by them for the Defence of the Country.'[65]

Merchant networks bound the Irish Atlantic together. Atlantic commerce was a risky business because of the hazards of oceanic travel between Europe and America; the possibility of fraud; and the fragility of credit structures if tragedy did strike. Trust between partners and investors on both sides of the ocean were a necessity if business enterprises were to flourish. As such, partnerships were often built upon common ethnicity and religion. The dozen or so expatriate Irish flax-seed merchants in New York during the 1750s displayed a great deal of cooperation in the purchasing and transportation of their product. These business networks served as conduits through which transatlantic communication between Scots Irish and Ulster Presbyterian communities was channelled. In 1768, Dr Francis Alison, the Ulster-born vice-provost of the College of Philadelphia, bought a collection of books at auction from the moderator of the General Synod of Ulster, Rev. James Macky, for £4 17s.[66] The transaction was administered through the Philadelphia-based partnership of Belfast merchants Orr, Dunlope and Glenholme. The partners agreed to have the books ported from Belfast to Philadelphia aboard one of their vessels for the sum of 11s 6d.[67] The Irish-born merchant Waddell Cunningham wrote from New York to his business partner in Belfast, Thomas Gregg, in September 1756. Cunningham asked Gregg to inquire after a bundle of pamphlets published in Belfast by local printer James Magee.[68] Cunningham intended to sell these pamphlets in New York.

Emigration sometimes led to a situation where Presbyterian immigrants in America became something akin to absentee landlords in their own right. James Caldwell, an Irish merchant in Philadelphia, made sure that his sister Sibella of Ballymoney was the beneficiary of the leases – signed in both of their names – rented on family property in Ireland. The renter, Nathaniel McDowell, owed the family biannual rents totalling 5s 6d on every pound earned on his returns from receivers fees on the properties. The rush to repopulate Ulster in the wake of seventeenth-century conflict bequeathed many benefits to future generations of tenants. Most obviously, it guaranteed inexpensive rents throughout the province well into the eighteenth century. Tenants in Ulster also enjoyed the freedom to sell unexpired terms in their holdings. This aided emigration by allowing families to cover the initial costs of relocation by raising capital beyond selling produce or personal property. But it also left proprietors with a problem. The original agreement between the landlord and the undersigned tenant held for the length of the term agreed upon; no matter who the property was later sublet to. This was an annoyance to those landlords desperate to get out of the cheap agreements made earlier in the century.

A typical lease in Ulster throughout the century lasted for the lives of three people listed on the lease. Once those three people died the lease would be renegotiated. In practice the average lease of three lives was about fifty years. What happened when one or more of those whose lives determined the length of a lease migrated? This became an issue on George Macartney's estate at Lissanoure in County Antrim in 1803. The previous proprietor of the estate before it came into the possession of the Macartneys had issued a lease in 1729 to 'Walter Lyle and Partners' at the annual rent of £11 5s 6d. The lease was for the lives of Walter's three young sons. Upon Walter's death, the tenancy passed to each successive son. In 1801 the Lyle family was paying the same rental rate as they had in 1729. In the meantime one of the sons, John, had emmigrated to America. When the second son, Walter Jr, died on 24 June 1803, Macartney believed that he could finally raise rents on the property. He was denied the ability upon hearing word from a returned emigrant that John Lyle was still alive in Pennsylvania. An affidavit was sworn by John Lyle himself on 7 November 1803 in Montgomery County, Pennsylvania, and Macartney was deprived of his chance. It is unclear when the lease finally expired, but at the annual rent of £66 12s 2d in 1816, the property was worth more than five times what it had been ninety years earlier.[69]

In 1753 the first guidebook for Irish emigrants, entitled *America Dissected*, was published in Dublin. The pamphlet consisted of three letters written by James MacSparran, an Anglican minister in Rhode Island, to friends in Ireland. MacSparran was born in the Parish of Dungiven, County Londonderry, to Presbyterian parents in 1683. He emigrated to Boston in 1718 after completing his studies for the Presbyterian ministry. MacSparran did not remain in Boston long. He sailed for England in 1719 and was ordained an Anglican minister by the Bishop of London in 1720. His decision to convert was perhaps owing to the harsh treatment he received at the hands of the Congregationalist establishment of New England. He returned to America in April 1721 as a missionary of the SPG to the parish of St Paul in Narragansett, Rhode Island.[70] The title-page of *America Dissected* advertised the reasons for its printing. It was 'Published as a Caution to Unsteady People who may be tempted to leave their Native Country'.[71] Readers would learn the truth about, among other things, the 'bad and unwholesome air', the 'Badness of Money' and the 'Danger from Enemies'.[72] Yet despite the negative images conjured up by the title-page, the pamphlet was not solely a polemic against migration. It also included useful information about the climate, demography and character of the various colonies. MacSparran admitted that those prepared to work could improve their lot in America. He observed that the people of Londonderry, New

Hampshire, were 'all Irish, and famed for industry and riches'.[73] He also conceded that while

> It is pretty true to observe of the Irish, that those who come here with any wealth, are the worse for their removal; though, doubtless, the next-generation will not suffer so much as their fathers; but those who, when they came, had nothing to lose, have throve greatly by their labour.[74]

Such objectivity was acceptable while annual migration remained steady. After the war Presbyterian emigration again began to rise to worrying levels. An American visitor to Dublin reported 'a vast jealousy of America here on account of the vast numbers that go to America from the North of Ireland, which they say will in the end rob them of their best Protestants and manufacturers'.[75] Fear over the negative ramifications of Protestant emigration from Ireland re-emerged and the passenger trade again came under fire as a result.

On 13 May 1763 the *News-Letter* published a letter from a migrant named John Smilie detailing his mistreatment aboard the *Sally* during a voyage from Belfast to Philadelphia during the previous year. John's father Robert added a preface to the letter in which he claimed that it was his 'Duty' to have the letter published as warning to his 'Friends and Countrymen' about to embark for the colonies.[76] The letter detailed the miseries brought upon the crew and passengers by the ship's captain. They had set out from Belfast grossly under-prepared and after a few months at sea the vessel had become a 'Spectacle of Horror'.[77] John described the scene in detail: 'nothing was now to be heard aboard our Ship but the Cries of distressed children, and of their distressed Mothers, unable to relieve them'.[78] The crew and passengers had no water and were unable to consume their dried food lest it led to further dehydration. 'Never a Day passed', John told his father, 'without one or two of our Crew put over board; many kill'd themselves by drinking Salt Water; and their own Urine was a common Drink'.[79] In all sixty-four of the crew perished before the ship finally anchored at the Delaware port of Newcastle on 4 September.[80] The publication of the letter was meant either to dissuade people from going or to educate those whose minds were set about the dangers that they might expect to face on the Atlantic passage.

The Seven Years War in America was itself an engine for Irish migration, as many soldiers and personnel attached to regiments sent to the colonies from the Irish establishment never returned. The military manpower siphoned from Ireland to fight the French in North America was immense. Of the fourteen regiments stationed in Ireland a total of nine were sent to America between February 1756 and spring 1757.[81] To make up for this loss two battalions were raised in Ulster, requiring a shift in official attitudes regarding the arming of dissenters.[82] The conflict saw perhaps as many as one in every nine or ten men of military age (16 and 50 years of age) in the British Isles serve in the British Army.[83] Computing the number of Irishmen, let alone Ulster Presbyterians, within this tally is difficult. Though technically barred from enlistment in the Irish establishment before 1780, there is clear evidence to suggest that Ulster Presbyterians served in the British army at a much earlier date. In the late 1750s the need for soldiers was such that the law was blatantly ignored by recruiting parties who received orders to 'inlist none but such as are certified by a minister of the church of Ireland, or by a protestant dissenting minister'.[84]

Officially, Irish recruits were not permitted into British infantry units on the island. Instead, officers were forced to send recruiting parties to Britain in order to augment Irish regiments. The reasons for this were obvious. Local recruitment meant the depletion of the Protestant interest on the island through death and transportation. Also, it opened up the possibility that Catholics, masquerading as Protestants, might find their way into the Irish regiments and gain access to arms and training. The fear of Protestant recruitment was especially strong in Ulster in the wake of the waves of migration to the colonies that began in the 1720s. Officers were expected to maintain regimental quotas of active men. Orders for embarkation to foreign countries were commonly met by widespread desertion. To maintain their quotas, officers either had to draft soldiers from other regiments or turn a blind eye towards local recruitment. As such, large numbers of Catholics and Irish Protestants found their way into British regiments going to America in the mid-1750s. In 1755 one British regiment recently arrived from Canada was said to be composed entirely of 'convicts and Irish Papists'.[85]

The ban against local recruitment was suspended at moments of international tension, particularly during the War of Austrian Succession (1740–8) and the Scottish Jacobite rising in 1745. The global strains put on the British military by the Seven Years War, and the necessity to employ Irish regiments elsewhere, again forced a change in Irish recruitment policies. The need to reinforce the local militia in the light of the possibility of French invasion and Catholic rising was a perpetual concern for government throughout the century. Between 1735 and 1756 they expended over £90,000 on arms for that purpose.[86] Locals, however, viewed these guns as personal property rather than belonging to their landlord or the militia. When the militia officers of County Antrim, wary of a possible French invasion, surveyed the stores of arms at their disposal in 1756 they discovered that one in ten weapons issued by the militia had been 'carried out of the kingdom' by men emigrating to America.[87]

In 1755 Protestant Dissenters were officially allowed to hold commissions in the local militia for the first time.[88] A year later, the Chief Secretary Henry Conway devised a plan to augment Irish regiments with 4,800 additional men through local Protestant recruitment.[89] The commanding officer was to ensure that a local clergyman and justice of the peace swore by each recruit's religion so as to restrict Catholics from enlisting. Recruitment parties were soon after sent to Ulster. At first their efforts bore little fruit, particularly as Presbyterians and Anglicans alike were already organizing themselves into volunteer corps in anticipation of an invasion or rising. In 1759 the Duke of Bedford suggested that recruitment parties publicize the threat of French invasion to encourage Protestants to enlist.[90] The regimental returns ordered by the British Commander and Chief in America, Major-General Lord Loudoun, in the summer of 1757, reveal that only 30 per cent of his force then serving in America were 'English' recruits, while more than 50 per cent were identified to be either Irish or Scottish.[91] To a large extent, the high number of Irishmen serving in the army can be accounted for by the fact that many of these men had served in Ireland in the years prior to the American campaigns but had in fact been raised in England. Still, a large percentage of units with regional ties to Ireland, such as the 27th Inniskilling Regiment of Foot, were made up of soldiers born in the country.[92] Thus, many of the units that arrived in America before the relaxing of Irish recruitment policy in 1758 contained a high proportion of Irish-born soldiers.

The ships that transported Irish regiments from Cork to America from 1754 to 1757 contained not only soldiers. British regiments required their own armies of civilians, including women, for their support. Soldiers' wives, for example, crossed the Atlantic with their husbands despite government discouragement from so doing.[93] Henry Joy thought government refusal to allow women and children to accompany the forces departing Cork in 1757 was a mistake. He reminded the readers of his paper that an 'embarkation to America ought to be considered as a very different thing from one to Flanders'.[94] If the government provided ships to take soldiers' families

> it might answer several valuable purposes, as the married men would go off more cheerfully by having their families provided for in a

plentiful country; and the colonies would gain a greater number of inhabitants, than they possibly could do, by having only men sent over, which would be of great advantage to them as they want hands, and have lands enough to maintain more inhabitants than these islands can send them for an hundred years to come.[95]

Joy's comments indicate that Protestant migration at mid-century, at least in some circles, was not seen as the threat that it had previously been. Indeed, it might be something to encourage rather than condone.

Other civilians apart from soldiers' families saw economic opportunity in the British operations in America. John Moore and his sister, whose journey from Larne to New York opened this book, left Ireland to earn money in the supply industries upon which the British military relied. Many of those soldiers who survived the war never returned to Ireland. Thomas Busby, who enlisted in the Inniskilling regiment shortly before it disembarked from Cork, stayed in Quebec as an innkeeper along with several other Irishmen after the regiment sailed for Ireland in 1767.[96] A Royal Proclamation in 1763 inviting disbanded soldiers to apply for cheap grants on fifty acres of land in America enticed many soldiers away from the prospect of returning to Europe.[97]

By the 1750s Irish migration to the British North American colonies underpinned the province's greater integration into the first British Empire. Commercial links born of the flaxseed and passenger trades sustained the growth of the linen industry, while simultaneously opening the door for the importation of imperial commodities such as sugar, tobacco and West Indian Rum.[98] The people of Ulster were not only bound to colonials by kinsfolk networks, they were sometimes also bound to them by law in the form of lease agreements. Transatlantic migration was not the novelty it had been in the 1720s. America and the reality of annual migration were now well and truly embedded in the everyday experience and world-view of ordinary Presbyterians.

2

The Press, Associational Culture and Popular Imperialism in Ulster, 1750–64

In August 1759, Hugh Montgomery, an officer enlisted in the British regiments deployed on the continent, wrote to his mother Catherine at their family estate in Greyabbey, County Down, from an infantry encampment at Paderborn in the German province of Westphalia. Hugh was the second son of the current Lord of Rosemont House on the largely Presbyterian Ards Peninsula. Montgomery, excited by his experiences on the frontline, gave his mother a dramatic first-hand account of the recent battle of Minden, one of the pinnacle engagements in Britain's *annus mirabilis* – or year of miracles. He told her of how he narrowly escaped death twice during the engagement. First, when a cannon ball tore through the rank of soldiers immediately in front of him, killing a few men from his regiment but miraculously leaving him unscathed, and then again when a French musket ball grazed his collarbone. He concluded the letter by stating that he regretted that he was unable to inform her of any substantial intelligence involving the overall state of the campaign, instead assuring her that 'Francis Joy', the founding editor of the *Belfast News-Letter*, 'will give you a better account, than I can at present'.[1] This brief statement – to a no doubt concerned mother – reveals several points about the place of the regional press in Ulster society during the Seven Years War. First, it indicates that the provincial broadsheet, a relatively new development in eighteenth-century Ireland, only really established in the previous generation, had by this time become a respected and legitimate source of news in the north of the island. Secondly, Montgomery's letter demonstrated public trust in the newspaper editor, in this case mistakenly identified as Francis Joy (ownership of the business had by this time passed to his two sons Henry and Robert), and his ability to cobble together a reliable product out of information gleaned from a dependable network of informants and sources.[2] Indeed, Montgomery assumed that the editor was better able to supply his mother with detailed information about the campaign in which he was an active participant than he could.

The *News-Letter* was more than simply a repository for foreign intelligence and local gossip, and its editors were not mere collectors of news later regurgitated to the reading public.[3] The paper was an agent of change; an instrument that, in the hands of its capable editors, actively moulded and transformed public opinion. John Caldwell claimed later in the century that he had 'often heard of the electrical effect of the first newspaper' founded in Belfast in 1737.[4] He stated that the paper had shaped the political consciousness of northern Presbyterians, encouraging them to participate in the reform movements that dominated national politics from the late 1770s onward. 'It raised the curiosity of the people', he recalled, and 'set them reading and from reading to thinking and from thinking to acting.'[5]

By the mid-eighteenth century, news journals had transformed Irish cultural life by enabling the quick and coherent spread of information across distance. The influence of these journals was felt well beyond the august surroundings of Rosemont House. It penetrated the lives of men and women of all backgrounds, merchants, weavers and tenant farmers alike.[6] This chapter evaluates how Irish newspapers propagated a greater awareness of the British Atlantic Empire during the Seven Years War. The war for North America sparked hitherto unprecedented levels of attention to colonial affairs within Ireland. This was due, in part, to the development of print networks and provincial newspapers across the kingdom. These networks bred a sense of imperial interconnectedness and collective destiny across the country that was sustained and strengthened throughout the lows and subsequent highs of the Seven Years War. While acknowledging the newspaper reader's active engagement with the text and its production, this chapter focuses on the role of the Irish press as an active agent in the formation of imperial consciousness in mid-eighteenth-century Ulster.

The press and Ulster Presbyterian imperial consciousness

Throughout the 1750s and 1760s the act of discussing the empire, in print or in conversation, allowed for the emergence of a British imperial identity among Ulster Presbyterians. In Ireland, as in Britain, the war sparked tremendous public interest in North American affairs. One in five books about American topics published in Britain between 1640 and 1760 were printed in the 1750s.[7] In Ireland printers throughout the country churned out cheap editions of London pamphlets on colonial issues. A reader took the time to write to Dublin printer George Faulkner expressing his approval of the Dublin edition of Ellis Huske's 1755 pamphlet, *The Present State of North America*. Printers, the reader declared, should publish more pamphlets of this sort, 'as all Informations relating to his Majesty's Colonies at this Time of the perfidious Encroachments of the French, are in the highest Degree interesting'.[8] In Ulster, widespread newspaper coverage of the war in America facilitated greater awareness of Britain's colonies among a community already heavily invested in colonial trade and accustomed to transatlantic migration. This press coverage did more than promote general awareness about the Atlantic world among Presbyterians. It forced them to weigh-up the costs and benefits of the emerging imperial system. But, perhaps most significantly, the press propagated the idea that Irish men and women were members of an imperial polity that included their fellow subjects across the Irish Sea and the Atlantic Ocean.

By the 1750s there could be no doubt that Ulster had become integrated into an expanding Atlantic economy. The linen industry was increasingly reliant on imported Pennsylvanian flaxseed, while Irish imports to America rose by 6 per cent in the years between 1756 and 1776.[9] Imperial luxury commodities such as tea, coffee, and sugar trickled into the northern countryside and had, by the late 1750s, become thoroughly imbedded in the day-to-day routine of many throughout the province – especially in the northeast. Arthur Young, for example, listed the communities who drank tea with sugar, in his tour of the province in the 1770s.[10] By the 1750s Ulster imported nearly all of the buckskin used in the manufacture of fashionable men's breeches from North America. By the end of the century the *News-Letter* printed notices of incoming cargoes of American buckskin as often as three times a month.[11] But it was press coverage and editorial commentary during the Seven Years War that really propagated the idea that Irish Protestants were members of a much larger community of 'free-born' British subjects within the extended polity of the Atlantic Empire.[12] Indeed, Ulster Presbyterians may have first articulated their sense of being 'British' amidst the patriotic fervour generated by the imperial victories of the 1750s and early 1760s.[13] The language of an inclusive British imperial patriotism (shared Protestantism, commercial and personal liberty, anti-Gallicism) certainly permeated Presbyterian political discourse in the north from 1760 onward.

Irish newspaper readers' thirst and enthusiasm for imperial news can be inferred from high wartime circulation rates, indicated by the increased space allocated to foreign news at the expense of local adver-tising.[14] More concretely, letters to the editor on American topics as well as reports describing public celebrations of British victories proved that the public enthusiastically absorbed imperial news. The Irish press illuminated the world beyond their readers' island and helped them comprehend the complexity and geographical immensity of the global conflict in which their country was immersed. Troy Bickham noted that the War of American Independence interrupted Britons' 'daily routines through the press, making the war-ravaged New York frontier seem closer at times than the next county'.[15] Press coverage of the Seven Years War in North America had a similar effect on Irish audiences, though, I would argue, it had particular resonance within one community. The annual migration of Ulster Presbyterians to those now bleeding frontiers had become an established, and rather mundane, reality over the previ-ous thirty years. It was, by the 1750s, as much a part of life in the north as the seasonal harvest. In this regard, the luxuries of blasé detachment and the safety of distance enjoyed by most British readers were not shared by their Irish Presbyterian counterparts. American news in Irish newspapers reinforced this sense of kinship between Presbyterians and colonials. At a more basic level, newspapers and other printed texts contained precise information that was difficult to find elsewhere. Some of this information, such as that contained visually in supplementary maps, was nearly impossible to transmit by word of mouth.

The proximity of geographically diverse and topically unrelated sto-ries on the pages of newspapers suggested commonality between them. This allowed readers to categorize individual events within larger narra-tive frameworks constructed overtime such as international war or provi-dential judgement. The formation of these narratives largely depended upon the structure of the newspaper medium itself, in the sense that the format of the paper dictated where stories were placed in relation to one another. The front pages of eighteenth-century newspapers were littered with seemingly random stories related only, in the words of Benedict Anderson, by the 'calendrical coincidence' of their occurrence.[16]

Sometimes, however, editors hoped that their arrangement would lead their audience to interpret events in a particular way. On 13 February 1760 Henry Joy printed a timeline of the decisive events in Britain's current war with France.[17] The timeline, which stretched back more than a decade and extended over three continents, condensed the mammoth conflict into a comprehensible format. It began in 1748 with the signing of the treaty between Britain and France at Aix la Chapelle, progressed through the 1750s and culminated with the events of 'the glorious 1759'. Readers could chart the progress of the conflict from its disastrous beginnings in the woods of North America through to Britain's current, though not yet unchallenged, position as the dominant power in the world. General Braddock's defeat in 1754 was situated a few lines above a brief segment about the black hole of Calcutta, while the fall of Quebec lay next to the Prussian victory over the Austrians at Maxen earlier in the year. By imposing a framework through which his readers could understand the events that his paper had covered over the course of the previous two decades, Joy provided them with a sense of their island's role within a larger, though seemingly shrinking, world. Joy's timeline represented his attempt to impose a unifying narrative over the stories previously printed in his paper. It suggested continuity between stories over time and asked the reader to compartmentalize events – present, past, and future – from a similar prospective.

Long-term examination of a particular paper's print run reveals the interconnectedness of its content, allowing larger narratives to be constructed.[18] The arrangement of events on the front pages of provincial newspapers poses unique questions about the construction of regional, national and imperial identity in eighteenth-century Britain and Ireland. Kathleen Wilson rightly posited the questions: whose community was represented in provincial and colonial (as opposed to metropolitan) papers; and who was 'imagining' that particular community's existence in the first place?[19] Applying these questions to regional Irish papers highlights added complications. The majority of the population was indifferent, or outright hostile, to the 'national' culture celebrated in the press. Furthermore, regional editors were suspended within the orbit of two metropoles – Dublin and London. By publishing material from their counterparts in both cities, regional editors disseminated hazy and disjointed messages regarding the boundaries of their readers' national community.

Yet Dublin, like all cities and towns in the empire, could not escape from the cultural orbit and political influence of London. Irish papers were all built upon a common foundation: they were utterly reliant on news from the imperial capital to fill their front pages.[20] It was common practice for provincial editors to lift stories verbatim from their London counterparts. Such editorial pilfering ensured an underlying uniformity of subject matter included in papers across the British Empire. This common language strung the Anglophone empire together, ensuring that people in Belfast, Philadelphia and Edinburgh were largely on the same page – as it were – regarding world events. This is not to discount the local flavour of the provincial press but rather to suggest that print regionalism should be understood within the context of contemporary editorial practice. While the news pages of any given paper were international in character – albeit with local stories scattered throughout – the advertisements sections were windows into the material, cultural and economic world of the immediate area. Editors in larger towns, especially ports such as Belfast, had a range of stories from an array of locations to print or exclude. The editor's selections were chosen to appeal to his local readership. Inevitably, however, his choices further embedded the region within the fabric of the wider British world through a shared vocabulary of stories.

The *Belfast News-Letter* and the provincial press in the north in the mid-eighteenth century

In 1750 Belfast's population was half that of Ireland's main Atlantic port, Cork. Yet, despite its small size, Belfast commanded disproportionate commercial and cultural influence given its strategic location at the heart of the highly literate linen country of the northeast. The town also boasted one of the two successful provincial papers that appeared in the first half of the eighteenth century, the *Belfast News-Letter*.[21] The paper was founded in 1737 by local Presbyterian Francis Joy and is the oldest continuously printed newspaper in Britain and Ireland. It emerged in the 1730s, a relatively prosperous inter-famine period in which demand for foreign news was high because of the possibility of Britain being dragged into the War of Polish Succession (1733–8).[22] The reasons for the *News-Letter*'s existence and enduring success boil down to its location and readership. The dissenter-dominated counties of the northeast were, like Dublin, an area of the country in which the preconditions for a viable, self-sustaining print industry existed. The population was largely English-speaking and Protestant and was therefore more receptive to the proliferation of print emanating from London. Also, literacy in Belfast and its hinterland was high as a result of the Presbyterian emphasis on education – particularly religious instruction.[23]

The *News-Letter* maintained stable circulation rates throughout the middle decades of the century. Although rare, data regarding newspaper circulation in the period does exist. Surviving information indicates that circulation revenues increased dramatically during times of war or international turmoil. The accounts ledger of London's *Daily Advertiser*, for example, shows that between 1765 and 1771 – when the Atlantic imperial crisis was intensifying – revenue from sales increased by nearly 50 per cent, while advertising revenue from the same six-year period only went up by roughly 33 per cent.[24] Irish papers were no exception. In 1794 Henry Joy placed an advertisement in the *Belfast News-Letter* for the sale of the paper that included circulation details for the previous five years. It revealed that by January 1789 the average print-run per issue exceed 2,100.[25] Joy's advert revealed that a spike in production occurred in 1793, the year France declared war on Great Britain. Similarly, stamp tax revenues from 1784 indicate that a drop in circulation of 14 per cent in Dublin and 27 per cent in the provinces occurred on the previous year's returns.[26] The year 1783 marked the Treaty of Paris between France, Britain, and the United States, which ended the war for American Independence.[27] Irish editors certainly profited from public interest in the Seven Years War as well. Between September 1758 and September 1760, for example, Dublin printer William Sleater printed three volumes of war news gleaned from assorted pamphlets and London journals.[28]

The lack of source material makes establishing circulation numbers for mid-eighteenth-century Irish newspapers difficult, though we can use information from later in the century to infer the size of earlier print runs. The *News-Letter* enjoyed consistent success during the first fifty years of its existence without the benefit of any substantial technological developments to the industry or advancements in distribution.[29] Relying on Stamp Tax returns, Robert Munter approximated that most Irish newspapers sold between 400 and 800 copies per issue before 1760, with the largest papers selling as many as 1,800 or 2,000 from the late 1720s.[30] The *News-Letter* was a middle-sized newspaper whose average print run probably fell between Munter's two ranges. It is therefore probable, based upon the information in Joy's 1794 advertisement and the aforementioned stamp tax figures, that the paper enjoyed perhaps the largest circulation of any newspaper outside Dublin: about 1,000 to 1,500 per issue. This print run almost certainly exceeded these numbers during the war years 1756–63.[31]

The *News-Letter* differed from the Dublin papers in subtle, but ultimately quite substantial, ways. The paper emerged from a different social and cultural environment than the southern journals. The town of Belfast was an emerging regional commercial centre in the 1750s and 1760s thanks to its position as one of the main centres in the lucrative Irish linen trade.[32] The linen industry was fed by regular imports of American flaxseed. This seed was then spun into thread and woven into linen cloth that was in turn sold in colonial, British and European markets. By mid-century, Belfast had become one of the premier northern ports, along with Newry and Derry, servicing Irish trade with the North

American colonies. Also, Presbyterians, a group that constituted a large percentage of the *News-Letter*'s readership predominated in both the city and its surrounding areas.

With the city's prime location on the British Atlantic trade routes came direct access to news from the North American colonies. This information made its way into the *News-Letter*, and from there was often picked-up by the Dublin papers.[33] Often the paper's American intelligence was gleaned from local correspondence with American merchants or Irish emigrants. The commercial networks that produced this correspondence were often the product of confessional business relationships underpinned by shared cultural values.[34] Trust between partners in the potentially lucrative, but risky, world of Atlantic commerce depended upon such trust as a form of credit, often in the absence of hard currency. The partnership between Belfast merchant Thomas Greg and New York Presbyterian Waddell Cunningham, formed in the late 1750s, was one example of this type of venture.[35] Aside from this correspondence, the *News-Letter* was the leading repository of breaking colonial news because mid-Atlantic North American shipping often made Irish landfall in Ulster ports. This was especially true between the months of November and February, when the American flaxseed fleet was anchored in the major ports along the northeast coast.

The commercial, outward-looking, character of Belfast manifested in the back pages of its newspaper in numerous ways. First, and perhaps most obviously, the advertisement pages reflected the character of the town's trades, namely, the production of linen, which so dominated the cottage industry of its hinterlands. The postings for cultural events and goods, so common in the Dublin papers during the social season, were less frequently included in the *News-Letter*.[36] Instead, announcements from the town's linen board and regional market associations abounded along with advertisements regarding the sale of flaxseed, linen cloth, bleaching implements and other tools of the trade.[37] Secondly, the advertisement section of the paper often revealed the degree to which the economy of Belfast was tied to Atlantic trade. The newspaper was an important tool for both those wishing to take advantage of, and discourage, the Irish Presbyterian propensity towards emigration. Shipmasters frequently used the journal to solicit passengers for outward voyages to New York, Charleston and the Delaware ports. American employers searching for skilled indentured servants also bought advertisement space from the Joys. The Presbyterian emigration craze that began immediately after the war ended in 1763 and climaxed in the early 1770s sent shivers through the Protestant establishment across the island. The *News-Letter*, hitherto one of the main organs through which the passenger trade was popularized, became a vehicle for those who wished to discourage it to air their concerns. On 13 May 1763 the paper published a letter from a recent emigrant named John Smilie describing the horrors of the Atlantic passage aboard the *Sally*, including poor treatment by the ship's captain and extreme shortages of food. In the preface to the letter Smilie committed the information to the editor begging that he 'may communicate it to the World, for the Good of Mankind, thro' the Channel of [his] very useful News-Letter'.[38] His account, he assured readers, was genuine but not unique. If they wished to find further evidence for mistreatment they need not look hard, for 'There are many Letters in the Country, from others, to the same purpose.'[39]

The reality of Presbyterian migration was impossible to miss in nearly every edition of the *News-Letter* from the 1750s and 1760s. The back pages were littered with eye-catching images of ships situated above advertisements calling for passengers to fill the hulls of outgoing vessels for the British colonies. Often these advertisements were published in the same editions as were stories of murder on the frontier. On 14 August 1764 five images of ships appeared in the back pages of the journal while the front pages were soaked in the blood of murdered settlers. These images, along with two of the four accounts of colonial atrocity are reproduced in Appendix 1. The numbers of ships advertised in this issue, although visually impressive, do not match the numbers published in the early 1770s when migration was at its peak. Vincent Morley has counted no fewer than sixteen advertisements in a single edition of the paper from that decade.[40] Even if readers were not emigrating themselves, the images of ships that punctuated the last two pages of the paper reminded them of the kinship and mercantile links between Ulster and the colonies and that many of their countrymen and women *were* risking the voyage despite the horrors that might befall them.

To claim that the *News-Letter* simply reflected the needs and opinions of the Belfast merchant community would be to underestimate the significant influence and circulation of the paper in other towns throughout the north. The lack of another regional newspaper before the emergence of the *Londonderry Journal* in 1772 meant that the *News-Letter* was the primary venue for local advertising in the region.[41] Its back pages demonstrate the geographic breadth of the paper's influence. One page of the advertising section of the paper in April 1756, for example, contained four advertisements for leases in counties Donegal, Down and Antrim; a declaration on behalf of a suspected criminal from

County Tyrone stating that he intended to turn himself in to the assizes in Derry; and an announcement regarding a meeting of the Patriot Club of Armagh.[42] The paper also held a near complete monopoly over the coverage of local news throughout the province, so much so that the Dublin papers seemed to rely on it for news from the north. This was especially true during periods when the eyes of the entire kingdom were centred on Ulster, such as during the Hearts of Oak disturbances in 1763 and Thurot's landing at Carrickfergus in January 1760. These factors show that the paper had extraordinary influence both over how regionalism was constructed in the north and how a wider national audience viewed the province.

The Joy brothers and their newspaper were very much a product of the cultural world of Belfast. The *News-Letter* became a sounding board for the General Synod and other Presbyterian groups who used it to announce their activities and resolutions. At the height of the 1740–1 famine, details of a Presbyterian alms-gathering mission organized in Belfast by 'the reverend ministers of the four congregations' was printed in the *News-Letter*.[43] In 1761, the paper published an address from the Presbyterian Ministers of the Northern Association to the new king, George III, expressing their hopes that he would maintain religious toleration and freedom of conscience for his Dissenting subjects.[44] Earlier in the year the Joys also inserted in the paper the full memorial presented to the General Synod on behalf of the Corporation for the Relief of the Poor Distressed Ministers in America in the hopes that such a move would encourage people to contribute to the subsequent Sabbath collection in Presbyterian meetinghouses for American frontier refugees.[45] Yet another example of the paper's underlying Presbyterian character can be found in a letter written by 'Irenicus' published in January 1764 with the expressed purpose of exculpating the Seceders of the north from charges of disloyalty.[46] These moves publicized a Dissenting agenda and, perhaps misleadingly, portrayed a relatively cohesive Presbyterian community, both at home and abroad, despite the many divisions that existed within the denomination.

Outsiders readily acknowledged the paper's Presbyterian character and reformist agenda, as well as the looming presence of America within its news and advertising sections. Owing in large part to the seventeenth-century Puritan migrations to New England, the North American colonies were seen as hotbeds of religious and political radicalism.[47] The reality that migration and trade had produced a sympathetic community in the north susceptible to American radicalism was obviously a concern among Irish conservatives and moderates from the mid-1760s onwards. James Hoey published a poem regarding Joy's partiality on American affairs in his *Dublin Mercury* on the 26 September 1775:

> The puritan-Journal, impress'd at Belfast,
> Exhibits the printer's complexion and cast;
> Whose partial accounts of each public transaction
> Proclaim him *the infamous tool of a faction.*
> ...
> But [Joy], the low scribe of a party quite frantic,
> With zeal for their Brethren beyond the Atlantic,
> Discreetly and piously chuses to tell
> No tidings, but such as come *posting from hell.*[48]

Joy was clearly amused by this poem as he chose to include it in his history of Belfast, which was comprised largely of clippings from the *News-Letter* and was entitled *Historical Collections Relative to the Town of Belfast.* It was placed within a lengthy section regarding the emigration scares of the early 1770s and near a selection of Patriot toasts originally published in the *News-Letter* in 1768, including one to 'The American Colonies, and may the Descendants of those who fled from Tyranny in one Country, never be forced to submit to its galling Yoke in another.'[49]

The *News-Letter* both reflected and propagated the economic and political outlook of northern Presbyterians and the mercantile interests of Belfast. The paper, by virtue of its wide-ranging circulation and readership, collapsed cultural and spatial distance within the province, all the while propagating a regionally particular variant of 'Britishness'. Crucially, the Joys's operation was based in the town of Belfast, a port heavily involved in trade with Britain and its mid-Atlantic North American colonies. The Joys collected foreign information as it flowed off the quays and out of the taverns and coffee houses that lined the town's entries. Often the information they gathered had ricocheted from port to port across the north Atlantic basin before it eventually passed into their hands. They discovered, for example, that an attack on Quebec was imminent in the autumn of 1759 from an 'Extract of a letter from New-York to a Gentleman in London, sent by a vessel to Bristol, where a Copy was taken and transmitted to a merchant in Belfast'.[50] Conversations with shipmasters docked in Belfast Lough also provided the Joys with much news from Philadelphia and other American ports.[51] The *News-Letter* plugged Ulster into the circuits of information that bound together the wider British Atlantic world.

Absorbing war news in eighteenth-century Ireland

The act of reading a newspaper, or any other printed work for that matter, in the eighteenth century was not necessarily the solitary experience that it would later become in the nineteenth and twentieth centuries. Nor was the information contained in them only absorbed by the literate. Cultural historians have warned against modern assumptions about the practice of reading anachronistically upon past peoples and cultures.[52] Orality – or, as John Feather has put it, 'the ability to absorb large amounts of information by *listening* once rather than by reading perhaps many times – actually extended the power and influence of the printed word' in the eighteenth century.[53] It was common for printed material to be read aloud at social gatherings: in clubs, while at work on the loom, or at the local coffee or alehouse. In a general introduction to a collection of essays on the act of reading in early modern Europe, Roger Chartier stated that the act of public reading 'invested the handling of the chapbook, the tract, the broadsheet, or the image with values and intentions that had little to do with those of solitary book reading'.[54] It was 'collective and postulated decipherment' in which groups of people jointly assigned meaning to the symbols on the page – whether they were written sentences or pictorial representations such as maps. Crucially, public readings and discussion gave newspapers a much larger audience than subscription rates would suggest. It also allowed for the wider circulation of news among the illiterate.

Not only were broadsheets and newspapers read aloud in public, they were dissected in lengthy discussions. The public consumption of news in eighteenth-century Ireland was often accompanied by the ingestion of coffee or alcoholic beverages in the convivial surroundings of the tavern or coffee house. Coffee houses spread to Ireland in the late seventeenth century, first to Dublin, and then to provincial centres across the country. By the 1750s they were a common feature in the Irish urban landscape.[55] While originally the reserve of the elite, by the middle of the eighteenth century the coffee house had become a place where men of all backgrounds could come to read the news journals and engage in conversation. This was partly owing to the fact that tea and coffee were relatively inexpensive commodities. Coffee house owners also subscribed to newspapers, pamphlets and other printed works in order to attract customers. Lengthy discussion and casual perusal of pamphlets and the latest journals could therefore be enjoyed at little cost to the customer.

There was no shortage of places in the north where people could congregate and read the papers.[56] Ale and coffee houses abounded throughout the country, especially in market towns and ports. In Belfast alone there were multiple such venues. In terms of alehouses, the George Inn on the Old Rope Walk became a favourite of the improvement-minded middling sorts, while the New Inn and Donegall Arms seemingly attracted a diverse clientele.[57] Those looking for coffee and tea could turn to Dunn's Coffee House, a place frequently advertised in the *News-Letter*.[58] Local establishments such as these paid an annual subscription rate of 4s 4d to stock the *News-Letter* (the paper sold for one penny an issue in the 1740s). In Derry, political debates inspired by newspapers raged in local coffee houses in the early 1770s, though coffee house culture surely existed in the city long before then.[59] As was the case in Belfast, customers in Derry and Newry had access to the regional paper. The Joys charged higher rates to subscribers outside Belfast, starting from 6s 6d in neighbouring towns and rising to as much as 7s 7d in Coleraine and Ballymoney.[60] Likewise, Dublin papers were more expensive in the provinces. A Belfast proprietor, for example, would have paid two crowns per year to carry *Faulkner's Dublin Journal*.[61]

Despite the *News-Letter*'s status as the only paper published in the north, it was certainly not the only paper available throughout the province. British, American and Dublin papers were also crucial to the development of the Irish Presbyterian world-view for a number of reasons. First, they provided the Joy Brothers and other provincial editors with much of the subject matter later reprinted in their papers. Second, foreign and Dublin papers, while less common in the north than the *News-Letter*, were available in ports and market-towns throughout the region. This was certainly true of the Dublin broadsheets. Across Ulster, coffee and alehouses stocked southern papers along with others from London and, occasionally, provincial English and Scottish titles. Urban Presbyterians, as well as those occasionally drawn to towns and markets, had ready public access to papers printed outside their province.

American geography in Irish newspaper supplements

The eye-catching images of ships that littered the back pages of Irish newspapers remind us that the printed word was not the only means by which the press cultivated public awareness of the empire beyond their shores. There was a visual element to mid-eighteenth-century papers that impressed information on the minds of readers. Printed maps were perhaps the most obvious media by which American topics found visual expression in the press. The widespread and regular inclusion of maps in British periodicals was a new phenomenon, and it was only from the late 1740s that maps became a regular feature in popular monthlies such as the *Gentleman's* and *London* magazines. The technology and resources were in place for the dissemination of cheap maps in newspapers and journals at the moment violence erupted between British colonial and French troops on the American frontier in 1754. Throughout the ensuing global conflict the British and Irish public had recourse to cheap printed maps as never before. The impact of these maps and other geographical texts on the spatial awareness of people in Britain and Ireland, as well as how they thought about their empire, was nothing short of revolutionary.

The capital was the only city in Ireland where printers possessed the resources to reproduce high-quality maps within the actual pages of a newspaper. Population density and the presence of an affluent middling and aristocratic readership ensured high circulation and subscription rates and made such a costly endeavour – involving the casting of individual date-specific plates – financially feasible. These maps should be placed within the larger context of Irish printed material devoted to describing American subjects in mid-eighteenth-century Dublin. In 1756, for example, the printer John Exshaw published an extraordinary – and expensive – map of the northern colonies along with the pamphlet, *A Description of the English and French Territories in North America*. Depending on how much they were willing to pay, customers could choose between three editions of the print. Exshaw sold the cheapest 'plain' edition for £1 0s 4d and the most expensive individually coloured version for £2 0s 2d.[62] The pamphlet was designed to explain the current war and, Exshaw promised, showed 'all the Encoachments of the French, with their Forts and Usurpations on the English Settlements'.[63]

Dublin editors printed map supplements on the front pages of their papers. The most notable surviving examples of front-page maps are found in *Faulkner's Dublin Journal*, where four such images were printed during the height of the conflict in Canada from 1755 to 1759.[64] It is significant that these four represent the entirety of such maps printed in the paper from 1754 to 1765. Indeed, the public's keen interest in North American news can be inferred by the fact that all the maps printed in the *Dublin Journal* in this period were of the northern British colonies and French Canada.[65] The paper published no maps of the European or Asian theatres of the conflict. The latter's absence is particularly striking given the public's greater unfamiliarity with the geography and culture of the Indian subcontinent. It seems to suggest the editor's preoccupation, perhaps shared by his readers, with the Atlantic rather than the Asiatic dimensions of the conflict.

For a brief period from 1755 to 1763, before the reality of paying for the upkeep of Britain's international military commitments had time to sink in, Irish Protestants were enthralled with the idea of empire. This popular imperialism spurred a desire to learn about the geography of British overseas possessions. At the very least, international conflict familiarizes the civilian population of the country conducting foreign campaigns with the place names and a general, often misrepresentative and reductionist, picture of the cultures living within the war zone. Maps, in the hands of the state, were also active tools of imperialism, quantifying resources, delineating sovereign boundaries and defining land ownership.[66] Maps were only one segment of a growing corpus of geographical texts including histories, travelogues and textbooks that legitimized and popularized Britain's overseas expansion. Literary scholar Martin Brückner argues that the 'geographic revolution' of the seventeenth and eighteenth centuries influenced literary education in North America and that this, in turn, fostered the emergence of American regional and national identities.[67] A similar process was at work in Ireland. As in Britain, the explosion of printed material during the Seven Years War represented genuine Irish interest regarding their empire intensified by war in America.[68] I say 'their empire' because pride in the British Atlantic system informed Irish Protestant patriotism, or what Eliga Gould and others allude to as their 'Greater British' identity, as much as it did their contemporaries across the Irish Sea.[69] It is certainly the case that greater awareness of the Empire encouraged greater engagement with it, and vice versa. The Empire increasingly infiltrated public consciousness as the British Atlantic system became more economically and politically unified as the century progressed. This awareness, propagated through printed media such as maps, increased the likelihood of Irish economic investment and trade in America, heightened the possibility of emigration to the colonies, and allowed for the formation of broad support for British military expenditure on foreign wars. But, perhaps most significantly, newspaper maps altered the way in which Irish men and women imagined the British Empire and their place within it.

Irish public opinion during the war gloried in the expansion of Britain's empire. Irish Protestants, like their fellow subjects in Britain and America, repeated the defining mantra of the empire; that it was 'Protestant, commercial, maritime and free'.[70] The proliferation of geographical texts about America during the middle decades of the eighteenth century broadened the Irish world-view while simultaneously propagating the patriotic discourse of imperialism. This process transformed ordinary men and women, largely within the Protestant population, into both active and passive supporters of British overseas expansion. They imagined Britain and Ireland inhabiting a privileged place at the centre of the imperial infrastructure. John Pue reported from Dublin in 1761 that the incredible expense of the war had been worth it:

> By a Termination being now put to the War in India and North America, the great Expences consequent in prosecuting it in those remote Parts, will be exchanged for uninterrupted Trade on our Parts, and Depression on that of the Enemy, which will tend to enable us to carry it on with still greater Vigour and Superiority, both at home, as well as among their unconquered Parts in the Western World.[71]

One author writing to the *News-Letter* in 1759 stressed the benefits of further expansion. He declared, 'I wish to call, [North America] *our Continent'* and stated that the seizure of Spanish Florida was necessary to make the colonial enterprise in America 'perfect and invulnerable'.[72] Yet another, writing to Joy under the name 'Brutus' about the prospect of peace in 1760, desired that Britain focus all of its efforts on the cultivation of its Atlantic empire and abandon its European commitments altogether. Now that Britain's 'colonies and commerce' were all but secure, Brutus warned, 'let us learn to take present and past examples of the ruinous tendency of continental connections, and never be the dupes of proud and ambitious courts'.[73]

Long before the fortunes of war had turned in Britain's favour, readers in Dublin and Belfast wrote to newspaper editors in reaction to pamphlets detailing the war in North America. Arguments abounded in the *News-Letter* stressing the commercial importance of the thirteen colonies on the mainland and those of the Caribbean to the mother country and the need to protect them with the full might of the British Army and Royal Navy. In April 1755 the Joys printed a reaction to 'the pernicious, narrow, selfish spirit' of a pamphleteer who claimed that the Americans should have to defend themselves from the threat of France without military aid from Britain. The author computed that the annual export value of American goods amounted to £4,800,000 and that 27,000 seamen were employed in the maintenance of British Atlantic trade.[74] He reminded the Joys's readers that Ireland too benefited from this trade, and that they should ask themselves, 'What an addition is made to the riches and power of this country by our colonies and plantations in America, and what numbers of industrious manufacturers and mechanics of all sorts must be employed and maintained on this island by providing for our people who inhabit that part of the world.'[75] American defence was not solely a commercial necessity, it was also a moral imperative. These people were, after all, fellow British subjects. They were, in the author's own words, 'our people'. Could Irish readers really accept a policy, in good conscience, that would 'leave all our back settlements exposed to the cruel ravages and plunder of the Indians'?[76] 'Surely', he concluded, 'we cannot suppose them able even to defend themselves, against the whole force which the kingdom of France may send thither if we do not prevent it.'[77]

The press was an important vehicle for the creation and consumption of empire in mid-eighteenth-century Ireland.[78] It is likely that newspaper maps not only provided an outlet to satisfy widespread curiosity regarding such exotic locales as Quebec or Iroquoia but also served as a channel for the consumption of empire as an ideological concept. Through geographical supplements in newspapers, Irish readers absorbed the idea that the imperial system that moored their island to these foreign lands was not only mutually beneficial for the constituent regions included within it but also absolutely necessary. They need only to look at the growth of the Irish economy across the century as a result of transatlantic trade in order to recognize the importance of continued imperial investment and advancement.[79] Unlike the majority of crude, re-usable images in the advertisement pages of most contemporary Irish newspapers, the maps contained in the *Dublin Journal* were highly detailed. The four maps printed in the paper were allocated prime positions on the front page immediately below the header and in three cases took up a third of the page. Each showed the location of important sites, invariably described in the news stories located below them, including cities, fortifications, defining landmarks and important natural resources. Three were coded with individual letters on the map corresponding to brief descriptions of the object or place in an adjoining legend. One map published in 1755 included groupings of dotted lines off the coast of Louisbourg and Nova Scotia that signified lucrative cod and herring fisheries.[80] These shoals could be lost to French fishermen in the advent of defeat and opened up to Irish vessels in the case of British victory. Mention of these resources reassured doubtful readers as to why their country was now immersed in an expensive war fought thousands of miles from home. Language contained within these maps also reminded them alongside and against whom they were fighting. A description of Nova Scotia in one map's legend read, 'Nova-Scotia, usurped by the French, who did not suffer us to enjoy any more of it than the Peninsula part'.[81] Use of inclusive words such as 'us' or 'our' alongside these images reaffirmed the bonds that drew together the constituent elements of the British Empire in opposition to an overarching French threat.

First and foremost these images were reference tools to help readers familiarize themselves with the geography of foreign terrain significant to the British war effort. A week after news of Quebec's capitulation brought jubilation to the streets of the capital, Faulkner printed 'A PLAN of *QUEBEC*' featuring the layout of the town and the topography of the terrain surrounding it.[82] The legend contained a list of the city's defences, including individual French batteries, along with the names of prominent landmarks and buildings, such as the Church of Notre Dame de Victoire and 'the Strand' separating the St Laurence and St Charles rivers.[83] As news of the battle trickled in over the ensuing weeks readers could refer to this map in order to more fully reconstruct and comprehend the event. Faulkner also included a brief history of the town leading to 'the 18th of Sept. 1759' when 'it was taken by Admiral Saunders and Gen. Townsend, in a Year remarkable for conquests made by the English'. He also included a brief note about demographics. 'Quebec contains 7 or 8000 inhabitants', he reported, 'and brings a Revenue of 53,000 l. yearly to France.' Like the inclusion of Canadian fisheries in Faulkner's previous map of the Gulf of St. Laurence, this statement put the expense of the conquest into relief by demonstrating the monetary value of the captured city if it were to be fully incorporated into the empire. Material of this kind later informed the robust public debate over the nature of an eventual peace settlement in the early 1760s.[84]

These images do not merely represent the preoccupations of George Faulkner acting out of step with the interests of his clientele. It is clear that he was responding to a wellspring of public interest in the region. In 1755 he printed his first map, 'A most Accurate and Correct MAP of *NORTH AMERICA*, the Seat of present Actions against the *French*', which rendered all of Canada, the Gulf of St Lawrence and northern Massachusetts.[85] The next week Faulkner reinserted the image, claiming that he had been forced to do so, 'At the earnest Requests of many of our Readers', who had also pressed him to include the degrees of north latitude. Faulkner acquiesced to public demand and printed more clearly defined coordinates along the sides of the map. The public's interest in the coordinates of the areas printed in these maps indicates a desire on their part to be place America in their mental geography alongside locations more immediately familiar to them. In June 1758, Faulkner printed a map of the Canadian town of Louisbourg detailing its defences and harbour in advance of the British offensive against it.[86]

Perhaps stating the obvious, Faulkner reminded his readers that the coordinates provided on this occasion were based upon distance relative to London – a fact he inserted in his subsequent maps. When news arrived two months later that the town had indeed fallen, the map was again inserted in the *Journal* so as to reacquaint readers with the layout of the town. Newspaper maps, then, were tools through which active readers could familiarize themselves with, and thus demystify, locations throughout the Atlantic empire.

The *Dublin Journal* also included visual depictions of North American battles. Throughout the war British regiments deployed in Ireland were redirected to frontlines in North America and Europe, leaving the Protestant public both anxious at the prospect of foreign invasion and curious about the location to which their defensive forces had been siphoned off. The first depiction was included in 1755 with the aim of helping readers make sense of the cacophony of information pouring into Ireland following the demoralizing defeat of General Braddock's force during the second offensive against Fort Duquesne. It showed three columns of British and colonial troops facing a force of 2,100 French troops with two bodies of 'French Indians in Ambuscade' on either side of the main British contingent.[87] The image was very crude, depicting the initial layout of the battle with no pictorial or geographic flourishes ('in Ambuscade' hinted at the landscape of the battle, referring to the well-circulated but false news that the British force had been surprised by French-aligned Indians waiting in the surrounding woods). The second diagram, 'A PLAN of the Battle fought ... between the *English* Army under General Johnson, and the *French* under General Count Diskau', published later in the year, was far more complex.[88] Like the larger map supplements, it incorporated geographical features, such as Lake George and the Hudson River, as well as symbols representing French and British forces and their camps. Battle maps embedded British troops within the landscape, planting the notion of the Crown's entitlement to that land in the mind of the viewer.

The expansion of Irish readers' knowledge of North America was further augmented by lengthy descriptions of the geography and natural resources of the continent. This was especially true where lack of money and/or equipment prevented editors from including in their papers maps of the quality enjoyed by the readers of the *Dublin Journal*. Henry Joy printed several geographical descriptions in the *News-Letter* in clusters at the beginning and end of the conflict. These vignettes were mostly positioned between the news and advertisement pages in what gradually became the 'supplements' section of the paper. They also contained other information not found in Faulkner's maps, including notes on the customs and cultures of the peoples of the continent.

The first cluster of supplements consisted of two French accounts of North America published at the beginning of the conflict in late 1754. Together, they highlighted a sudden curiosity in imperial affairs resulting from heightened tensions between French and British interests on the colonial frontier. The first account, entitled 'a *Geographical Description* of Louisiana', was lifted from a memoir of Monsieur le Page du Pratz, an employee of the French West India Company who had resided in the area for seventeen years.[89] It lingered on the area's environment and its natural resources, often with the underlying assertion of their strategic and economic usefulness. Joy concluded du Pratz's observations with a chiding comment, stating that 'when the French have a settlement in the corner of any uncultivated country unpossessed by any nation, they never fail to reckon all that country within the limits of their settlements'. Using this logic, the British had just as much right to claim territory west of the Appalachian Mountains as did the French. 'No nation', he claimed, 'ought to appropriate to itself more land in America than it is first possessed of by actual cultivation and inhabitation.'[90] Joy's solution was to commit French maps to the scrutiny of British cartographers in order to nullify their claims to lands that, by right of occupation, would soon be incorporated into the British Empire through settlement anyway.

The second French account of the continent, entitled '*Reflections* on the English colonies of North America', was printed in December 1754.[91] After a brief discussion of the British colonial resources, the author described the geographical placement of British possessions relative to territory claimed by France. 'Our possessions', he claimed, 'are of a larger extent [and] may be said to form a kind of bow' to which the English colonies 'are the string'.[92] He then exposed a few weaknesses in the British American imperial infrastructure, particularly regarding defence. He noted the independence of each colony's legislature, claiming that 'it is not the authority of the governors, or even the king himself, which without the consent of the assembly of a colony' can provide military aid to other colonies in wartime. The author concluded that the 'military power of a country, where there is such a slender subordination is little to be feared' and that French American military might was 'vastly superior to the English'. This account was printed at a time when British military superiority over the French in America or elsewhere was far from certain. Irish readers were aware that French attempts to militarize the Ohio Valley could result in war, and with war came the attendant possibility of a French invasion of their island. Interest in imperial geography, therefore, partially stemmed from the realization that events in America could very well affect the domestic stability of Ireland.

Reflections did not paint an entirely negative picture of British North America. The author did praise the British on two points. First, citing the example of William Penn, he noted that the 'flourishing settlement of Pennsylvania' was a 'singular instance in what a private person is capable of achieving, when seconded by government'. Ministers, he followed, should not discourage the zeal and talent of such people when their efforts 'may render capable of doing good service to their country'. Secondly, he claimed that the diversity of British America was one of its strengths. The continuing immigration of Palatines to the middle colonies, for example, 'cost the English but few men' but increased the strength and wealth of their settlements. 'This encouragement to foreigners of all kinds to resort to its colonies', he wrote, 'is a wisdom in the government of England, which can not be too much commended, being an acquisition of an additional wealth, power, and subjects.'[93]

The second cluster of geographical supplements were printed between 1762 and 1765, after the myth of French Canada's invincible martial culture had been demolished by the conquest of Quebec. These accounts interspersed discussions of the customs of the peoples of North America alongside descriptions of its geography and resources. They, like Faulkner's maps, were tools through which readers could better comprehend the peoples and places now under British rule and how their country might benefit from the new imperial order. The longest American supplement published in the *News-Letter* in the aftermath of the war, a selection taken from Major Robert Rogers's *A concise Account of North America*, was printed over the course of several issues in December 1765.[94] It contained descriptions of the customs of the Native Peoples of the Great Lakes region. Like the information found in the legends of Faulkner's maps, each of Rogers's descriptions reads like an inventory or census – informing the reader of the usefulness of, or threat posed by, the individual groups of Indians in the vicinity of British-controlled territory. Nearly all of his descriptions of the Indians bordering the Great Lakes were followed by a tally of the number of warriors each group could furnish in the event of war and the degree to which they traded with the English or French. For example, Rogers informed his readers that the Attawabas could 'raise about 12,000 fighting men' and had 'considerable commerce with the French'. This information was accompanied by notes on their seasonal migration and detailed accounts of their homes and communities:

> They live in houses or huts that are built in the form of cones; the base is generally from sixteen to twenty feet wide, containing commonly ten or twelve persons; the top of the cone is left open for about two feet, which aperture serves them both for a chimney and a window, their fire being kindled in the centre.[95]

Such descriptions showed readers a different picture of American Indian culture than that provided to them over the previous decade of bloody conflict on the frontier. Here was a domestic portrait of Attawaba life meticulously documented and mediated through the eyes of a British officer. These descriptions demystified Indians to a European audience and, simultaneously, quantified the degree to which they remained a threat to British interests.

One Canadian supplement published in 1762 reminded readers that Ireland was attached to America by a web of communication left dangling across the ocean by thousands of departed Ulster Presbyterian migrants. It was a declaration from a committee of sixteen Irish migrants regarding the quality of land in Nova Scotia.[96] They testified that the land reserved by Colonel Alexander McNutt – an agent in the trafficking of Irish passengers to the colonies – along the Minas Basin was of the quality advertised to them prior to their departure from Derry. The point of this supplement was to attract more migrants, and thus more tenants, to McNutt's holdings of land previously owned by French Arcadians before their forced relocation in 1755. In order to do this, the declaration included a description of Nova Scotia and the fertility of its land compared to that other colony most familiar to Ulster Presbyterians, Pennsylvania.[97] The signatories of the document certified that the soil of Nova Scotia was 'equal in goodness to the best lands in Ireland' before stating, '(as some of us have been in the province of Pennsylvania) that the soil of this country is much richer, and bears every thing larger and in greater abundance than that of Pennsylvania'. Furthermore, McNutt's land, or so he claimed, was situated near navigable waterways, making the transportation of goods inexpensive and quick. Available holdings in Pennsylvania, by contrast, 'are more than two hundred miles within land' so that 'carrying the produce to market there [*sic*] costs as much as the several species of grain are worth at market'. McNutt realized the difficulty of redirecting migrant traffic away from Pennsylvania and exaggerated the lures of Nova Scotia. Indeed,

proof of his stiff competition is found in the form of a shipping advertisement printed on the same page as his declaration for 'the good ship
Sally' bound for Philadelphia.[98]

The image of early modern Ireland as a subject of British imperialism looms so large in the popular and scholarly imagination that it
sometimes obfuscates the reality of the Irish as enthusiastic imperialists
in their own right. While scholars examining the Irish contribution to
overseas empire-building have rectified this to some degree, much work
remains to be done on public opinion regarding the empire at home.[99]
The middle decades of the eighteenth century, before the age of revolution and imperial consolidation redefined Irish political culture and the
island's relationship with England, remain especially neglected. Printed
ephemera – such as newspapers, maps and pamphlets – that included
American subjects produced during the Seven Years War indicates profound Irish curiosity in the continent that instigated Britain's most
successful war of the eighteenth century. This material then, can tell us
a great deal about Ireland's engagement with the British Empire at the
height of its power in the eighteenth century.

Associational culture and America: the ritual of toasting and imperial awareness in Ulster, 1755–63

Community celebrations for British victories abroad occurred alongside
other dates within the Irish Protestant calendar.[100] In all, commemorative celebrations were widely observed on twenty days throughout
the year in the early years of George III's reign.[101] Victory celebrations
were short-lived additions to the rhythm of the commemorative year.
While never possessing the degree of local significance needed to jos-
tle their way onto the pantheon of dates revered by Protestants across
the kingdom, they were still clearly important expressions of national
identity. The spontaneous celebrations that occasioned news of British
victories both temporarily reinforced and broadened the significance of
other annual commemorations. The patriotic fervour of the early 1760s
energized Protestant observance of anniversaries such as those held in
honour of the Battle of the Boyne (1 July) or the Relief of Derry (31 July).
Victory celebrations and other associational gatherings in which the
American campaigns were mentioned injected an imperial flavour
into the calendar. This altered the character of many common annual
commemorations. The patriot societies of the mid-1750s, for example,
routinely met on days of special significance and used those occasions
to mark their support for the British war effort. The Patriot Society of

Downpatrick met on 10 November 1755 to celebrate the birthday of George II. Alongside the usual toasts in honour of the reigning monarch and to the memory 'of the great King William', its members also raised their glasses to 'Gen. Johnson, and Success to his Majesty's Forces in America'.[102] New anniversaries were also briefly introduced into the calendar as a result of the war. The *News-Letter* reminded its readership that 7 September was the birthday of their 'gallant countryman' and hero of Minorca, General Blakeney.[103]

Associational culture provided northern Protestants with another vehicle to express patriotic sympathy and affinity for groups beyond their shores. Taverns, inns and coffee houses, as mentioned in the last section, were locations where patrons imbibed information as well as alcohol, teas and coffee. They were places where people went to read and discuss newspapers and where they congregated to toast British victories and mourn defeats. They were also the favoured meeting spots for formal organizations and associational societies. Political and economic organizations across Ulster met at taverns and inns to conduct business and to hold dinners. A crucial component of these gatherings, indeed a defining characteristic of eighteenth-century communal celebration in general, was the ritual of toasting. Often the centrepiece of the evening, toasting was a declaration of the shared commitments and common principles of those present. It was an act of affiliation that publicly bound each participant to one another.

At its heart, the act of toasting was more than a bonding exercise between those participating in the ritual. The toasts themselves were often expressed in the form of an appeal directed into the ether, to a force beyond the participants, in a fashion not unlike a secular prayer. Participants couched their political desires and opinions on international events in the form of a request spoken out loud and affirmed by the group, either through vocal restatement and/or the communal consumption of alcohol. In the spring of 1756 one northern patriot club decreed, 'Protection and Succour to our American Colonies against our perfidious Enemies.'[104] This statement was not only a display of the club's inclusive imperial patriotism; it was an earnest plea for the object of the toast – that is, the safety of their fellow American subjects – to be realized.

The bonds established at the actual toast extended to others far beyond the site of the celebration – both geographically and temporally. Lists of toasts were often published in newspapers afterwards, thus extending their audience far beyond the room in which they were initially drunk. The Patriot Club of Downpatrick, for instance, immediately upon completing their toasts at meetings in February and June 1756, resolved to have a list of them 'printed three Times in the Belfast News-Letter'.[105] Similarly, the Antrim patriots agreed to print their resolutions, including a list of thirty-eight toasts drunk at a recent meeting, in both the *News-Letter* and the *Universal Advertiser*.[106] This practice not only broadcast the agenda and ideological platform of the group who composed and drank the toasts but also gave a far-flung reading audience access to them. In his study of political celebration and the construction of American nationalism, David Waldstricher argues that the printing of toasts and newspaper coverage of popular festivity 'gave them extra-local' meaning.[107] He further claims that the reality of early American national identity lay not in ideological consensus but 'in the gathering of people at celebratory events, in the toasts and declarations given meaning by assent, in the reproduction of rhetoric and ritual in print'.[108] The same could be said about the construction of imperial identity within the Protestant nation through the vehicle of mid-eighteenth-century Irish newspapers.

Martyn Powell points out that the 'politico-ritualistic' consumption of toasts offered eighteenth-century Irish patriots 'a degree of unity and purpose, a collective bonhomie, an awareness of a shared past and a common set of goals in the present, and allowed the identification of friends and enemies in public'.[109] The toasting ritual usually set the tone of an evening of celebrations including the lighting of bonfires and other illuminations and the ringing of bells, providing a conceptual framework from which participants could derive meaning from such enjoyments. Publication of these toasts in periodicals expanded the audience and popularized patriot agendas beyond the original drinking circles and revellers. During the Seven Years War two groups published lists of toasts in the *News-Letter*. Northern patriot societies published their toasts during the parliamentary elections and the aftermath of the Money Bill crisis between 1754 and 1757 and the Belfast linen drapers advertised toasts between 1761 and 1762. These lists began with references to the King and the Royal Family and were followed by invocations of important dates in the Protestant and patriot calendars. Toasts to the memory of the Battle of the Boyne on 1 July 1690, or the Duke of Cumberland's victory over the Jacobites at Culloden on 16 April 1746, for example, were drunk. In this way the clubs established both their loyalty and their place within the Whigish national narrative. The next grouping on the lists was comprised of toasts either celebrating or cursing contemporary events or people on the Irish political scene. With a few exceptions, toasts regarding American and European topics fell into this section.[110] Publication of these toasts in Irish newspapers further strengthened fraternal good will towards American and European Protestants.

American affairs did not factor into patriot toasts throughout 1754 when reports of violence were just beginning to reach Ireland. This changed the following year when reports of French and Indian aggression on the British American frontier flooded back to Europe. The Antrim Club listed a commonly made toast, 'Support and Protection to the British Colonies in all their Rights, Liberties and Possessions', in the nineteenth place on their advertisement (interestingly, the 'Linen Manufacture' was included much further down this list, at number twenty-three).[111] These toasts prefigured those drunk in the heyday of the volunteer movement during the Imperial crisis of the following decade. As the year progressed, the clubs' references to American events became more specific. The Down and Killileagh Patriots toasted 'our American forces' in the campaign against the French in western New York. William Johnson, the Crown's northern Superintendent for Indian Affairs, who was, the *News-Letter* bragged on several occasions, 'descended from a very ancient and worthy Family in Ireland', organized this operation.[112] Lists of published toasts reveal that colonial news was absorbed within patriot circles and incorporated, albeit temporarily, into their historical timelines. By 1756 stories from the frontiers had become so common as to influence the Londonderry Patriot Society's toasts. They proclaimed, 'May paternal Aid, and a firm united Spirit in the British American Colonies, become an effectual Security to them, against French and Savage Treachery.'[113] Toasts therefore became another media – alongside the newspaper settler victimization narratives examined in the next chapter – through which Euro-American suffering at the hands of Native Americans was propagated in Ulster.

The focus of patriot toasts shifted after a European theatre of operations was opened by the declaration of war in 1756. Again, foreign invasion accompanied by domestic insurrection became a legitimate fear for Protestants. This anxiety is apparent in the records of club celebrations, as best demonstrated by the fourteenth and fifteenth toasts of the Down Patriots on 24 June 1756:

> 14 May every Protestant and loyal Subject in the Counties of Down and Antrim speedily enjoy his natural and constitutional Right of being properly armed and in a state of Defence against all foreign invasions. 15 May those who despise or neglect the Protestants of the Counties of Down and Antrim, never stand in need of assistance against a French or any other invasion.[114]

While references to the American conflict continued throughout 1756 and 1757, toasts extolling Britain's European allies became increasingly

common. Prussia, in particular, was routinely celebrated at Patriot dinners. Frederick II was toasted several times in 1757.[115] On one occasion
the Antrim Patriots included a toast in his honour fourth on their list,
immediately below the British Royal Family and above 'the glorious
memory of king William'![116]

The fear of French privateers and the ravages of war on the agriculture of the middle colonies interrupted the transatlantic flaxseed trade
during the war. This affected the livelihoods of weavers throughout
the northern countryside and temporarily depressed the linen industry. Improving landlords and members of the linen board in Dublin
and Belfast were quick to make the point that increased domestic flax
production would free Ireland from its dependence on foreign imports.
They argued that such a move would cut-out the costs of transporting
foreign flaxseed and make Ireland more resistant to the economic dam-
ages of war. Derry merchant William Kennedy wrote to George Faulkner
arguing that domestic flax production would be of 'utmost advantage to
this kingdom' by cutting 'the immense annual expence [of] importing
it from America or the Baltic'.[117] This would alleviate, he claimed, 'the
danger we are, in some years, threatened with a total failure of this our
staple manufacture'.[118]

Both the linen drapers of the early 1760s and patriot associations
of the late 1750s championed the political and economic interests of
Ireland. Because of the narrow professional nature of the drapers' association, their toasts revealed a more pointed economic agenda than
the earlier patriot lists. The Linen Board in Dublin and Belfast arranged
meetings in opposition to the Linen Bill, which they argued would
have restricted the sale of Irish linen on the imperial market. The board
subsequently published the toasts of these meetings in order to dis-
seminate their position within the community at large. North America
again appeared in the drapers' lists, but unlike patriot club toasts their
support was not magnanimous. The toasts drunk at their 1762 meeting revealed a civic pride in the town of Belfast and scepticism regarding the equity between imperial trading partners. This scepticism was
apparent in the drapers' tacit support of the colonials for which they
proclaimed, 'Prosperity to our American colonies but not at the expence
of this deluded country.'[119] Again, the reality of Protestant migration
could not have been far from the minds of the audience for these published lists. The toasts were printed on the same page of the *News-Letter*
as several shipping advertisements, including a call for passengers to
embark from the port of Larne to New York. Another list of toasts from
the linen merchants of Newry published in the summer of 1762 bore

a similar sympathetic tone to the patriot toasts from the beginning of the conflict. It also linked the commercial success of Ireland to the fortunes of America and the international expansion of Protestantism: '16. The Linen Trade of Ireland ... 18. Prosperity to our American Colonies ... 27. The Protestant Interest over all the World'.[120]

Historians of late eighteenth-century Ireland have long been preoccupied with the topics of mass politicization and the evolution of the various strands of Irish nationalism. The counter-narrative of popular imperialism within an expanding British-dominated polity has, in contrast, received comparatively less scholarly attention. Historians examining public opinion during the age of revolutions and those interested in the politics of consumption in late eighteenth-century Ireland have begun to redress this balance.[121] It remains, however, that the complex relationship between Irish imperial enthusiasm and national belonging has yet to be appreciated. This is especially true for the period between 1750 and 1765, before the breakdown in the transatlantic relationship between the thirteen North American colonies and Britain led to a wholesale re-evaluation in Ireland of the country's place within the larger imperial framework.

3

He Never Wants for Suitable Instruments: The Seven Years War as a War of Religion

In late spring 1756 news arrived in Belfast that the country was, again, officially at war. On 28 May the *News-Letter* printed the king's declaration of war, and the province braced itself for yet another round of hostilities with Britain's arch-rival, France. At noon on 1 June the declaration was read to the inhabitants of Belfast at 'the several public Places ... in the usual Manner'.[1] Over the course of the summer, as the other European powers fell into one camp or the other, it became clear that this conflict was different in character from its most recent predecessor. The belligerents were now largely divided along confessional lines. Britain's alliance with Austria, negotiated by the Duke of Newcastle earlier in the century to contain French ambitions on the continent, had fallen by the wayside. A powerful Bourbon-Hapsburg bloc emerged that included Austria, France and – from 1762 – Spain. Britain now found itself treaty-bound to several small, largely Protestant, German states – most notably Prussia and, of course, Hanover. From the beginning, this war was to be about religion as well as empire. From 2 July onwards the *News-Letter* routinely made mention of Britain and its allies as 'the Protestant Powers'. Correspondents to the paper used similar language. One observer, for example, hoped that 'Rome may receive a fatal blow, in consequence of the coalition between France and Austria to oppress or ruin the Protestant cause.'[2]

The arrival of war in 1756 took no one in Ireland by surprise. It had already been raging in America unofficially for two years. A year before the declaration was read aloud in Belfast's Market Square, a Philadelphia correspondent wrote to local merchant Daniel Mussenden, optimistic about the British war effort in North America. He bragged of General Mockton's victories over the French in Nova Scotia and ended his report by stating that 'we every day expect to hear of Genl Braddock's possessing himself of the fort on the Ohio'.[3] On this final point, his prediction was dramatically off the mark. On 9 July 1755, two days after the letter to Musseden was posted, the British army sent to capture Fort Duquesne was decimated on the banks of the Monongahela River by a combined force of French regulars and their mainly Ottawa and Ojibwa Indian allies. Two-thirds of the expedition were killed or wounded. A week later Braddock himself was dead, his body ingloriously buried in the middle of the road and the site trampled upon by his retreating army in order to ensure that the General's remains were not mutilated by the French and their Indian allies who they believed to be in pursuit. Braddock's defeat left the western settlements of the British mid-Atlantic Colonies undefended. Immediately thereafter, Delaware war parties, many of them driven into a French alliance by Braddock's contempt for Indian political customs, attacked the length of the Pennsylvania, Maryland and Virginia frontiers. Within months, accounts composed by surviving Irish soldiers of the battle and bloodletting that followed flooded into Cork, Dublin, and Belfast. On 30 July one veteran, Matthew Leslie, instructed an anonymous merchant in Philadelphia to 'communicate [his] sad intelligence to our friends in Ireland'.[4] 'We have lost gallant officers and generous friends,' he claimed, 'not in battle, for that we can bear, but by murder, by savage butchery.'[5] Leslie could not shake the memory of his first experience of Indian war: 'the yell of the Indians is fresh on my ear, and the terrific sound will haunt me until the hour of my dissolution'.[6]

This is how Britain's war began – with two regiments of its professional army routed by a motley force of French regulars, Canadian militia and American Indians.[7] The disappointments of that day were later mirrored in the defeats at Minorca, Calcutta and Fort William Henry. This string of disasters led to a feeling of dread and despondence throughout the British world. In 1757 Lord Chesterfield proclaimed that Britain was on the brink of total defeat and was to become a dependency of France. He remarked to a friend 'we are undone ... The French are masters to do what they please ... We are no longer a nation.'[8] Samuel Blacker, a lawyer from County Armagh, wrote to Sir Archibald Acheson, 5th Baronet of Gosford, in 1762, claiming that if the Bourbon monarchs were to emerge victorious then 'we and all our Settlements, trade etc. etc. are undone'.[9] Defeats in America, Europe and India brought with them a sense that all British subjects throughout the empire were united in loss and dejection. This was especially manifest in printed literature prepared for fast days. Yet ultimately the Seven Years War ended in a near total victory for Britain. The prevailing optimism and celebratory mood of the late 1750s and early 1760s were in sharp contrast to the air of doom that hung over the empire during the first few years of the conflict. The jubilation that greeted British victories on the streets of Irish cities from 1758 onward infused Irish Protestant patriotism with a sense of imperial accomplishment.

This chapter seeks to understand how public culture, imperial aware-ness and a sense of a shared wartime experience contributed to Irish Presbyterian identification with the other peoples of the Atlantic world. First, however, it might be helpful to define the term 'public culture' as it is used here. In this particular context, the term encompasses collective gatherings or communal activities in which the participants articulate a national or international identity through expressions of empathy for, or affinity with, other geographically distant groups. Ulster Presbyterian imperial empathy was based upon the understanding that the inhabit-ants of the 'greater Britain' encompassing the Atlantic empire shared similar cultural values with themselves. Primarily, they envisioned the empire as a Protestant polity. Furthermore, this chapter asks whether it is possible to ascertain Irish Presbyterian attitudes towards the empire by examining the relationship between religion and the rites of empire such as community fasts for American defeats, or the celebration of American victories. Ulster Presbyterians, like most Protestants through-out the Atlantic world, believed that the wealth of the empire and the success of the nation were reliant upon their community's good stand-ing with God. Providence provided Irish Protestants with a template for comprehending both British defeats and, later, victories during the war. In times of crisis, Ulster Presbyterians, especially within the Old Light, Seceder and Covenanter wings of the denomination, were ever on the lookout for divine messages in the world around them. Their attentive-ness to God's hand in world affairs bred a greater understanding of the Atlantic empire and with it a greater willingness to empathize with those who suffered as they did.

Imperial defeat, fasting and national commiseration, 1754–8

It concerns you all seriously to reflect upon your Sins, and the Sins of your Land, which have brought all these Calamities upon us. If you believe that God governs the World, if You do not abjure him from being the Ruler of Your Country, You must acknowledge that all the Calamites of War, and the threatening Appearances of Famine, are ordered by his Providence; *There is no Evil in a City or Country, but the*

Lord hath done it. And if You believe that he is a just and Righteous Ruler, you must also believe, that he would not punish a righteous or a penitent People. We and our Countrymen are Sinners, aggravated Sinners: god proclaims that we are such by his Judgments now upon us, by withering Fields and scanty Harvest, by the Sound of the Trumpet and the Alarm of War.[10]

In early April 1756 Henry and Robert Joy republished this popular American sermon in Belfast for the price of three pence per copy.[11] The author, Samuel Davies, was a young Presbyterian clergyman and future president of the College of New Jersey. He had been at the head of several fledgling congregations in western Virginia when his ministry was interrupted and his congregations scattered by the arrival of war. Davies based his sermon on 2 Samuel 10.12: 'Be of good courage, and let us play the men, for our people, and for the cities of our God: And the Lord do that which seemeth good.' At that particular moment, the pamphlet's message of providential judgement and divine displeasure with Britain was as relevant in Ulster as it was in Virginia. God, it seemed, was angry with the British Empire as a whole, and Ireland certainly had not escaped his wrath. Bad harvests had resulted in a shortage of grain throughout the country and several Dublin banks looked to be on the verge of collapse. In a thanksgiving service after the war, James Bryson, a New Light licentiate from Armagh who was later ordained minister at Lisburn, looked back upon the dark days of the 1750s.[12] He recalled that early British failures including Braddock's defeat, the fall of Minorca and the alleged misconduct of Admiral John Byng 'were thought by many to be the prelude to our Destruction'.[13] He remembered that 'At Home was scarcity and Dearth, abroad Shame & Loss, in our Armies Dejection and loss of Spirit ... among the People Consternation and Discontent.'[14] 'These Evils', he added, 'were heightened by continual Alarms of a home – Invasion.'[15] Davies's sermon arrived in Belfast at a moment when there was no end in sight regarding the domestic and foreign problems besetting the island. Its call for repentance and its underlying assertion of God's sovereignty offered Irish Protestants an explanation for the hardships afflicting the British Empire.

The urgency of Davies's message was underpinned by the threat of invasion that hung over Britain and Ireland throughout the late 1750s. Widespread Protestant anxiety about a possible invasion cannot be attributed solely to baseless paranoia. The French actually had been planning an invasion of Ireland in 1759 that was to include a regiment of Irish Catholic troops headed by the exiled Lord Clare.[16] Dublin bookseller William Bruce described the mood of the city to a friend in the spring of 1755: 'We are all in constant expectation of intelligence concerning our fleet, which at present is the principal object of our solicitude.'[17] Invasion hysteria hit Belfast that April. Reports abounded in the papers that the new Lord Lieutenant's arrival in the kingdom was hastened by the immediate threat of invasion and rebellion in Munster. Simultaneously, news arrived that the Brest fleet had sailed with 20,000 men and had 'steer'd toward the West of Ireland'.[18] The Joys tempered these reports with information gleaned from a 'Letter of good Authority', which claimed that the Duke of Bedford's hasty departure from England was no more than a precaution. Still, there was no telling where the Brest fleet was heading and it was 'more than possible' that a 'Diversion may be intended in Great Britain or Ireland, the better to accomplish the Designs of the French in America'.[19] The following year, the town was still on edge over the prospect of a French landing. A petition signed by eighty-nine residents was sent to the Lord Lieutenant requesting that a new volunteer unit be raised with Hill Willson at its head. The petitioners warned that this force was immediately necessary, 'as a sudden invasion is apprehended, and likely to be attended with every evil Consequence that may be dreaded from our most inveterate Enemies'.[20]

Well into the 1760s Catholics accused of aiding the enemy or actively recruiting men for French service faced trial and execution. The last recruiting officer to be sentenced to death in the period was Dillon M'Namara in 1764.[21] As late as 1758 the Lord Lieutenant warned Whitehall that the French could easily take Cork and land a force in 'those popish and disaffected counties' so as to 'transfer the seat of war from their own coasts into the south-west of Ireland in the wild parts of Munster and Connaught'.[22] Even in 1759, when the French seemed unable to carry on the war on land or sea for much longer, the fear of invasion remained. One observer warned that the French 'tho' a wise Nation' may yet decide to invade: 'Despair of success in the ordinary methods, will put men to extraordinary efforts, which tho' they will probably miscarry, yet possibly may succeed.'[23] In the past, the author stated, the French had caused 'insurrections in our natives, by throwing up small parties of men by stealth'.[24] They may yet, it was widely feared, attempt such a strategy again.

Like the vast majority of British and Irish Protestants, Ulster Presbyterians believed that God was active in the world and that his sovereignty was absolute. God favoured the reformed religion and had entered into an implicit covenant with its adherents. In periods of war and famine his presence was terrifyingly immediate. Historians of the eighteenth century have long asserted the need to take into consideration the religious convictions of their subjects alongside the increasing popularity of Enlightenment rationalism and humanism.[25] While Enlightenment thinking increasingly percolated into Ireland as the century progressed, many, if not a majority, continued to rely on religious or folk explanations to make sense of human history and natural phenomena. The Enlightenment was not a zero-sum game in which everyone who came into contact with sceptical literature became a confessed deist or even atheist. Many took what they wanted from imported works from Britain and the continent, reprinted by Dublin printers and in such periodicals as the *Dublin Magazine* and Limerick's *Magazine of Magazines*, without abandoning their religious understanding of historical causation.[26]

For many Irish Presbyterians – especially those on the Old Light, Seceder or Covenanting wings of the denomination – every natural occurrence and human action affecting their communities revealed either divine contentment or displeasure with his chosen people. It was up to Presbyterians, acting in the spirit of the biblical prophet Jeremiah, to interpret the 'signs of the times' in order to decipher God's messages regarding their community's moral standing.[27] In the late 1750s God was clearly displeased with his chosen in Ireland. Dearth, British military defeat and natural disaster were all signs of his discontentment and were perceived as judgement for the corporate sins of the local community, nation, or, in the case of the Seven Years War, the empire. France and its allies were unwitting tools by which God punished Britain and its empire – like the Babylonians and Assyrians against the Israelites. The hand of God himself was evident in the crop failures of 1756 and 1757 and in the terrible earthquake that destroyed Lisbon, the capital of a British allied nation, in 1755. In order to alleviate God's anger and avoid further punishment, Protestants had to first correct wrong behaviour and demonstrate their communal piety. Fasting was a means to do so. It also afforded individuals the ability to reassert human agency in an otherwise uncontrollable world. Andrew Holmes explains that a providential world-view provided Protestants with 'a way of explaining what was happening, a means of changing the situation through humility and prayer, and, failing that, a conviction that no matter what occurred, God was still sovereign'.[28]

God's providence was not only evident in grand diplomatic narratives and dramatic natural phenomena. It extended to the everyday lives of individuals. The Calvinist jeremiad tradition informed the day-to-day lives of Ulster Presbyterians, practically at important points in the agricultural or religious calendar. The condition of the harvest commonly led to either a fast or a day of thanksgiving. Between 1691 and 1777 the General Synod of Ulster appointed forty-three fast days.[29] On top of these, congregations within the bounds of the synod also observed government fast days. Sometimes, as was the case in 1757, northern Dissenters complied with both official and synodical announcements of a fast in one year. Rev. Thomas Clark, the Seceding minister of the Ballybay congregations appointed a fast on 27 April 1755 'to plead with the Lord that for Jesus' sake he forgive the many sins of Britain Ireland and the dominions'.[30] In doing so he clearly conceived of the judgements then befalling Ireland in retribution for the corporate sins of the empire. Adherence to the fast re-inforced community solidarity in the face of local hardship. Fast days were solemn occasions in which observers were expected to attend public worship, keep private devotions and, of course, fast. In so doing, they brought the community into better standing with God. Individuals were aware that breaking the fast could adversely affect the 'Protestant cause' and were thus under immense social pressure to show proper reverence.

The act of fasting fostered Ulster Presbyterians' sense of shared experience with Protestants throughout the empire and their feeling of belonging to a national Protestant 'interest' at home. Notices of general fasts to be observed in both Britain and Ireland were published in newspapers across the island. They called for all of the King's subjects to supplicate God in order to avert 'those heavy judgements' that their 'manifold sins and provocations have most justly deserved'.[31] These published proclamations, read aloud in towns and from pulpits, made it clear that Irish Protestants were united in purpose with their co-religionists throughout the King's dominions and that all loyal Britons were engaged in the same ritual activity to ensure divine approval. It was common for newspapers to print royal decrees for national fasts and to list the Irish and Scottish days of observance at the end of the declaration. The approximate simultaneity of public fasts across Britain, and those issued slightly later by the Lord Lieutenant in Ireland, reinforced a shared sense of national belonging and imperial unity among Irish Protestants and their fellow subjects in Britain.

Often local clergymen composed sermons on the occasion of the government fast. On occasion, these sermons were diffused beyond the congregation in cheap printed editions. The *News-Letter* advertised one such sermon on 11 June 1756. The document was printed by James Magee, then the largest printer in Belfast, and distributed by sellers in Newry, Armagh and Coleraine. Unfortunately the sermon has not survived and the author remains unknown.[32] The sermon was probably authored by either Robert Higinbotham at First Coleraine or Charles Lynd, the Seceding minister at Coleraine New Row.[33] Regardless of its authorship, the advertisement provides us with some indication as to the nature of the content and the reasons for its publication. It read:

> Just published ... A persuasive to learn Righteousness when the judgements of God are on the Earth; a sermon preached at Coleraine the 6th of February, 1756; being a Fast appointed by the Government, on Account of the Earthquake in Lisbon and other Places; and our being Engaged in a War with France.[34]

The reasons given for the fast in the title reveal that natural disaster and war were interconnected in the minds of the Presbyterian clergy in the north.

But public fasts were not enough to ensure divine good will. In February 1757, the *News-Letter* reprinted a letter written under the pseudonym 'Hibernicus'. Its author offered his own private prayer, claiming that others should take his example and pray for forgiveness. He wrote that whereas public devotion on fast days was 'the cry of an whole people, with their king at their head, directed to the mercy seat of God', individual prayer was 'the private atonement of each particular person, for his share of the national guilt'.[35] As many of the above examples suggest, the great Lisbon earthquake weighed heavily on the minds of those Protestants who feared Ireland could be subject to the same judgement.[36] On 1 November 1755, when many of the city's residents were in church celebrating the Catholic holiday of All Saints' Day, Lisbon was destroyed by a powerful earthquake and subsequent tsunami. A disaster of this magnitude received much attention from ministers and philosophes alike. Voltaire, for example, attacked the idea that the disaster was an act of divine intervention, in both his *Poèm sur le désastre de Lisbonne* (1759) and *Candide ou l'optimisme* (1759).[37] Unlike Voltaire, however, the majority of the Irish population held firmly to the idea that God was the ultimate source of historical causation and that the Lisbon earthquake was a clear sign of his displeasure.

The Lisbon disaster troubled Irishmen and women across the denominational divide. Protestants were eager to ascertain God's reasons for initiating the disaster because Portugal was a staunch British ally. They wondered what God might next have in store for Britain and Ireland. Yet Portugal was a Catholic country, a fact that the Irish Catholic population, who also largely viewed the episode as an act of God, found equally worrisome. Newspapers reported that several Irish clerics lost their lives in the tragedy.[38] Both Protestant and Catholic places of worship were packed to capacity on the day of the government fast.[39] Everyone, it seemed, was awed and saddened by the monumental loss of life. Throughout the British Atlantic people waited for further judgement and the catastrophe initiated a wave of anxiety with the *News-Letter* reporting tremors in Switzerland, Boston and Philadelphia.[40] In Dublin, shocks from the Lisbon quake inspired bad poetry that urgently stressed the need for national atonement:

> Britons! Attend, Ierne! mind the Call
> Of Voice Divine, proclaim'd aloud to all.
> …
> Twice hath Albion totter'd like a Wall,
> That Ruin threats, and ready for its Fall.
> Lethargick Natives of this Northern Clime,
> Awake! awake! reform, repent in Time;
> With inmost Dread observe the last Alarm;
> Wrath is gone out, th'Almighty lifts his Arm.[41]

Two years later, Ireland was in the grips of a subsistence crisis and the British war effort was in shambles. Through all of this, the fate of Lisbon continued to inspire dread and anxiety among Ulster Protestants. The image of God, with his arm tensed, preparing to shake the earth in righteous fury, still haunted the national imagination. It appeared ad naseaum in much of the printed ephemera from the period. A prayer published in the *News-Letter* during a downturn in Britain's fortunes in 1757 called for repentance:

> I with dread, acknowledge thy Almighty arm, in lately shaking terribly the earth about us; and in now hanging famine and the sword of our enemies over our heads: with the deepest sense of gratitude for thy mercy, in hitherto staying the hand of the destroying angel.[42]

A reprinted selection from London's *General Evening Post* attempted to account for the tragedy by claiming that effeminate and luxurious nations often fall prey with time to other nations but 'when the Sins of a People are exceedingly numerous and abominable God himself arises, and strikes the final blow'.[43] The author added, 'Various are the Methods of punishing a guilty Nation, by Famine, War, or Pestilence: but of all the judgements of the Almighty, an Earthquake is the most tremendous.'[44] The disaster came in the wake of Braddock's defeat in the colonies and the beginning of the bloodletting on the frontier. Urgent steps needed to be taken in order to avert further punishment. The British government immediately declared a fast day on 30 December 1755 and the Lord Lieutenant of Ireland followed suit a week later.

In the proclamation of an Irish fast after the quake, the Lord Lieutenant emphasized the 'blessing of the Protestant religion' and called upon loyal subjects to 'tender the favour of Almighty God' so as to avoid the unhappy fate of the Portuguese. Another commentator compared the reaction of George II, who immediately called a national fast out of 'paternal concern' for his people, to that of France, 'whose wisdom is artiface; justice, oppression; and whose great moderation proceeds only from a want of power'.[45] The report that the Pope had also declared a fast led to the reprinting of a poem in the *News-Letter*, written by 'a Protestant':

> An earthquake Rome's conversion works at last;
> For lo! her priests adopt our solemn fast;
> Blest Shock! That gradually unites us thus,
> As now they fast, they soon will pray – with us.[46]

The positive consequence of the disaster, from the view of some particularly callous British Protestants, was that it might advance the reformed religion among continental Catholics.

For Irish Presbyterians, the outbreak of international war and natural disaster were interconnected. British military defeats, Indian raids on the American frontier, and the devastation brought upon an ally in the form of an earthquake were all symptomatic of divine displeasure with the Protestant peoples of the British Empire. It is crucial to understand that these times of suffering helped to foster imperial consciousness among Ulster Presbyterians. The trials of war and threat of judgement affected their understanding of community. On the one hand, their concerns were obviously local. They were concerned about French invasion and Catholic insurrection, crop failure and disruptions in the linen industry because such developments directly impacted upon their lives. On another less tangible, but no less relevant, level, the events of the 1750s encouraged Presbyterians to see their community suspended within the larger context of the British Empire. The discourse of providential judgement was another means through which Ulster was further integrated into the Atlantic world. This, coupled with Atlantic emigration and the expansion of colonial trade, increased the likelihood that

Ulster Presbyterians accepted their cousins across the oceans as fellow Britons whose fortunes were intricately linked to their own.

Imperial victory, thanksgiving and national celebration, 1759–63

From 1758 onwards those in Ireland who revelled in the good fortune of British arms found a great deal to celebrate. This was especially true during 1759, the *annus mirablis*, in which Britain and its allies appeared invincible following a string of victories that culminated in the fall of Quebec. News of each of these triumphs brought jubilation to the streets of Irish cities. In July the printer John Pue reported that news of Prince Ferdinand's victories on the continent were greeted with bonfires and cannon rounds in Dublin. Throughout the night, he claimed, 'there were the greatest Rejoicings that could possibly be made throughout the whole City and Liberties'.[47] On 15 October 'there were great rejoicings' in Belfast following word of Quebec's capture. Henry and Robert Joy reported that, 'At night a great number of the principal gentlemen of this place assembled at the Market-house (before which was a large bonfire) to celebrate this great event; and the night concluded with illuminations and other demonstrations of joy.'[48] Crowds congregated at the shores of the Lough to watch ships with their colours on display fire their guns until well after dark. The situation was similar in Dublin where news of General Wolfe's death was initially met with volleys fired in Phoenix Park, while 'at Night the City was most beautifully illuminated, which concluded with Bonfires, Ringing of Bells, and other Demonstrations of Joy'.[49] Exactly a year later another large bonfire was built in front of the Market House in Belfast to celebrate 'the reduction of Montreal, and with it of all Canada'. The gentlemen of the town again gathered there to toast the King and the providential success of his forces on land and water, while 'at the same time the four companies of major General Stroude's regiment quartered [in the town] were drawn up under arms, and fired 24 vollies, in answer to each toast'.[50] The conclusion of peace in 1763, one Dublin minister remarked, was a wonderful moment, 'the greatest indeed that ever *England*, or its Dependents, or those who wish well to the *Protestant* Cause in *Europe,* ever had for Thankfulness'.[51]

Just as providence provided Irish Protestants with a prism through which they could understand British defeats in the early years of the war, it was also a tool through which they could comprehend British victories near its end. Similarly, natural phenomena that benefited the

British cause were seen to be indicative of divine power in the same way as those that hindered it. Thus the wind taking General Loudon's regiments to the new world in February 1756 was described as 'a Protestant wind', an example of divine benevolence in the tradition of Elizabeth's delivery from the Spanish Armada or William's landing at Torbay.[52] On 26 October 1760, Dublin castle issued a prayer of thanksgiving that was to be read aloud in all the places of worship in the kingdom. It asked the King's Irish subjects to give thanks for 'the Overthrow of our Enemies, and the Tranquility of our Fellow subjects in North America, through thy blessing on the Conduct of our Generals, and the Valour of our Soldiers'.[53] The author intended that the prayer be read aloud following the morning and evening services held at all Dublin churches on the thanksgiving fast ordered following the capitulation of Canada.

Ministers reminded their flocks revelling in British victories to remember the dark days that the nation had weathered at the beginning of the conflict. Rev. William Fletcher, the Church of Ireland Archdeacon of Kildare and Rector of St Mary's in Dublin, chose to base his 1759 thanksgiving sermon delivered before the House of Commons on Psalm 11.11, 'Serve the Lord with fear and rejoice with trembling.' Fletcher's overriding message was that the nation should not be so carried away in the euphoria of the moment as to neglect their obedience to God. He reminded his parliamentary audience that the godly and patriotic subject should reflect upon the reasons for God's benevolence towards his country and must conclude that 'although the present generation may reap some benefit from [providence], he fears, lest it should prove a snare, and by their adding more ingratitude to the measure, it should overflow'.[54] To put it bluntly, Fletcher claimed that the righteous subject 'blesseth GOD *with fear, and rejoiceth with trembling*'.[55] Fletcher imagined the dread felt by the 'natural man' converted to the gospel when he recollects his former condition: 'He looketh back to the dangers he hath escaped with a heart divided between pain and pleasure: so that Fear is the very foundation of his Joy, and in the words of my text, he *rejoiceth with trembling.*'[56] 'In respect to such as are *National*', he told his congregation, the citizen naturally rejoices at God's benevolence towards his country. Yet the present generation might forget God's benevolence and slip into sin, thus the citizen 'fears, lest it should prove a snare, and by their adding more ingratitude to the measure' that 'God may retract his bounty'.[57] The victories of 1759 demonstrated that Britain's costly investment of men and money in far-off places like America and India was not in vain. Britain and Ireland were in the midst of a righteous war fought against an enemy with designs 'against the very being of Protestantism itself'.[58]

Thanksgiving fast days were less frequently appointed by the General Synod than those issued to placate an angry God. Only four were sanctioned before 1777.[59] Thanksgiving fasts brought the world to Ulster Presbyterians in a similar fashion to those days sanctioned for repentance during the war. They too invited Irish Presbyterians to imagine that they belonged to a larger national and imperial community. Now, however, they were united not in commiseration but in celebration. Thus both the low and highpoints of the international war were weathered and celebrated in turn by Irish Protestants in the belief that they were sharing similar experiences with their coreligionists throughout the empire.

The celebratory air of the early 1760s extended beyond designated Thanksgiving fasts. Ministers who had previously warned their flocks that the military's misfortunes were the result of the nation's sins now asked them to thank God, in his benevolence, for the success of British arms. Speaking before his Usher's Quay congregation, Presbyterian Thomas Vance commented, 'Victories have followed Victories, and Conquests Conquests, with almost uninterrupted Rapidity' over the course of 1759.[60] By the grace of God Britain had become the dominant power in the world. Vance chastised earlier French arrogance: *'How art thou fallen from Heaven, O Lucifer, Son of the Morning! O Lewis,* who didst pride thyself in outshining all the Kings of the Earth!'[61] William Boulton, a Dublin Baptist minister, preached a sermon upon the death of George II in which he compared the deceased monarch to David. Like David he had led a sinning people to righteousness and was 'the blessed Instrument, of hitherto defeating those who unjustly rose against us [and was responsible for] procuring considerable Advantages to us, in our Trade and Commerce; and we trust, of laying a Foundation for a Peace, that will be honourable and lasting to these Realms'.[62] The late King had been instrumental in holding together the Protestant coalition and had 'united with his faithful Subjects of these Kingdoms, and his Protestant Allies abroad, in carrying on that just and necessary War'.[63]

Just as the French had been the instrument of divine punishment for the sins of British Protestants in the early years of the war, British arms were now tools of his righteous vengeance for the transgressions of France. Writing to a friend in Ireland, an officer in Boston declared his dismay at 'the dreadful Alarms of an Overture of Peace' in 1758.[64] The officer sincerely hoped that this news, which had arrived 'by the way of Corke', was false and was nothing 'more than Munster News'.[65] The British could not yet sue for peace, not with all of Canada within their grasp. 'Like the Divine Vengeance, we shall be terrible at last', the officer claimed, 'The Paltry Advantages the French have had hitherto in America have had no other consequence, but that of inspiring an implacable Resentment for their base Murders, and their perfidious Breach of Capitulation; a proper Vengeance is near at Hand.'[66]

For some, British victory over the coalition of Catholic powers was significant to the eschatological future of humankind. Throughout the conflict Arthur Dobbs maintained a belief that both the war and the expansion of the British Empire were preconditions for the coming Millennium and the implementation of the rule of the saints in a New Jerusalem. In a message sent to the North Carolina Assembly in December 1754, Dobbs claimed that the House of Bourbon had over the previous 'Two centuries, laid a plan for enslaving *Europe*, by ruining the liberties of the *Germanick* Body, and Protestant Interest of *Europe*'. He warned North Carolinians to take heart in these uncertain times: 'God Almighty, who by his Providence under the conduct of his *Messiah*, hath, in many remarkable Instances, defeated all *Popish* Schemes, when the Protestant Interest and Liberties of *Britain* seem'd to be at the Brink of Ruin.' By 1761, with British victory imminent, Dobbs had become convinced that he too was an instrument of providence. Writing from North Carolina he confided in a letter to his cousin, Dr Alexander McAuley, in Dublin, that he was glad to have lived to witness the French driven from North America. The conversion of the Indians living under British domination could soon begin in earnest without competition from Jesuits and Canadian priests. 'And what is a great addition to my pleasure', Dobbs claimed,

> is that I have been Instrumental in so soon entering into this American War by my [obtaining] the grant to the Ohio Company which was the means of bringing on the War before the French were prepared to begin their attack against our Colonies and according to my explanations of the prophecies all these surprising events coincide with all the prophecies at this surprising era, as the Time of the end approaches and the Dawn of the Philadelphian Church and Sabbatic Millenium is far advanced.[67]

British and Irish Protestants found some reasons for celebration in the late 1750s despite the overall mood of doom and gloom that characterized those years. While the British campaigns before 1758 provided Irish audiences at home with little to celebrate, the same cannot be said for the battlefield performances of Britain's strongest continental ally, Prussia. King Frederick II became a national hero throughout the

British world in lieu of home-grown idols. Ulster Protestants of all types shared with their British neighbours in the adulation of Frederick as the Protestant figurehead *du jour*. This pan-Protestant affinity emerged within the context of the dramatic reconfiguration of European alliances in 1756. It was a manifestation of an inclusive form of confessional patriotism that made space for their European coreligionists.

The conflict elevated Frederick II of Prussia to celebrity status throughout the British world. He was already seen as the liberator of the Silesian Protestants and was cast as a brave underdog by the British and Irish press. His exploits and early victories against the Austrians and Russians were celebrated at a low point for the British campaigns in North America. The *Dublin Gazette* even reported that an Irish Catholic unit was soon to be organized within the Prussian Army.[68] They therefore energized a public in need of good news. In 1757 Joy bragged that 'the king of Prussia hath declared that he will march 80,000 men against one empress, and if occasion requires 80,000 men against the other, and doubts not but by God's assistance, to beat both their imperial majesties'.[69] An indication of his status can be inferred from the Joys' coverage of British privateers. The names of these ships symbolized the cause for which their actions were supposedly justified. It is therefore telling that from 1758 onwards the exploits of the sloop *Oliver Cromwell* were joined by those of the *King of Prussia,* the latter of which also ferried emigrants across the Atlantic, thereby further strengthening the link between current international politics and the process of migration.[70] On 31 May 1759 the *News-Letter* reported that the sloop sailed from Newry two days prior: 'Capt. M'Glastiry, sailed out of the harbour with 225 passengers for, Philadelphia. They were all in high spirits on account of the goodness of their accommodations.' This advertisement reveals that many potential migrants – even if they were not as optimistic as the posting suggests – were indeed eagerly waiting for Britain's military fortunes in North America to improve before making the decision to sail themselves. After 1759 migration resumed as if it had not been disrupted by the war.

An anonymous poet writing under the name 'A Protestant' eulogized Frederick as the ideal enlightened, masculine ruler:

> To Rome and Greece two distant ages gave,
> Caesar the sage, and Ammon's son the brave;
> But Rome and Greece must now resign their fame,
> And cede to Germany the juster claim,
> Where nature forms a FREDERIC complete,
> And in one breast the sage and hero meet.

In so doing, the author, unknowingly challenged the popular French view that their nation was the guardian of European civilization against Anglo-Saxon (i.e., Prussian and English) barbarism.[71] Though he still enjoyed a great deal of popularity among Irish Protestants after 1758, the changing fortunes of Britain's war made him a less appealing celebrity. Figures such as Generals Robert Clive and, most significantly, James Wolfe filled the void left vacant by an absence of domestic heroes at the beginning of the war.[72]

On the morning of 21 February 1760, Protestant Ireland confronted the nightmare scenario of a French invasion. A French force under the command of Commodore François Thurot landed near Kilroot, County Antrim, and captured the nearby garrison of Carrickfergus. Initially, Thurot's expedition had been designed as a diversionary raid in support of major operations in Essex and western Scotland. The destruction of the French fleet at the Battle of Quiberon Bay in late November 1759, however, meant that assaults on British soil never materialized. Thurot's squadron of eight ships and 1,110 men were therefore left to complete their now pointless mission alone.[73] Thurot's aim was not invasion and it was never the intention of the French to raise an Irish rebellion in 1760. The tiny fleet had been at sea for four months over which time they had been reduced to three sail by a near constant onslaught of bad weather. By the time the fleet arrived off the coast of Ireland, Thurot faced dissension among his officers, and his crew were desperately low on supplies. The raid on Carrickfergus was a desperate attempt to secure some much-needed supplies for his men in order to stave off a mutiny.

The weary French force managed to take the under-defended garrison then under the command of Lieutenant-Colonel John Jennings. Thurot immediately sent a message to nearby Belfast stating that the town would be burned if its inhabitants did not provide his force with a list of provisions. Thurot held Carrickfergus for five days despite harassment from an ever-growing number of Volunteer units, ultimately totalling about 2,000 men. By the time reinforcements of dragoons from Dublin arrived in Belfast at midnight on 27 February, the French had abandoned the garrison and the squadron was leaving Carrickfergus Bay. The next morning they were attacked off the coast of the Isle of Man by three English ships commanded by John Elliot. Thurot died in the ensuing battle and his remaining force totalling 432 men was taken prisoner and brought to Belfast.[74]

Thus disaster had been averted. There was no Catholic uprising, nor was there much appetite for one in the first place. Thurot's landing too became a cause célèbre throughout the kingdom in the optimistic atmosphere of the early 1760s. On 10 June 1761 a piece simply entitled *Thurot's trip to Carricfergus* was performed at Dublin's Theatre Royal.[75] A year and a half later, the Joys printed advertisements for a play entitled *The SIEGE of CARRICKFERGUS. A tragical, comical, historical, operational, farsical, dramatic Satire on the French.* The preface of the poem was included in the paper. The author bragged that the failed landing showed 'to the World, the Vanity of Those; Who try (in vain) to be Britannia's Foes!'[76] As for Ireland:

– Hibernia – viewing, without Fear,
A wretched Fleet – commanded by Monsieur!
Let 'em call Anchor – weigh – and quit the Shore
Bet – net by Elliot – trouble 'em no more
[By] Hearts of Oak our Song – the Ladies Dance;
The Fair One's Triumph – And, the Fall of France![77]

Irish Protestants, no longer fearing an invasion, were now free to indulge in a bout of self-congratulation in the belief that their country too had been an active theatre of conflict in the closing years of the war.

A month before Thurot's landing, Dublin was rocked by a riot on 3 December 1759 in reaction to rumours circulating through the city that the Parliament at College Green was about to debate union with Britain. Immediately the usual suspects were blamed for the disturbances, including Catholic clergy and French emissaries.[78] The Duke of Bedford wrote to William Pitt from Dublin castle claiming that 'new light Presbyterians, or Twadlers' from the city's liberties were as much to blame for the riot as were their disaffected Catholic neighbours.[79] 'Their tenents both here, and (I am sorry to say it) in the North of Ireland', Bedford explained, 'are totally republican and averse to English government.'[80] Was there something to Bedford's remarks? Were the majority of Ulster Presbyterians in the winter of 1759, at the height of British imperial glory, really harbouring resentment towards the British connection? To be sure, agitation throughout the 1750s and 60s revealed a strong aversion to London's meddling in Ireland's political fortunes. The patriot clubs of the north did actively campaign against the possibility of union. After the Tyrone elections of 1761, for example, the Omagh patriots drank toasts to 'short Parliaments and no Union'.[81] But surely Bedford's insistence that northern Presbyterians, at that time, were anti-establishment and republican was misguided. Such accusations probably stemmed from deep-seated English prejudices regarding Presbyterian loyalty. The spontaneous celebrations that accompanied news of British victories in towns across Ulster told a different story than the one related in Bedford's letter. They indicated both popular enthusiasm for the British connection under Pitt's ministry and the Protestant public's tacit approval of imperial expansion. As is the case in the history of early America, the chief narratives of late eighteenth-century Irish history – the evolution of both mass politicization and emergent national self-awareness – need to be examined alongside the island's accelerated imperial integration from 1759 onwards.

4

Sorrowful Spectators:
Ulster Presbyterian Opinion and
American Frontier Atrocity

> [N]ext Spring, if we furnish Niagara abundantly with
> powder and trade goods, we can unleash nearly three
> thousand Indians on the English colonies. What a
> scourge! Humanity shudders at being obliged to make
> use of such monsters. But without them the match
> would be too much against us ... What can one do
> against invisible enemies who strike and flee with the
> rapidity of light? It is the destroying angel.[1]

Louis Antoine de Bougainville's thoughts regarding his American Indian
allies, cultivated while on campaign as the Aide-de-camp to the Marquis
de Montcalm, betray both his revulsion towards, and captivation with,
American Indian warfare.[2] His remarks, while indicative of the prevailing euro-American condescension towards the culture of the Native
peoples of America, provide us with a glimpse into how contemporary
European observers understood Indian combat. British observers also
made the comparison between Indian raids on European settlements
and the 'destroying Angel' of the book of Exodus. In the month of
Braddock's defeat, the Ulster-born Presbyterian minister, Francis Alison,
did so in a sermon delivered in Philadelphia, in which he claimed the
bleeding frontier was nothing less than judgement from an angry God.[3]
As noted in the last chapter, news concerning the war in America had
special significance for Ulster Presbyterians that made these stories more
popular with northern audiences than those in the south of Ireland.
In particular, stories of American Indian violence and brutality held
a macabre allure among a population that had grown accustomed to
colonial emigration over the previous two decades. The violent frontier captivated Irish audiences. So many local families had left to make

a better living on the cheap land promised in that bountiful country, only now to find the wilderness surrounding their settlements lashing-out either to destroy or envelop them. From 1754 onwards graphic stories depicting the murder and kidnap of settlers became a staple on the front pages of Irish periodicals, especially in the north. These atrocity narratives were central to the construction of the image of the Native American as a 'skulking', bloodthirsty savage.

At best, we possess only a partial understanding of how people in the north of Ireland imagined the Native Peoples of America throughout the eighteenth century. Literary scholars have excavated a fairly positive image of the American Indian from the writings of Irish reformers of the last quarter of the century.[4] Even in their praise of the American patriots, the Irish pamphleteers of the 1780s hinted at the dark reality hidden behind American revolutionary rhetoric. They recognized where the revolution failed to live up to its promise to protect the god-given equality of all. Joseph Pollock, in trying to convince his readers of the attainability of Irish independence, pointed to the hurdles overcome by the Americans in their struggle against Britain. Not only did they face the might of British arms but also 'the incursions of Indians (perhaps too justly enraged) on their rear'. In the south the revolutionaries also confronted the threat of slave insurrection 'whose dispositions to revenge must have been expected to burst on their more immediate oppressors'.[5]

Luke Gibbons notes that many leading figures within the United Irishmen movement of the 1790s were uncomfortable with the survival of the institution of slavery and the treatment of Indians in the supposed land of liberty across the ocean. His examination of anti-colonial themes in the rhetoric of the United Irishmen sheds light on how educated Presbyterians imagined the American Indian during the closing years of the century.[6] Specifically, he stresses the influence of the Scottish 'ethnographic Enlightenment' on the movement's conception of the intrinsic rights possessed by all human beings. The Seven Years War raised public awareness of the American Indian, and forced many intellectuals to re-examine their thoughts of societal progression, leading to the gradual refinement of the stadialist theory of human development.[7] The Scots philosophers' re-evaluation of the state of nature, from a 'state' to a 'process' in which nations rose or fell from one stage of development to another over time, altered prevailing views about the Native American society and culture. They, along with Irish peasants and Gaelic Highlanders, were no longer thought by all to be immoral by nature. They simply required the light of Anglo-British civilization to guide them away from their barbarous ways and onto the next step in the hierarchy of civilization. The incipient romanticism of the 1790s further elevated the image of the American Indian in the British and Irish imagination. Indians were now invested with innocent nobility as a consequence of their cultural distance from the corrupting influence of European luxury and decadence. They were moulded into the ideal paradigm of masculinity and restraint, if not virtue. These mythic images of the Native American were, however, largely absent from Irish popular discourse on British imperialism in the 1750s and 60s. Newspaper readers were bombarded with negative representations of the American Indians in which, to give one example, they were alleged to be cannibals capable of the most inhumane cruelties. In some cases they were even accused of devil worship.[8] It was this image of the Indian with which the people of mid-eighteenth-century Ireland were most familiar, and who dominated the front pages of Ulster newspapers during the period.

Linda Colley has explored the influence that American Indian captivity narratives had on the shaping of Britain's imperial consciousness and has pointed out that popular interest in the war sparked wider curiosity in American affairs. This curiosity, like the wars earlier in the century, increased newspaper circulation.[9] Indian captivity and atrocity narratives were subsumed within a flood of printed material on North American topics resulting from public interest in the war.[10] Colley claims that most British captivity accounts 'lingered on the pornography of real or invented Indian violence, in part because such lurid passages attracted readers even as they allowed them to feel properly repelled'.[11] What Colley describes as the pornography of Indian violence, the American historian Peter Silver has recently dubbed 'the anti-Indian sublime'. In his study of the role such stories played in the shaping of colonial identity, or the construction of American 'whiteness', Silver claims that 'Pamphlets, sermons, petitions, newspaper accounts, private correspondence, poems and plays – all were transformed by a horror-filled rhetoric of victimization, intent on the damage that Indians had done to colonists' bodies and families.'[12] This rhetoric 'proved all but unanswerable as political discourse' for those who, like Philadelphian Quakers, challenged it, and allowed a new artificially uniform Euro-American identity to develop from mid-century onwards.

Irish editors across the country included Indian atrocity narratives to attract readers. Henry Joy was no exception, and the *News-Letter* printed dozens of stories that lingered on violence against defenceless non-combatants. Tales of Indian cruelty had specific resonance among Ulster Presbyterians because their communities had for the last fifty years supplied large numbers of emigrants to settle the very frontiers now under attack. Those American victims on the edges of European settlement were not as distant to the reading public of Belfast and its hinterland as they were to the average newspaper consumer in London, Norwich or Birmingham. The 'pornography' of Native American violence had a more profound emotive effect on their community than it had on most Britons for a number of reasons. First, the victims of Native American violence were, in large part, Irish Presbyterian immigrants or their progeny. Secondly, the perpetrators of these attacks were portrayed to be puppets of the French and were in many instances identified as Catholic converts.[13] The British and Irish press frequently remarked on the inroads made by Jesuits in the conversion of the Native Peoples bordering the Great Lakes and New France.[14] Ulster Presbyterians were a religious minority surrounded by disenfranchised Catholics who had, in the past, supported French invasion, and who might do so again. Stories of Native American savagery roused memories of earlier Catholic atrocity and the mythic past of Irish Protestants.

American Indian violence and colonial victimization in the *Belfast News-Letter*

On 26 August 1760 an ex-soldier wrote to Henry Joy under the name 'Americus' regarding his encounters with American Indians while under the command of General Oglethorpe on the Georgia frontier two decades earlier. In his introduction he claimed, 'We have received many accounts of the barbarous ravages and the massacres of the Indians in America during the course of the present war.'[15] He hoped that his balanced portrayal of Native American customs, particularly their conceptions of justice and fairness, might help readers better understand the conflict and correct the misinformation spread throughout Ulster regarding frontier warfare. He argued that French emissaries, popularly believed to be spreading popery and hatred for 'heretics' among the tribes neighbouring British settlements, were not primarily responsible for the Indian war on the frontier. Rather, the 'impolitick treatment of [Britain's Indian allies] for many years past' and the 'corrupt measures pursued by a late ministry' brought about the current deplorable state of the North American borderlands. Yet, despite the assertion of British culpability and the author's promise to gloss over the details of his story that were 'too gross, and too affecting for your readers ears', the letter still contained the hallmarks of the savage Indian stereotype common on the front pages of the *News-Letter*.[16]

Americus described the destruction of a fort in Georgia in 1740 and the scalping of its defenders while also devoting considerable attention to the abuse and eventual murder of a defenceless mother and child. By choosing to focus on graphic violence and settler victimization, the author undermined his proclaimed objectivity. As a result, his readers were perhaps left better informed about the reasons that underlay Indian violence but unsympathetic to the plight of native peoples in their dealings with land-hungry settlers and duplicitous colonial administrators. The Indian remained violent and cruel, the unforgiving antithesis of European civility and reason. As well-intentioned as Americus may have been, his account only fostered the image of the bloodthirsty savage, lurking on the western fringes of the Empire. His letter indicates that tales of Indian savagery were a common topic of conversation in the north of Ireland throughout the war. Indeed, the thirst for such stories was great enough to merit the publication of decades'-old memories from well-informed retirees eager to contribute insights on the topic *du jour*.

A general awareness of war in America within Ulster Presbyterian communities is evident in the few surviving emigrant family letters and merchant correspondence from the period. In 1758 David Lindsey received a letter from his two cousins, Thomas and Andrew Fleming, who had previously emigrated to Pennsylvania. In his reply he claimed, 'I expected an account oftener from you, only times being troublesome in that country with wars that we were assured that you were all ded or killed.'[17] The recent wars and the dearth of correspondence did not deter Lindsey who declared 'these things does not Disourage me to goe only we Depend on ye for Directions in the goods fitting to take to that place'.[18] The New York and Belfast merchant Waddell Cunningham wrote to potential clients in Newry about the American flaxseed crop of 1756. 'The Season is very favourable both for a crop of grain and flaxseed', Cunningham claimed.[19] Unfortunately 'The Province of Penselvania will fall short of Both, as a great Part of the province is now deserted.'[20]

As a matter of course, Irish editors, following the example of their colonial counterparts, favoured gruesome narratives over level-headed coverage of the war on the frontiers. That this was often a conscious decision on the part of the editor, is demonstrated in a story lifted from the *South Carolina Gazette* and printed in an April 1760 edition of the *Dublin Courier*. The selection described the details of a recent Cherokee raid and consequent 'murders, rapine and devastation, such as would melt the heart of any human being, except that of an Indian'. It ended abruptly with the sentence, 'Other advices represent things in a more favourable light.' Not surprisingly, these alternative portrayals were not published alongside the more gruesome accounts in either the original publication or the *Courier*. Both Irish editors and the colonial news-papermen that they relied upon for subject matter knew what type of stories appealed to their audiences. Positive portrayals of the American Indian did not sell papers on either side of the Atlantic, or at least not as many as did the image of the warlike savage.

From 1754 to 1764 a minimum of 142 accounts of American Indian violence were published in the *News-Letter*. Figure 4.1 below shows annual totals of these accounts printed in the paper alongside statis-tics from two Dublin papers: *Faulkner's Dublin Journal* and the *Dublin Courier*. In all probability, the overall total from the *News-Letter* is low, as some editions of the paper from these years have been lost. Survival rates for the years 1755–7 are the worst in the sample, for which approxi-mately 20 per cent of the issues printed are lost. These three years saw the escalation of hostilities between British and French regulars on the mid-Atlantic frontier, frequent Indian raids on colonial settlements, and a relative lull in the British campaigns on the European continent. It is therefore very likely that more accounts were printed at that point than are represented on the chart. Annual averages for the frequency of Indian violence narratives across these eleven years would be misleading as the genre was far more popular at some points than it was at others. In 1762, for example, only one such story was printed, while in 1760 thirty-two were published, averaging one account printed every other

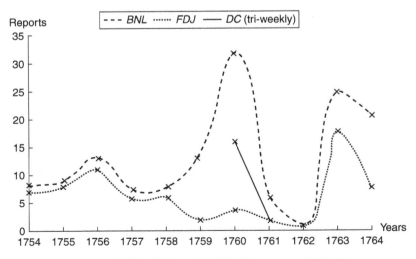

Figure 4.1   American Indian Violence in Irish Newspapers, 1754–64.

week. Even this incredible statistic, however, is misleading as these stories were often – though certainly not always – printed in clusters. As a result, some issues were inundated with tales of Indian cruelty. The Joys, for example, published three such stories on 2 January 1756 and four on 14 August 1764. With the exception of a few lulls, however, the paper provided a fairly regular coverage of war on the American frontier.

The accounts depicted in Figure 4.1 constitute a particular genre of story that displayed the supposed characteristics of Indian warfare as it was defined and understood by contemporary European observers. References to 'savage' violence including scalping, burning or kidnapping are included while descriptions of pitched battles between Indians and British soldiers without these exotic accoutrements are not. It is worth mentioning that this list also included incidents in which white soldiers behaved in a 'savage' manner, using techniques commonly associated with American Indians. This scenario was common in the coverage of the Cherokee War of 1759–60 and occasionally occurred during Pontiac's rising of 1763–4. Fourteen accounts of this type were printed in the *News-Letter* and four in the *Dublin Journal* between 1757 and 1764.

The majority of examples represented in the chart are brief descriptions that provided little detail other than bare, matter-of-fact reports of what supposedly occurred. Many were simply lists of atrocities committed such as those related to the *News-Letter* in a letter from Virginia on 17 October 1755 in which a gentleman claimed that a group of Indians had in a recent attack 'scalped some, beheaded others, drank their very Blood, ript up the Women; and left them in a Posture to shocking to be related'.[21] Some were even shorter, simply stating that a family or person had been scalped. Others, however, were lengthy vignettes that described individual incidents in great detail. The *News-Letter*, for example, printed a graphic account of the decapitation of a captured highland soldier in Georgia: 'The Indian directs the forceful blow with skill, the discontinuing blade glides, swift as lightning, between the vertebrae: *the head assists the deception by continuing some moments on the trunk: then tumbles* with it on the ground; *and rowls away in everlasting separation.*'[22] By evaluating the significance of a common negative stereotype, I do not mean to imply that there were no positive portrayals of American Indians in the *News-Letter* during these years. There were many instances in which the valour of friendly Indians was celebrated, especially in the case of the southern Cherokees before 1760. Coverage was, however, overwhelmingly negative. Taken together, the large number of these accounts reveals that American events were very much on the minds of Irish Presbyterians and that the welfare of British colonials did trouble the Ulster reading public.

Before delving into their content the discrepancies between the numbers of these atrocity narratives published in the *News-Letter* and the Dublin papers requires explanation. The Joys continuously printed more stories from the American frontier across the period than did their Dublin counterparts. Sometimes they printed quite a bit more. That they did so, can be attributed to two interrelated factors: Ulster's intimate commercial and familial ties with the colonies and a resulting local interest in American affairs – especially as they related to the frontier. Ulster's strong commercial ties with the colonies meant that American news was readily available in local ports and market towns, while familial connections in America increased demand for such information across the province. The north's distinctly strong attachment to the North American frontier is evident when compared with Dublin papers in the chart during the years 1759–60. The greatest statistical variation between the *News-Letter* and the *Dublin Journal* manifests during these two years. In 1759, the total numbers of atrocity narratives published in each journal diverge for the first and only time in the period; with the genre becoming more common than the previous year in the *News-Letter* and less so in the *Dublin Journal*. The number of Indian atrocity narratives then explodes in the *News-Letter* over the course of the subsequent year. When one looks at the *Journal*, however, there is only a modest upsurge in the popularity of these stories in 1760. The difference between the size of the 1760 spike in the *News-Letter* and that in the *Dublin Courier* is not as dramatic, but it is still significant. The *Courier* was printed on a tri-weekly basis rather than the bi-weekly schedule of both the *News-Letter* and the *Journal*. Its editor was, therefore, more likely to include information overlooked by Faulkner at the *Journal* because of the need to fill a greater number of pages on a more frequent basis. Despite publishing a third more papers in a given year, the *Courier*'s total in 1760 was still half that of the *News-Letter*. Nevertheless, the paper's print run from this year does demonstrate that atrocity narratives continued to circulate in Dublin despite the general shift in editorial interest towards the European theatre of the conflict.

Why did the *News-Letter* print so many of these stories between 1759 and 1761 compared to the Dublin papers? What happened in the colonies during these years that encouraged the Joys to publish so many accounts of frontier violence at a point when their Dublin colleagues were shifting their focus eastward? The answer to these questions is tied to Ulster's unique relationship with the particular region then under attack. The last large migration to America occurred in the early 1750s and was to the Carolinian backcountry. In 1759, Cherokee war parties began raiding the western fringes of European settlement in earnest. This conflict within a conflict later became known as the first Cherokee War (1758–61). The *News-Letter* contained a large number of Indian atrocity narratives in these years because many of its readers had recently witnessed people from their communities sail from Ulster to the very areas now under attack. These were not faceless colonials. They were former friends, neighbours and family members. Many Presbyterians in the north-east devoured information concerning the Carolinian frontier, as it arrived in the province. The stories presented to the public were grizzly but mostly devoid of the facts needed to establish a link between frontier victims and people readers knew. Few accounts, for instance, divulged the names of victims. Thousands of miles from the Carolinian interior, many readers suffered in the knowledge that something horrible might be happening, or had happened to, the people they had once known in person. The stories that were diffused through the paper into the Antrim countryside, where the most recent migrations had originated, must have haunted those who could not help but imagine the faces of their acquaintances among the mutilated dead left abandoned and unburied in the woods of America.

One of the primary land promoters for migration immediately before the war, and the first of three major agents investigated by R. J. Dickson in his seminal book on the subject, was the wealthy County Antrim landowner and author of *Essay on the Improvement of Ireland*, Arthur Dobbs.[23] Dobbs had been keenly interested in colonial affairs and in 1745 purchased 4,000 acres of land in North Carolina. Between 1751 and 1753 at least six ships ferried migrants from Dobbs's County Antrim estate to North Carolina. On 4 June 1754 Dobbs and his chaplain Alexander Stewart published letters in the *News-Letter* extolling the virtues of North Carolina, namely, the comparably high wages enjoyed by colonial weavers and their free practice of religion.[24] The optimistic image of America championed by Dobbs in the early 1750s was shattered in the second half of the decade. His speech to the colonial assembly, printed in the spring of 1755 after many emigrants had already embarked for America, was far less optimistic and celebratory. It was delivered in a time of uncertainty following a confrontation between Virginian troops led by a young George Washington and French regulars in what would become western Pennsylvania. In it he spoke of how the French had already sent their Indian allies to 'massacre in cold blood, and scalp' North Carolinians. He urged solidarity with neighbouring colonies claiming that the 'religion, liberty, and property' of Carolinians were at stake if they did not. These warnings from a man well known and trusted in the north of Ireland were among the first received by many Presbyterians who had recently witnessed many of their kin sail with their landlord for what they assumed was a better life in the colonies.

The most detailed sub-category within the Indian atrocity genre emphasized violence against helpless colonials and European captives. Printed depictions of American Indian brutality often centred on the victimization of women and children. The gendered violence of these accounts, real or fictitious, demonstrated to readers throughout the British Atlantic world the alien nature of Native American violence. Thus the *News-Letter* printed a letter from Philadelphia regarding recent Delaware raids on western settlements in September 1764:

> [A] woman named Cunningham, big with child, was going from her house to one Justice M'Dowell's, about two miles below [Fort] Loudoon, she was met with by the Savages, who murdered, scalped, and otherwise most horribly abused her, ripping her belly open, and taking out the child, which they left lying beside her; [and] that another woman named Jameson, was missing supposed to be carried off.[25]

The letter highlighted the particular brutality of the murder and mutilation of a pregnant woman and her unborn child. This story and the brief allusion at the end to the kidnapping of another woman represented the worst affronts to the patriarchal model of the European family, and thus highlighted the supposed savagery of American Indians while simultaneously providing the opportunity for the Irish reading public to sympathize with colonial victims.[26] Another reprinted letter from New Hampshire five years earlier highlighted the tragedy of a man who was forced to watch helplessly while Abenaki warriors killed his wife. Phillip Call and his son were returning from the fields when they spotted 'a number of Indians, supposed to be of the St François tribe, enter his house, where his wife was, (a woman of about seventy years of age) whom they hauled out, killed and scalped before the door; the husband being hid in the bushes, was a sorrowful spectator of the tragedy'.[27] The stated advanced age of Mrs Call reinforced the brutality of the crime. The scene was made more pathetic by Mr Call's inability to protect his wife in front of his home and in the presence of his son, leaving him utterly emasculated.

The affidavit of George Casper Heiss, taken in Northampton County, Pennsylvania, on 18 December 1755 was reprinted in the *News-Letter* the following January. Heiss recounted how he had rushed to his neighbour's house upon hearing screams. When he arrived he discovered that the entire family had been murdered by a Delaware raiding party. When he returned home he found that the same party had visited his house. He was greeted by screams from his wife who, before being dragged into the darkening woods, yelled, 'Casper, Casper, ah my dear Casper! farewell, I shall never see you more.'[28] Such emotive flourishes highlighted the tragedy of these stories, giving them a human element and increasing their appeal to readers.

The *News-Letter* published a letter from Augusta County, Virginia, in June 1764, depicting the murder of planter David Cloyne's family. While Cloyne was away on business a small party of ten Indians stormed his house, tomahawked his wife and sons, and stole over £700 in cash. Mrs Cloyne survived the attack notwithstanding the fact that she was 'an antient woman, and was very much hacked and mangled'.[29] Another brutal account emerged following the French capture of Fort William-Henry in 1757. On 21 October Joy published the account, stating that 'The following is printed here by order.'[30] The selection told of how the English force had surrendered only to be massacred afterwards:

> That the French immediately after the capitulation, most perfidiously let their Indian blood-hounds loose upon our people … [the fort's defenders] were despoiled of their arms; the most were stript stark-naked; many were killed, and officers not excepted. All the English Indians and Negroes in the garrison were seized, and either captivated or slain. The throats of most if not all the women were cut, their bellies ript open, their bowels torn out and thrown upon the faces of their dead and dying bodies; and, it is said, that all the women were murdered in one way or other: That the children were taken by the heels, and their brains beat out against the trees or stones, and not one of them saved.[31]

Again, it was clear that those brutalized by French treachery in America were 'our people'. This closeness between the residents in the north and distressed colonials was reinforced by periodic letters from the frontier to correspondents in Belfast that were then passed on to the Joys for publication. One such letter to find its way into the paper was dated 1 March 1757 and arrived from Lancaster, Pennsylvania. It described several scalpings and the subsequent exchange of dismembered human remains among different parties of Indians and white rangers near Fort Duquesne. The author of another letter begged 'the stingy mother country' to send presents in order to sate the Indians and 'spare the effusion of her children's blood, who are butchered in a manner shocking to all civilized people'.[32]

Presbyterians continued to emigrate to America throughout the war despite reports of carnage from the frontier. Port agents and advertisers competed among themselves to show that their ship offered the most comfortable journey across the Atlantic in order to combat the falling numbers of willing migrants. These cheery advertisements were often printed in the same editions as stories of American Indian brutality. On 14 August 1764, for example, five ships for America were advertised in the same issue of the *News-Letter* as four different reports depicting murder and violence on the frontier (see Appendix 1). Even if readers were not emigrating themselves, the images of ships that peppered the last two pages of the paper reminded them of the kinship and mercantile links between Ulster and the colonies and that many of their countrymen and women *were* risking the voyage despite the horrors that might befall them when they arrived. References to Irish migration were scattered among the first reports of Indian raids on the New York frontier in the winter of 1754, including the burning of a village near Albany, and a refugee crisis that resulted from it. Joy translated news that the Massachusetts Assembly had 'granted lands for four townships, (each to contain 120 families) in order to encourage Foreign Protestants settle in that Government'.[33] It also debunked rumours that had apparently spread throughout the town and country regarding a shipwreck carrying Irish soldiers and passengers. 'We can by Authority, positively assure the Publick', the paper claimed, 'that the Story of one of the Transport ships bound for America, having been lost near Falmouth, is without Foundation.'[34]

Migrants were not the only Irish men and women directly affected by Indian attacks on the American frontier. As the Americus letter suggests, Irish soldiers were often involved in the British campaigns against the French-allied Indians. These soldiers required a vast body of men and women for their upkeep while on campaign and were often serviced by people who, sensing an opportunity to make money from government contracts, followed the Irish regiments across the ocean. Any triumphalist notions that the Irish reading public may have had regarding the superiority of British regulars over disorganized Indian war parties were shattered early in the conflict by Braddock's defeat. It was clear these 'savages' actually posed a threat, not only to amateur colonial militiamen but also to European soldiers as well. Concern for the safety of British soldiers, many of whom belonged to the Irish home regiments, was certainly shared by Irish Protestants. The 27th Regiment of His Majesty's Foot, an infantry unit raised in Inniskilling, County Tyrone, was involved in the British offensives against Fort Ticonderoga, Crown Point and Montreal. The unit's exploits were celebrated in newspapers and at public dinners across the country. Its Irish commander, Lord William Blakeney, was already a hero famed for his earnest, though unsuccessful defence of Minorca in 1756. The Friendly Sons of St Patrick honoured him with a statue in Dublin.[35] Letters to Ireland revealed that men from the regiment were also present at the massacre at Fort William Henry, where many of them were murdered or taken into captivity.[36] News of their captivity was later diffused throughout the province in the *News-Letter*.[37]

Many stories printed by the Joys reminded readers that those suffering in the woods of America were people of their own religion and ethnic background, often their former neighbours and relatives, and were not faceless colonials. In January 1756, within months of Dobbs's harrowing speech before the North Carolina legislature, the paper reported that war had indeed erupted on the Pennsylvania frontier and that 'Two Presbyterian clergymen in Cumberland county have marched in quest of the enemy, at the head of two considerable parties of their hearers ... for the defence of their country, and safety of their families.'[38]

The names of both the victims of Indian violence and the places in which these atrocities took place also suggested ethnic links between distressed colonials and Irish readers. Often the victims' surnames hinted at their Scottish or Irish ancestry. This was true in the case of a man named McSwin, whose dramatic escape from a Shawnee war band made the front page on 2 January 1756 and was featured in a report from Fort Bedford after an attack during Pontiac's War in which 'one M'Cormick, two women, and a child, were murdered'.[39] The names of places in these accounts were sometimes familiar to Irish Presbyterians. The site of the massacre of two families in Ulster County, New York, during the winter of 1759, for example, had obvious resonance with readers from the province after which the county was named.[40] A printed selection from Ulster County outlined the terrifying situation faced by frontier inhabitants across the colony. In the winter of 1757 the packets from America brought more tales of misery to Belfast. The first line of one story from New York City printed in the *News-Letter* in early December 1757 read, 'We are in a dreadful Situation here! every moment expecting to be murdered by Indians.'[41] It went on to say that 'Patrick Car, who lived about 18 miles from Hudson's river, was shot lying in his bed, and his wife and five children, who resided in the same house, were carried into captivity by the Indians.'[42] The author complained, 'We, more than any other part of the province, have felt the direful effects of an Indian war: nothing has yet been done to succour us; the frontier settlers are all coming in, having abandoned their little habitations, to preserve their lives.'[43] The British military commander in New York, William Johnson, established two Irish colonies in western New York in 1740–1. Johnson was born in County Meath and was celebrated across the country as an Irish hero.[44] His first New York Irish colony, settled in 1740 near Fort Hamilton, was composed of forty families and the second, founded a year later, contained sixty. In 1754 Johnson published an advertisement for willing immigrants to join these settlements.[45] Many Ulster Presbyterian communities had recently witnessed emigration to New York prior to the war. For many throughout the province, violence on the New York frontier was therefore deeply unsettling.

By the early 1760s the French war was near its end and the frontier was, it was assumed, returning to a state of normality. Warnings from across the ocean published in Irish journals over the previous five years were either forgotten or deemed no longer relevant by prospective migrants eager to take advantage of the well-publicized availability of affordable land in the colonies. Such optimism was ill founded, as unprepared migrants sometimes found themselves in the midst of a warzone. The most direct example of Irish migrant victimization published in the *News-Letter* during the war detailed an instance where recent arrivals, alone in the Carolinian backcountry, desperately sought protection from hostile Indian raiding parties. The paper printed a selection of stories from Charleston South Carolina in the spring of 1763 regarding the arrival of '69 Irish Protestants from Belfast', who had been lured across the ocean by the colony's offer of land and free farming implements in a bid to bolster the colony's white Protestant population. The article reported:

> The lands allotted for them to settle on, we are informed, are some of the best in the province, and equal in any on this continent. And we are told, that, upon the accounts these people will translate[?] to Ireland, some hundred families of these useful settlers may be expected to follow them.[46]

Unfortunately for these immigrants, they arrived immediately before violence erupted on the Carolinian frontier during the multifaceted conflict known as Pontiac's War. A year after their ship sailed into

Charleston harbour, the *News-Letter* reprinted a harrowing account of the fate of these once optimistic immigrants, from the colonial papers:

> By Letters from the Frontiers we learn, that the Irish who came over last year are in great distress, the people round them have left their settlements, but they cannot do the same, because they have neither horses nor waggons [*sic*] to remove their children and provisions, and have neither firearms nor ammunition to defend themselves; they have applied to Mr. Mayson, at [Fort] Ninety Six, beseeching him to fetch them away.[47]

Readers were left to ponder the fate of these Irish families. Surely previous tales of murder, abduction and disfigurement, published in grisly detail within the pages of the *News-Letter* informed their conclusions.

American atrocity and the historical memory of Irish Protestants

The Seven Years War heralded uncertain times for northern Protestants. The late 1750s were a period of invasion scares and anxiety about the potential state of the Atlantic flaxseed/linen trade if the war were to go in France's favour. Domestically, the island was rocked by bouts of rural insurrection in the form of the Whiteboy and Oakboy disturbances. It was also a worrying time for those concerned about the fate of their American compatriots. Multiple factors contributed to how Irish Presbyterians reacted to the bloody stories from the American frontier and the meaning that they attributed to them. Their reactions were informed both by the dominant cultural discourses that held sway within the larger English-speaking world as well as by the local webs of historical memory and tradition in which their communities were suspended. Two factors were particularly important in this respect. First, the popular anti-Catholicism and the historical memory of past Catholic atrocities infused tales of American Indian brutality with historical and localized meaning that transcended the current conflict. Newspaper coverage of frontier atrocities in the north routinely blamed the French for misleading their Indian allies. These stories therefore fit within the familiar didactic between Roman Catholic cruelty and Protestant civility. Secondly, evolving Enlightenment conceptions of sensibility transformed how the reader digested and reacted to these gruesome narratives. The emerging cult of sensibility allowed for the consumption of material that might otherwise be deemed taboo as long as the subject reflected the moral consequences of reading tales of suffering. It is the first point that is the focus of this section.

The memory of past atrocities cast a long shadow over cross-community relationships in Ulster. The 1641 Catholic rising was particularly significant to the historical memory of Ulster Protestants. The physicality and proximity of the locations significant to the rebellion kept its memory alive in Irish Protestant communities. The stylized victims' narratives made popular by Sir John Temple, in his often reprinted seventeenth-century collection, *The Irish rebellion: or, a history of the general rebellion raised ... together with the barbarous cruelties and bloody massacres ensured thereupon*, guaranteed that the mental images of past violence recalled in the mind of the Protestant viewer by the sight of such places were formulaic and relatively devoid of historical accuracy. Such sites became ghostly tutors, asking both Catholic and Protestant passers-by: what happened here and why? Each had remarkably different memorized responses to these questions prepared. For Protestants, such catechismal reinforcement of past Catholic violence could be brought to the surface and transformed by similarly structured victimization narratives from alien contexts. This is apparent in the language invoked by the wealthy Belfast merchant John Black Senior in a letter to his sons Alexander and James in August 1766. In it, Black described a family property in Balintagert, County Armagh, claiming that the site had been the scene of extraordinary carnage during the 1641 rising. He informed his sons that '150,000 damned heretics men and women and children and usurpers' had been 'slain and extirpated' on the spot, and that 'some of the houses and places where these butcheries were then committed appear in ruinous heaps of stone to this day, a proper warning to the present generation to prevent for the future such Cherockee machinations of Roman profession to commit such horrid crimes of inhumanity'.[48] Black's choice of the word 'Cherockee' to describe past Irish Catholic violence is revealing. The word had apparently seeped into the Protestant vocabulary after more than a decade of intense press coverage of the wars on the American frontier, and was now interchangeable with words such as 'barbarous' or 'savage' to describe the cruel behaviour of those deemed uncivilized by European standards of the day.

The new vocabulary and imagery of Native American savagery was so pervasive at mid-century that it affected how some Protestants described their disempowered neighbours and the dangers posed by them. Travelling north from Dublin in 1759, the English circuit judge, Lord Chief Baron Edward Willes wrote to his friend the Earl of Warwick. Willes was struck by the poverty of Catholics in the Mourne Mountains.

They appeared to him 'upon rank with the American Savages' inhabiting tiny cabins he equated to 'Indian huts'.[49] He further stated that the peasants of Tipperary live in worse conditions 'than you read among the Creeks and Cherokes [*sic*] in America'.[50] In 1763 Andrew Stewart wrote of his detention at the hands of a group of agrarian protesters, or 'Green Boys', near Cookstown, County Tyrone. There the mob demanded that he take an oath to maintain stable rents at rates no higher than a penny per acre and that he not levy warrants for higher church dues. In humiliation, he exclaimed that any 'Gentleman in this Country' should 'prefer and immediately look for a Settlement in America than be subject to such barbarism'.[51] Here, Stewart inverted the rhetorical binary separating European civilization from American barbarism in order to highlight domestic problems. He was certainly not the first to do so. Jonathan Swift employed the same technique to address widespread poverty in the introduction to his infamous 1729 satirical pamphlet *A Modest Proposal*. In it, the anonymous author first contemplates the slaughter and preparation of Irish babies to feed local landlords and English consumers after a discussion he had in London with 'a very knowing *American*'.[52]

How should we interpret these references? Are they mere hyperbole? Did mid-eighteenth-century Irish Protestants literally equate their Catholic neighbours with the exotic and unfamiliar American Indian, with whom the vast majority of them had no personal experience? Gentry observers, such as Willes, almost certainly used the language for dramatic effect in order to register their shock at the destitution of poor Catholics. Comparisons between Irish Catholics and oppressed peoples such as African slaves and American Indians have attracted the attention of post-colonial scholars eager to emphasize the imperial imaginings of Ireland's colonial elite.[53] Ian McBride has recently warned against allowing such spectacular examples to drown 'out the more humdrum social vocabulary that framed contemporary discourse'.[54] Such remarks, after all, were exceptional. Most observations made by self-styled Anglican gentlemen regarding rural Catholics lacked racialized comparisons, and instead reflected the well-established view that both poorer Catholics and Protestants occupied different social strata from that of the observer. References to American Indian savagery were used figuratively, for effect, in order to distinguish between respectable behaviour and uncultivated barbarity.

Yet there was something to this language, especially in the manner in which John Black employed it in the example above. It meant something deeper to those who used it, something that is difficult for us, with our modern understanding of historical agency and causality, to grasp. Black found similarities between seventeenth-century Irish Catholic violence against Protestants and Cherokee raids against euro-American settlers because he was looking for a common denominator that underpinned both. That denominator, or the active historical force acting on both groups was, in Black's mind, the 'machinations of Roman Profession', or Catholic intrigue. Early modern Europeans spotted conspirators everywhere. As Jill Lepore has noted in a study of alleged slave conspiracy in colonial New York, nothing 'just happened' in the eighteenth century.[55] There 'was always a villain to be caught, a conspiracy to be detected' and reasonable people routinely 'spotted plotters lurking behind nearly every shadow'.[56]

This was a paranoid world in which the memory of past atrocity and fear of conspiracy routinely informed peoples' everyday lives. In Ireland, it was also an era characterized by frequent outbreaks of international war in which the attendant dangers of domestic insurrection and French invasion were a very real possibility.[57] Even though Catholic and Protestant communities lived alongside one another peacefully most of the time, Protestants remained aware of past Catholic atrocities and maintained guarded apprehension that another insurrection was imminent. The Ascendancy elite may have adopted a more tolerant stance towards Catholics through the 1750s and 1760s despite the threat of invasion.[58] It is, however, questionable as to whether their newfound tolerance was widely shared among Protestants further down the social hierarchy. At the beginning of the war, Archbishop Michael O'Reilly of Armagh was brought before a magistrate on the charge of an informer that he had been assisting the French.[59] Presbyterians cultivated a suspicious world-view in which the tentacles of the Roman Anti-Christ lurked behind the scenes to promote discord abroad and at home. American Indians, Irish Whiteboys and Louis XV himself were all instruments of papal power.

Many Protestants feared that a domestic rising, spurred by foreign influence, could result in the widespread slaughter of Protestants, as they believed had been the case in 1641. Across the Irish Sea, George Whitefield warned audiences of the threat of invasion in 1756, by reminding them of past Catholic atrocities. The French had proven what they intended for Britain in their treatment of

> our fellow subjects in *America*, by the hands of savage *Indians*, instigated thereto by more than savage Popish priests, Speak *Smithfield*, speak … Speak *Ireland*, speak … And think you, my dear countrymen,

that Rome glutted as it were with Protestant blood, will now rest satisfied, and say 'I have enough'.[60]

In 1766, charges of a possible link between the French and Whiteboy rioters emerged during a trial of men involved in the disturbances. Rumours also circulated that French money was found on the persons of captured Whiteboys and, more ominously, that the houses of Protestants had been marked in Waterford and Kilkenny on Good Friday Night 1762.[61]

Several factors contributed to the outbreak of the Catholic Whiteboy disturbances, in which it was reported that upwards of 14,000 people participated, across Counties Tipperary, Cork, and Kilkenny between 1762 and 1766.[62] Prices for beef and woollen goods rose as a result of increased demand from British Army personnel serving in America. Rising beef prices stimulated increased rates of enclosure among landlords wishing to take advantage of the situation by devoting more of their land to the rearing of cattle. Subsequently, rents in these counties went up. Conacre rents were also a point of contention that contributed to the protests. Like those many Presbyterians who also rose in limited insurrection during the 'Oakboy' campaigns of 1763, Whiteboys resented the farming of tithes for profit towards a church they did not support.[63] For many Protestants, however, foreign intrigue lay at the heart of the disturbances. William Fant, an attorney from Limerick, warned the Lord Lieutenant in 1762 that he had seen the Stuart Pretender 'disguised in woman's apparel' at a meeting of Catholics in Cork.[64] Another claimed that the mythical Queen Sieve Oultagh, whom the Whiteboys claimed as their symbolic leader, was actually a Spanish friar or priest.[65] The fact that the most prominent figure hanged for his involvement in the protests had been a priest, Father Nicholas Sheehy, did little to comfort panicked Protestants.

Larger historical narratives regarding the forces perceived to be responsible for both American Indian violence and Catholic rebellion – meaning Roman Catholicism and French intrigue – made it possible to transpose the language of American savagery onto domestic concerns among Irish Protestants. Such language was particularly powerful and suggestive in the period before the British naval victories at Lagos and Quiberon Bay in 1759 destroyed the possibility of a large-scale French invasion of the British Isles. Before 1759, allegorical comparisons between past Irish Catholic atrocity and contemporary American Indian violence became more real at each alleged sighting of a French ship off the coast and every report of increased activity at the port of Brest. This haze of panic that periodically fell upon Ulster Protestant communities clouded residents' judgement, making it possible for them to imagine potential Catholic violence bearing the hallmarks of American Indian warfare. It was easy enough for Presbyterians to cast themselves in the role of the American settler surrounded by angry natives. The dour outlook and anxiety that accompanied news of British defeats during the first few years of the war coupled with fear of invasion and a simultaneous Catholic insurrection added weight to such a comparison.

A line in the *News-Letter* regarding the discovery of '208 gross of *scalping knives!*' among the trophies taken from captured French ships in 1758 exposed popular paranoia regarding invasion and how the resident Catholic community could be imagined to act in the light of such an event.[66] This news accompanied reports from Brest about a possible French invasion 'not for America, but for a secret expedition much nearer at home', a theory – though accurate – debunked later in the paper by information received by the Joys.[67] It was unlikely that this cargo, if it existed at all, was destined for anywhere other than the New World. Nevertheless, the immediate proximity of the two stories in the paper and the use of the rare editorial exclamation mark undoubtedly unsettled a community who lived under threat of invasion and the possibility of Catholic unrest. Their suggestive editorial arrangement and punctuation choice undermined subsequent level-headed conclusions on the matter. In this way, they could benefit from the heightened sales that accompanied sensational journalism while also preserving the paper's reputation for truth and honesty. French strategy in America (i.e., arming natives and instigating frontier conflict) could be, it was feared, just as easily employed in Ireland.

Links between Irish Catholics and Native Americans may, to some extent, have been established earlier in the century.[68] Richard Burton's seventeenth-century chapbook entitled *The English Empire in America* was reprinted in Dublin in 1729 and 1735, and a Belfast edition was listed on an advertisement page within a 1750 edition of Robert Russell's *Seven Sermons*.[69] The Belfast printing was undertaken by James Magee, the foremost Belfast printer of the eighteenth century and the man responsible for the majority of the affordable literature peddled in the northern countryside, including most of the material sold to rural Presbyterian schools. Burton claimed that the Indians of New England were cannibals 'as were formerly the heathen *Irish*' and that they howled 'at their funerals like the wild Irish, blaming the Devil for his hard-heartedness'.[70] This chapbook literature instilled a bias against American Indians in Ulster Presbyterian society by juxtaposing them with the familiar other and sometimes enemy, Irish Catholics. Such sources may have had broader implications beyond Ireland. Whether this bias led to violent anti-Indian behaviour on behalf of Irish migrants upon arrival on the American frontier is difficult, if not impossible, to ascertain. It is, however, beyond doubt that those emigrants who left for America after 1763 had been programmed – by newspaper media, letters from American kin, casual conversation on imperial affairs and even colonial material read aloud by their ministers at the meeting house – to think about American Indians in a negative light.

Given their own historical experience, news of Protestant victimization in other contexts naturally roused empathy within Irish Presbyterian communities. In this respect, the juxtaposition of the literature born out of the 1641 rebellion and the Seven Years War on the American frontier is not as strange a comparison as would first appear. According to Ian McBride, modern Irish Protestant loyalism has been 'constructed upon a grid of talismanic dates', including the outbreak of rebellion in 1641, the Siege of Derry in 1689 and the Battle of the Boyne in 1690. These dates underlined 'the durability of ethnic antagonism in Ireland, the unchanging threat posed by Roman Catholicism and the ultimate assurance of providential deliverance'.[71] Combined with other British anniversaries such as 5 November and the reigning monarch's birthday, they ordered the Protestant year and also served a didactic purpose in that they reminded Protestants to remain ever vigilant in their dealings with their Catholic neighbours. The eighteenth-century Irish Protestant calendar, though perhaps not as static and codified as it would become following the rise of unionism in the following century, informed the Presbyterian sense of community and history. The memory of 1641 in particular provided Ulster Protestants with a useful template to make sense of American violence for a number of reasons. First and foremost, the victims in both scenarios were Protestant; more specifically, they were imagined to be Irish Protestants. News coverage of the war in Ireland often hinted at the Irish ancestry of many settlers on the frontier. The American charitable campaign that visited Ireland in the aftermath of the war on the Pennsylvanian frontier also made explicit reference to the Irish heritage of euro-American victims. Secondly, the short colonial vignettes recalled the gruesome stories from the 1640s and were later popularized by John Temple, in the *Irish Rebellion*. The similar content and style of the published accounts of 1641 and American settler victimization stories further conspired to unite the two contexts in the minds of Ulster Protestants by triggering the historical memory of past atrocities.

The remembrance of past Catholic violence against Protestants was a cornerstone of the world-view and identity of British subjects throughout the Atlantic world. Time itself, it would seem, perpetuated anti-Catholic feeling among Protestant Britons. The way in which the passage of time was marked throughout the British Empire reaffirmed its inhabitants' sense of communal unity through the celebration of their common Protestantism. Annual commemorations recalling past Protestant deliverances from Catholic intrigue fragmented the year and regimented time while simultaneously reinforcing a providential cosmology through which Protestants could interpret both local and global events.[72] Crucially, the British national calendar perpetuated a belief in Roman conspiracy and in the divine favour of Britain and its empire. In 1764, Bostonians marked the anniversary of the discovery of the Catholic conspiracy to destroy Parliament on 5 November 1605 (the infamous Gunpowder Plot) by parading two papal effigies through the streets of the north and south ends before throwing them on a bonfire on Boston Common.[73] In Ireland, the outbreak of the 1641 rising and Dublin's deliverance from the divine judgement later cast upon the Ulster Plantation were remembered well into the nineteenth century on 23 October in a national day of thanksgiving during which the various Protestant communities on the island routinely heard sermons warning them to remain strong in their faith and vigilant in their dealings with their Catholic neighbours lest God, in his wrath, should raise another rebellion.[74] Dublin Presbyterian minister, Samuel Bruce, used the anniversary of the rebellion to remind his congregation of the importance of individual conscience in 1761 and 1765. He warned that those who sacrificed personal judgement on manners of religion 'would always be in the power of those to whom the right is given up to make use of such instruments to execute their most abominable and wicked designs'.[75]

By the end of the sixteenth century, the narratives of Protestant victimization and providential deliverance held such sway over the British calendar that new colonial additions to it were understood in those contexts. During the first fifty years of the Virginia colony, for example, anniversaries of American Indian raids became public days of thanksgiving for divine deliverance, a practice that demonstrates the malleability and pervasiveness of the trope of Protestant victimization in British North America. Popular enthusiasm for these regional holidays waned in the eighteenth century despite an official decree that these solemn occasions be kept 'in perpetual commemoration'.[76] In their place, colonial Virginians rediscovered traditional British holidays, like the anniversary of the discovery of the Gunpowder Plot, as a way of reaffirming their cultural connection to the mother country. The Protestant calendar, therefore, was also a unifying marker of identity throughout an expanding Atlantic empire.

In the larger European context, the British calendar was an expression of an international Protestant culture celebrating martyrdom and deliverance. A literary industry marketing collected tales of Catholic aggression and Protestant victimization developed in Protestant strongholds throughout Europe from the sixteenth century onwards. Popular English translations of these European collections allowed English and Irish Protestants to imagine that they were a part of a larger religious community which, despite its perceived geopolitical weakness, stood in adversity and righteousness against the attacks and expansion of a corrupt Roman Church. Events from the history of the Huguenots, for example, were incorporated into the British and Irish Protestant mythology. The St Bartholomew's Day Massacre of French Protestants on the streets of Paris in 1572, Louis XIV's revocation of the Edict of Nantes – which had secured toleration for French Protestants – in 1685 and the brutal repression of the Camisards in the south of the country through the first decade of the eighteenth century reinforced both Irish Protestants' sense of kinship with their continental coreligionists and the need for the current generation to guard against Catholic treachery. In particular, the St Bartholomew's Day Massacre, and the tracts compiled in its aftermath, had a strong hold over the eighteenth-century British and Irish imaginations.[77] Similarly, Frederick II of Prussia had established his credentials long before the war as a protector of the reformed religion when his armies 'liberated' the Silesian Protestants from Austrian – and thus Catholic – domination during the annexation of the province in 1740.

Ulster immigration to North America was not the only movement of Protestants reported in the *News-Letter* at mid-century. A fear of the Catholic imperial powers and the belief in the comparative geopolitical weakness of international Protestantism led northern Presbyterians to empathize with their coreligionists in different countries. This was reinforced by the presence of small communities of continental Protestant exiles in Ireland. From the late seventeenth century onwards Ireland became home to significant numbers of these refugees, with a significant Huguenot presence in Ulster – particularly in Lisburn and Castleblaney – and Dublin, and a sizeable Palatine community in County Limerick.[78] The continued transnational movement of Huguenots and Germans from regions along the Rhine therefore received steady coverage throughout the 1750s and early 1760s.[79] More often than not, the paper hinted that these migrations were motivated by persecution. One author jokingly stated that while still in France Protestants would be 'hanged, burnt, [and] butchered, rather than neglect their Service', but when they arrived in Ireland 'where no body prevents them from going to Church, they never think of it'.[80] Reports of Catholic oppression on the continent were commonly printed. Austrian attempts to secure a Catholic elector over Ratisbon and the Protestant exodus that accompanied these efforts, for example, became a running story between January and March 1755. By following the fortunes of these groups the *News-Letter* expanded upon the theme of Protestant victimization. Such persecution narratives, as well as printed letters from the American frontier, reinforced Ulster and Ireland's place within the wider Protestant world.

Many examples from British and Irish history were incorporated into the international Protestant martyrological tradition. John Foxe's collection of stories detailing the executions of English Protestants during the reign of Mary, entitled the *Actes and Monuments of these latter and perilous dayes ...* more commonly known as the *Book of Martyrs*, was a prominent fixture of the Protestant canon. It was first published in 1563 and was continually printed in the form of cheap pirated editions throughout the eighteenth century.[81] Out of the maelstrom of religious violence in mid-seventeenth-century Ireland emerged another work that quickly established itself alongside the *Actes and Monuments* in the martyrlogical canon. It was a history of the 1641 rising and collection of the depositions of Protestant survivors of the rebellion edited and compiled by Sir John Temple, the Master of the Irish Rolls at Dublin Castle. This 1646 collection, *The Irish rebellion*, ignored violence directed towards Catholics and claimed that culpability largely lay with the Catholic clerical establishment who inflamed hatred for 'hereticks'.[82] Like the Marian vignettes made famous by Foxe and frontier victimization narratives, Temple's depositions detailed the torture and murder of unarmed Protestants – often women and children.

For obvious reasons, the Irish rebellion of 1641 held more sway over the Irish Protestant imagination than contemporary continental or English massacres. Temple's collection was wildly successful, a fact born out by its publication record over the next two centuries. Between its initial printing and 1812 it was reprinted at least ten times: two of these editions (1746, 1766) emerged in the middle of the eighteenth century.[83] This total does not take into account the myriad cheaper pamphlets that plundered Temple's account and made the stories contained within it available to a wider audience who were unable to afford the high price of the original.[84] The points of republication are significant because, as Toby Barnard has remarked, the printing of the *Irish rebellion* throughout the eighteenth century 'offers a useful barometer to rising protestant anxieties'.[85] The Bagnell family of Cork published the 1766 edition at a point when local Protestant concern over the possibility of Catholic insurrection was high because of the recent Whiteboy activity in south Munster and Tipperary.[86]

The memory of 1641 was very much alive in mid-eighteenth-century Ireland. Its legacy drew frequent comment from both foreign and domestic travellers in Ulster. The author of the 1744 pamphlet *The Antient and the Present State of the County of Down* often commented how individual localities in the county were affected by the rebellion and how the legacy of Catholic atrocity continued to inform daily life across the county.[87] On his first tour through Ireland in 1747, a young John Wesley remarked:

> I procured a genuine account of the great Irish massacre of 1641. Surely never was there such a transaction before, from the beginning of the world! More than two hundred thousand men, women, and children, butchered within a few months, in cool blood, and with such circumstances of cruelty as make one's blood run cold! It is well if God has not a controversy with the nation, on this very account, to this day.[88]

The spectre of the rebellion was again recalled to serve contemporary ends in the 1750s. In the same year as Wesley's first Irish tour, a young Dublin doctor named John Curry resurrected the arguments made by Catholic apologists after the Restoration regarding culpability for the excesses of the rebellion.

Curry was a Catholic whose family had lost land during the seventeenth-century confiscations. Writing under the guise of a concerned Protestant, Curry composed *A brief account from the most authentic protestant writers of the causes, motives, and mischiefs, of the Irish rebellion ... 1641* (London, 1747), in which he set out to expose the irregularities and inconsistencies in the Protestant record of the rebellion. His pamphlet caused uproar, inciting outrage within Protestant communities across the island. Its publication even provoked Walter Harris, the leading Irish historian of the day, to publish a lengthy retort, *Fiction unmasked: or, an answer to a dialogue lately published by a popish physitian ... wherein the causes, motives, and mischiefs of the Irish rebellion and massacres in 1641 are laid thick upon the protestants* (Dublin, 1752). The nerve struck by Curry was apparently still raw a decade later, and the topic of the Irish Rebellion again caught Wesley's attention on his second Irish mission:

> I read an account of the Irish Rebellion wrote by Dr. Curry, a Papist of Dublin, who labours to wash the Ethiop [*sic*] white by numberless falsehoods and prevarications. But he is treated according to his merit by Mr. Harris, in a tract entitled, *Fiction Unmasked*.[89]

Wesley's remarks on this occasion illustrate how precious the traditional tropes of victimization and Catholic cruelty were to Protestants throughout the Atlantic world.

Six years after Wesley's last tour the significance of the St Bartholomew's Day massacre and the Irish Rebellion were again contested in Dublin pamphlets.[90] By this time the political atmosphere had changed as a result of the intensifying debate over the imperial crisis in America. Arguing that contemporary Catholics should not be penalized for the misdeeds of their ancestors, Irish patriots of the 1770s were more likely to sympathize with Curry – though not necessarily agree with him – and to criticize Temple as a government 'jobber' who purposely distorted the numbers of those killed during the rebellion.[91] Still, these patriot authors found it difficult to convince Irish Protestants to alter or abandon the sacred memory of the martyrs of 1641.

The temporary incorporation of atrocity narratives from the Seven Years War within the Protestant martyrological tradition in Ireland was made possible primarily because of the confessional division between the two sets of European belligerents. The age-old enemies of the reformed religion, namely, Catholic France and, later, Spain, were at war with a new Anglo-Prussian coalition. Thus, the same French hand allegedly guiding the Whiteboys in the early 1760s was routinely spotted behind native violence and colonial unrest. In 1754 the *News-Letter* printed a fiery sermon preached before the governing council in Boston in which the speaker, Dr Matthews, claimed to foresee 'the Slaves of *Lewis*, with their Indian Allies, dispossessing the free-born subjects of King GEORGE'.[92] Throughout 1764 the paper reported that French Canadian partisans, bitter at their province's subjugation to British rule, had used Indians as vehicles for their vengeance. In March Joy reported that Pontiac had revealed his accomplices as part of his overtures for peace. Among them were 'discovered the names of near 40 Frenchmen, some of them men of consequence at Montreal, who were concerned in fomenting this war'.[93] A letter from the besieged Fort Detroit printed widely across Ireland revealed that the French offered more than just tacit support for the rising; they were often present in the midst of massacre. The author recollected the horror of the siege and of his dealings with deceitful French intermediaries:

> Was it not very agreeable, to hear every day of cutting, carving, boiling and eating our companions? To see every day dead bodies floating down the river mangled and disfigured, and Frenchmen daily coming into the fort with long wry faces telling us of most shocking designs to destroy us.[94]

In July of that year Acadian refugees, who had been forcibly relocated from the recently renamed province of Nova Scotia to other mainland colonies by the British government, were blamed for poisoning the breakfasts of eighty residents at the College at New Haven, Connecticut, because several scholars had offended them.[95] The following month, news from Georgia revealed that a Frenchman had led a notorious raiding party responsible for the deaths or captivity of one hundred British colonists in Augusta County.[96]

Stories in the press often claimed that the American Indian penchant for cruelty did not match that of their European allies. In fact, Native barbarity was often attributed to Gallic influence. One particular incident from General John Forbes's western campaign received prolonged attention in the *News-Letter* in early 1759 and illustrated the inhumanity of the French by shedding light on their barbaric activities in America. In the winter of 1758 British troops on the fourth and final British assault against Fort Duquesne were shocked at what they found when they arrived on the site of Braddock's defeat five years earlier. The bones of British soldiers killed during the Braddock and Grant offensives were left scattered across the field and neighbouring woods. The French, it appeared, had only buried their own dead and left the bodies of British soldiers exposed without the honour of a proper burial. Two accounts of this episode were printed in the *News-Letter* on 30 January 1759 in tandem with several accounts of Indian attacks on the frontier. The first witness noted: 'We have found numbers of dead bodies within a quarter of a mile of the fort, unburied, in many monuments to French humanity.'[97] Another soldier told of how a detachment was sent to Braddock's Field after the capitulation of the fort. He informed readers that this group went back in order

> to bury the bones of our slaughtered countrymen, many of whom were murdered in cold blood by (those crueler than Savages) French,

who to the eternal shame and infamy of their country, have left them lying above ground ever more. The unburied bodies of those killed since, and found round this fort, equally reproach them, and profess loudly, to all civilized nations, their barbarity.[98]

A week later, Joy printed another soldier's account elaborating the gruesome discovery that the bodies from General Grant's offensive 'strewed the ground for three miles, and to within 100 yards of their very fort'.[99] Like the earlier printed accounts, the author was shocked by the fact that French soldiers could go about their daily routine in and about the fort while in the near vicinity of rotting British corpses. He continued with the gruesome revelation that, prior to the fort's fall, captured British soldiers from the Highland units 'were burnt on [the] parade, the French officers beholding the cruel sight, and laughing at the unhumane scene'.[100] As was the case in the previous week's letters from America, the author ended with a declaration: 'From this time let the applauded titles of polite and humane, no more honour the savage Frenchmen.' Furthermore, a selection from the *Pennsylvania Gazette* printed later in the issue asked for a charity to be raised to bury the bones left bare in the foot of DuQuesne's ramparts. It compared the task faced by the British regiments now stationed there with that of the Roman legions under Germanicus who, upon visiting the site of the battle of Teutoburg Forest in the year 15, were moved to bury the remains of their massacred comrades left to rot in the open air by German warriors five years earlier.

The British, by contrast, were portrayed as the liberators of French-aligned Indians. The British Army brought civilization with it and each site of victory was a place 'which providence decrees for the protection of innocence and virtue'. A soldier serving under General Blakeney at Crown Point in 1759 wrote to a gentleman friend in Cork claiming that British successes had ushered in an era of peace on the frontier: 'The cries of infants cease, and the laborious planter now can rest secure from that barbarity with which the world sounded.' He further implied that Indians previously 'employed in the savage service of a most Christian Turk', had since learned the errors of their ways and were now 'the avengers of his cruelty'.[101] The avaricious and decadent French lacked the civility and virtue to take their imperial mission seriously and their hapless Indian allies suffered as a consequence. The French, it emerged, were in fact more barbarous than the Native peoples under their tutelage. In August 1761, James Potts, the editor of the *Dublin Courier,* printed a letter from one of the London papers warning against the prospect of establishing an 'unsafe' peace with France. The letter claimed that a French toehold in North America would endanger the mainland British colonies in the future because any peace inevitably would be a 'breathing-time from hostilities' in which the French could regroup. Britain, he argued, could have 'no dependence upon the good faith' of France 'which even the most savage Indians in America, till they were debauched by her, took an honest pride in cultivating'.[102] Not surprisingly, the Protestant Irish press attributed French barbarity to their religion. As a result, Indian war on the frontier was blamed on the activities and provocations of those 'incessant Disturbers of the Peace, and Invaders of the Right of Mankind, and necessary Tools of tyranny and arbitrary Power' – the Jesuits.

Indeed, Irish editors obsessively published stories detailing Jesuit conspiracies on the frontier. Early in the war, George Faulkner printed an accusation that, 'under the Pretence of making the Eastern Indians good Catholicks', the Governor of Canada had used missionaries to broaden an anti-English coalition.[103] Priests were sent to Indian towns and villages designing to 'pervert their native Honesty, and prejudice them against the English Hereticks, by all the sinister Means that [the Jesuits could] possibly invent'. In 1757, Peter Williamson, a soldier and former Delaware captive, published a hyperbolic account of his captivity under the title, *French and Indian Cruelty*.[104] Three years later, with Britain now at war with the Cherokees in the Carolinas, a Dublin editor found it potentially profitable to regale his readership with lengthy excerpts from Williamson's pamphlet, including the assertion that 'Those [Indians] whom the French have had the opportunity of tutoring' were induced to believe that 'the Son of God came into the world to save all mankind, and destroy all the evil spirits which now trouble them, that the English killed him, and that ever since; the evil spirits walk unmolested and disturb them'. These French tutors posited the only clear solution: the Natives had to 'massacre all the English, in order that the Son of God would come again, and banish all evil spirits from their land'.[105] Pontiac's rising showed that Catholic missionaries among the Indians wielded dangerous influence even after the capitulation of Canada. One informant declared that 'All these rambling Monks, Jesuits, &c.' ought to be 'banished, and if they return hanged'.[106]

It was easy for mid-eighteenth-century Irish Presbyterians to draw comparisons between violence directed at Irish settlers on the fringes of European settlement in America and violence against their British forerunners on the Irish frontiers a century earlier. This did not translate into a literal juxtaposition between American Indians and contemporary Irish Catholics. Rather, the subject matter contained in printed frontier victimization narratives, so similar in form and function to those woven into the mythic tradition of northern Protestants, suggested that the grisly violence that haunted the Irish past now lurked in present-day America. This violence was directed against, and affected the lives of, thousands of Irish migrants. Local press coverage of the war and the two interrelated forces of northern migration to the colonies and the greater mercantile interdependence between Ireland and North America resulted in a recalibration of community consciousness and geographic awareness among Ulster Presbyterians. Their understanding of this larger world and their place within it was filtered through the webs of cultural meaning created by local experience and history. In other words, Presbyterians relied upon the Irish past to make sense of the Atlantic present and vice versa.

The culture of sensibility, Irish empathy and American Indian violence

Colley's comment that the graphic frontier vignettes that flooded British newspapers at mid-century constituted a 'pornography of violence' mirrors a description employed by the Irish historian Roy Foster in reference to a conflict that occurred a century earlier. Foster stated that the depositions taken from Protestant survivors of the Irish rebellion of 1641, detailing the experiences of refugees in lurid detail, and later made popular in printed edited collections, most notably John Temple's *The Irish Rebellion*, 'resemble a pornography of violence'.[107] What exactly does this phrase mean in the context of the eighteenth-century cult of sensibility and sentimentality?[108] Commentators on modern genocide have used the phrase to describe the 'marketing' of massacre, particularly how constant exposure to textual, visual and oral recollections or displays of human suffering have led, in the late twentieth century, to a crisis of empathy in the form of widespread emotional numbing.[109] The phrase is loaded with sexual meaning and implicitly suggests a link between violent and sexual victimization. It also implies the moral impoverishment of the actors or subjects depicted in the work as well as its consumers.

Often stories of Indian attack focused on gendered violence perpetrated by Indian men against women and children while the enduring popularity of the captivity narrative was underpinned by the suggestion that Indians might gain sexual access to European captives.[110] In this way, the use of the word 'pornography' to describe popular representations of Indian violence seems apt. The phrase undoubtedly takes on a different meaning, however, when employed, as both Foster and Colley have done, against the distinctive backdrop of early modern warfare and print culture. In her seminal article on the topic, Karen Halttunen claimed that the popular revulsion to pain that accompanied the rise of sentimental literature, particularly the reformation of manners that accompanied it in the nineteenth century, also produced an oppositional phenomenon. 'The pornography of pain', she stated, 'represented pain as obscenely titillating precisely because the humanitarian sensibility deemed it unacceptable, taboo.'[111]

Throughout the eighteenth century the imposition of pain was increasingly seen as a marker of barbarity in opposition to the restrained comportment that defined polite – and civilized – behaviour. It was also offensive to the sentimental outlook so common of the men and women of feeling in the third quarter of the century. This did not mean that depiction of bodily pain and suffering were, at this point in the 1750s and 60s, taboo; far from it. Printed and oral victimization narratives depicting torture in lurid detail were not an underground phenomenon in eighteenth-century Ireland. In fact, they were remarkably commonplace. Tales of past Catholic violence and supposed treachery formed an integral part of Irish Protestant identity; one that found expression in sermons, annual commemorations, as well as printed memoirs and histories. Pain visited on the bodies of ancestors fed the siege mentality of Ulster Protestants and became a didactic tool to teach new generations to be wary of, and remain separate from, their Catholic neighbours. Violence as an instructional tool was also illustrated in the public execution of criminals and the printed gallows speeches that accompanied them.[112] Instructional or didactic violence, therefore, remained an important and highly visible aspect of life in eighteenth-century Ireland.[113]

The elevated respect owing to the virtues of compassion and restraint in eighteenth-century culture and society actually spurned a fascination with acts of cruelty and those who, out of a lack of humanity, committed them. In his lectures on moral philosophy at the University of Glasgow, Francis Hutcheson, inspired by the 3rd Earl of Shaftesbury's attacks on the dour Hobbesian claim that human nature was cruel and self-serving, posited the existence of a moral or sympathetic sense inherent in all human beings that forced them to engage with the emotional states of others. This sense, he argued, promoted a 'fellow-feeling' in those who witnessed the suffering or jubilation of their peers.[114] The moral weight attached to the internalization of others' pain by the cult of sensibility ascribed new meaning to the reading of victimization narratives. Hutcheson's successor to the chair of Moral Philosophy at Glasgow emphasized the centrality of imagination to the formation of sympathetic emotion. Adam Smith held that the 'fellow-feeling' between a person experiencing pain and someone observing it resulted from the latter's ability to imagine themselves in the same position. He claimed, 'that it is by changing places in fancy with the sufferer, that we come either to conceive or to be affected by what he feels'.[115] The power of the imagination to inspire sympathy was so great that the onlooker need not actually witness the pain of others to feel sympathy for them. Thinking about the suffering of others, even if the person reflecting on the suffering has never met the tormented, was enough to inspire fellow-feeling with the imagined subject.[116] Witnessing others' misery exposed the viewer's humanity and virtue in the sense that they were spurred to alleviate the subject's suffering. Thus, the reflexive quality of others' pain allowed for a positive reaction in the viewer. This encouraged the development of the sentimental spectator outside the confines of direct experience.

In 1757 Edmund Burke articulated a different system of sensibility from those espoused by his Scottish contemporaries. In Burke's model, the sensory stimulation that accompanied the realization of another's pain projected upon oneself actually excited a feeling of pleasure in the subject. In his *Philosophical Enquiry into the Origin of the Our Ideas of the Sublime and the Beautiful* he claimed that humans take 'a degree of delight, and that no small one, in the real misfortunes and pains of others'. However, his reasoning was not as sadistic as it would first appear: 'terror is a passion which always produces delight when it does not press too close, and pity is a passion accompanied with pleasure, because it arises from love and social affection'. God, he claimed, had twisted delight and pain together in one package, because the pain of bearing witness to another's misery without an attendant feeling of pleasure would force the observer to 'shun with the greatest care all persons and places that could excite such a passion' as pity and thus allow the sufferer to languish in misery.[117]

Like their counterparts throughout the empire Ulster Presbyterians were exposed to an onslaught of graphic Indian atrocity narratives over the course of the Seven Years War. Reactions to these stories in each context would have ranged on a spectrum from horror at one end, to macabre curiosity in the middle, and to utter indifference among some readers at the other end. Average reactions would have varied between each of these regions as well. Obviously the threat of Indian war was more pertinent to American readers than it was to their European peers. Within the European context, however, Ulster was somewhat unique.

The ties that bound Ulster Presbyterian communities to the very frontiers then under attack meant that audience reactions to Indian war in Belfast or Derry were likely to have been stronger than the popular responses among Dublin or London readers. Through constant migration Ulster Presbyterians had an emotional investment in the security of the American frontier in ways that others in Britain and Ireland simply did not. The persistent popularity of these stories in the *News-Letter* on a level that far exceeded other Irish journals provides a case in point. The paper's coverage of the Cherokee War, a conflict largely ignored by the Dublin editors who had by that time diverted their gaze eastward towards the European theatre of the war, further indicates a unique fascination with Indian war in the north. Both folk memory and mid-eighteenth-century theories regarding morality and the internalization of others' suffering provided Ulster Presbyterians with templates through which they could interpret the bloody vignettes of American Indian violence that flowed into the province from 1754 onwards. Anti-Catholicism and the memory of domestic insurrection coloured their understanding of what was happening in America within the framework of their own historical experience. They subsumed Indian warfare within the eschatological struggle for the very survival of Protestantism. By setting out clear guidelines regarding how the compassionate subject should feel about such stories, emerging conceptions of polite sensibility also dictated how Irish audiences should react to them.

5

'An Infant Sister Church, in Great Distress, Amidst a Great Wilderness': American Presbyterian Fundraising in Ireland, 1752–63

The clearing of French privateers from north Atlantic shipping lanes from 1760 ensured the resumption of trade and seasonal traffic between the mother country and the American colonies. It also presented American institutions and charities with the possibility of securing investment after being cut off from metropolitan patronage during five long years of war. These cash-strapped organizations sent emissaries across the ocean as soon as possible in order to capitalize on the perceived public goodwill and imperial enthusiasm generated by the war and the conquest of Canada. Throughout the early 1760s a legion of colonial agents scrambled into Britain, competing among themselves in the race to obtain patronage and support from what they perceived to be a fickle public in a game of diminishing returns. Often these agents made the short trip across the Irish Sea in their quest for funding. At least six such campaigns visited Ireland in the 1750s and 1760s, four of which toured Ulster. Five of these missions were for the benefit of seminaries and colleges, including the College of New Jersey (later Princeton, 1754), the College and Academy of Philadelphia (later the University of Pennsylvania, 1763), King's College New York (later Columbia, 1763), Wheelock's Indian School (later Dartmouth College, 1767) and the Baptist College of Rhode Island (later Brown University, 1767).[1] The other fundraising tour was for the Corporation for the Relief of Poor and Distressed Widows and Children of Presbyterian Ministers (or the American Presbyterian Widows' Fund, 1760).

Popular support for these campaigns demonstrates unambiguous public engagement with colonial causes among Irish Protestants.[2] Here, charitable giving to colonial causes represented a form of imperial activism in which the contributor understood that their personal offering advanced and stabilized British civilization in North America. Often, as is the case of the campaigns endorsed by the General Synod of Ulster, American agents made it clear that donations would benefit colonials of the same ethnicity and religion as the potential donor. Between 1760 and 1762, in particular, ordinary Presbyterians throughout Ireland demonstrated their sympathy and compassion for their beleaguered kinfolk on the other side of the ocean in their enthusiastic support of the American Synod's campaign for the establishment of a Widows' Fund.

This chapter focuses primarily on the fundraising tours for the benefit of the College of New Jersey (1753–4) and the Presbyterian Widows' Fund (1760–2). The reasons for this are simple and twofold. First, they were the only missions to seriously build Ireland into their overall strategy. Both were Presbyterian campaigns organized by Irish immigrants with links to the various Presbyterian bodies across the island. The June sitting of the General Synod of Ulster was one of the few dates around which both campaigns' itineraries were organized before agents disembarked from Philadelphia. We can therefore follow the success of each campaign in the records of the General Synod. Second, each campaign visited Ulster either immediately before the outset of the Seven Years War or after 1759 when popular support for the war in America was at its height. They thus provide a gage through which we can track public enthusiasm for American causes overtime.

As for the other campaigns: William Smith, the primary representative of both the College of New York and the Philadelphia Academy, never made it beyond Dublin due to an episode of sickness and because he believed that the Presbyterians of Pennsylvania had turned their co-religionists in the north against his mission.[3] Two American campaigns arrived in Ulster during the summer of 1767, both for the support and establishment of colonial schools. By this time it was clear that the wave of imperial euphoria that crested in 1759 had fully dissipated due to the increasingly bitter dispute between Whitehall and the colonies over parliamentary sovereignty. Rev. Morgan Edwards was entrusted by the colonial assembly of Rhode Island to solicit funds 'from the Friends of useful Literature and other well-disposed Persons' for the support of the recently established Baptist college (subsequently renamed Brown University).[4] Edwards was later joined by two ministers campaigning on behalf of the missionary Eleazer Wheelock's Indian School in Connecticut, later to bear the name of one of the institution's most powerful benefactors, William Legge, 2nd Earl of Dartmouth. Its two agents were the famed Mohegan minister Samson Occom and Philadelphia minister Richard Whitaker. Neither of the campaigns received the sanction of the General Synod of Ulster because they missed the sitting of the Synod in June. Occom and Whitaker did not leave Scotland before 15 July. When they arrived in Belfast they found it difficult to secure any support whatsoever, let alone a Sabbath day collection, because of Edwards's presence. They therefore decided to abandon Ireland and concentrated their efforts on parts of England that they had not yet visited.[5] Edwards sent James Manning a list of all the money collected in Ireland and where it came from. He explained that he had the list printed and distributed while on tour in the country in frustration at popular suspicion regarding foreign charity drives. He explained, 'the design was to let every one of them [the donors] see that I gave time – for what I have received', and had previous colonial agents 'done so they would have prevented suspicions very injurious to themselves and to those that come after them on the like errand'.[6] In an indication of how the transatlantic relation had soured by 1767, Edwards claimed that a London benefactor had been called a rogue for aiding the American charities because of the crisis then enveloping the British Atlantic world.

The first half of this chapter explores the Irish campaigns on behalf of the College of New Jersey and the American Presbyterian Widows' Fund. It examines their methods of raising funds, the success of their campaigns and, briefly, their political ramifications in the middle colonies. The second half of the chapter is dedicated to fleshing-out the economic world into which these two charities entered in order to demonstrate that, while small compared to London standards, the Widows' fund total Irish collection of nearly £430 was a success. Ulster Presbyterians maintained limited disposable incomes throughout the century despite the fact that their province was the richest in Ireland. Their ability to give to charitable causes, either foreign or domestic, was further curtailed during the economic downturn of the late 1750s. Taking these factors into account, the Widows' fund campaign still managed to raise a sum comparable to those collected for similar domestic initiatives. That he was able to do so testifies to the depth of feeling and concern among Irish Presbyterians for their kin across the ocean in the aftermath of a devastating war in the colonies.

American collections in Ireland before the war: Gilbert Tennent and the College of New Jersey, 1754–6

On 1 June 1754, near the end of a successful fundraising tour of Britain for the benefit of the recently established Presbyterian seminary in Princeton, New Jersey, the prominent American evangelical minister Gilbert Tennent left his travelling companion Samuel Davies in Edinburgh and headed for the country of his birth.[7] Three weeks later, Tennent attended the meeting of the General Synod of Ulster at Antrim where he was welcomed as a member of the body and had his petition read aloud before the assembly. According to the petition, the 'Colledge of New Jersey' was 'necessary to answer the exigencys of Church & State in those parts of His Majesties Dominions'. These pressures were caused, in no small part, by the stress put upon colonial Presbyterian institutions in the wake of the migratory waves of Ulster Dissenters in 1718–19 and 1729–31 as well as the constant stream of immigrants arriving in Philadelphia and New York throughout the 1730s and 1740s.[8] Until this point, American Presbyterian congregations largely relied on European, specifically Irish- and Scottish-trained ministers or local clergymen schooled at the colleges of Yale and Harvard in the Congregationalist tradition of New England. This situation became inadequate by the 1720s as a result of the growth of a non-English Presbyterian immigrant community demanding ministers trained in their particular brand of Calvinism. Consequently, demand for divines massively outweighed supply.[9] Ideally, the College of New Jersey would perform an invaluable service in the propagation of American Presbyterianism by training local clergy and thus easing colonial reliance on British trained ministers. The New Jersey campaign also attempted to galvanize support by intimating that their institution would benefit both the mother country and future migrants. It would, they claimed, help 'enlarge the *British* Dominions upon a vast Continent, whither the industrious Poor may transplant themselves, and find a comfortable Subsistance'.[10]

Several issues influenced the decision made at the joint meeting of the Presbytery of Antrim and the General Synod to appoint a collection for the College. First, Gilbert Tennent was among family friends and relatives on the floor of the General Synod. His cousin, Rev. Gilbert Kennedy Jr, a well-known New Light minister at Tallyrush, was present and actively involved in the overseeing of the recently established Irish widows' fund. Secondly, the Church of Scotland's endorsement of the mission a few weeks earlier legitimized the campaign, almost guaranteeing that the Presbyterian churches of Ireland would appoint collections on its behalf. Unsurprisingly, the General Synod voted unanimously to appoint a collection among all congregations within its bounds. The establishment of an American seminary was also welcome news for the Irish Synod which had frequently paid the cost of training new ministers only to see them answer a call from an American congregation shortly after finishing their studies. The petition required that the Synod render assistance as it 'shall think proper, particularly one Sab. days Collection'. The Synod, judging the 'Seminary to be of great importance to the promotion of the Interests of Religion & Learning in several Provinces of N. America', unanimously acquiesced to Tennent's appeal and 'ordered that public Collections be made in all the Congregations under their care' by the following November. In the meantime, ministers were encouraged 'to excite by proper exhortations their several Societies to this important Charity'.[11]

Nineteenth-century historians of early American religion and colonial education repeatedly asserted that Tennent's campaign in Ireland was a success. The common consensus seems to have been that he raised a total of £500 over the course of his solo four-month tour between June and October 1754.[12] If this were true, his mission to Ireland would have certainly been a triumph, with Irish donations constituting one-eighth of the total £4,000 collected by Davies and Tennent in Europe.[13] This achievement would have been all the more remarkable given the general lack of specie in the Kingdom and that Ireland was in the midst of an economic depression brought about by both a banking crisis in Dublin and bad harvests throughout the country.[14]

There are several reasons to suspect Tennent's Irish total. First, the sum of £500 is both suspiciously round and highly speculative. We simply do not know how much Tennent collected in Ireland as the sources where this information was likely to have been recorded have not survived. The College of New Jersey's early treasury books were destroyed when university buildings were damaged during the Battle of Princeton in 1777, or they were lost in the Nassau Hall fire of 1802.[15] Existing tallies of donations from the drive do not mention Ireland. Samuel Davies, the other representative of the College during the campaign, listed some totals in his journal, but he did not accompany Tennent on his travels through Ulster and therefore did not record Irish donations. Other totals are listed in published campaign literature, namely, the *General Account of the Rise and State Lately Established in the Province of New-Jersey*. However, all three editions of the *General Account* were published before Tennent sailed from Glasgow to Ulster. The closest indication of the size of Tennent's haul comes from an account of money collected in England presented before the Synod of New York, on 24 September 1755. It does not shed light on Tennent's mission in Ireland and only hints at limited Irish support for the initiative in London. The total compiled in that account was £296 17s, of which £1 1s was given on behalf of a 'Mr. Lunel in Dublin'.[16] Second, even if Tennent did manage to collect £500 after parting with Davies, it is uncertain how much of this total was gathered in Ireland. He also toured the west of England during the solitary leg of his journey, making it likely that English donations from a region heavily invested in colonial trade constituted a large portion of his 'Irish' collection.

Also significant is the fact that the Old Side wing of American Presbyterianism opposed the New Jersey campaign in the first place and that many anti-evangelical ministers, particularly Rev. Robert Cross and the Vice Provost of the Philadelphia Academy, Rev. Francis Alison – both Irish born – had allies within the General Synod. The Old Sides had actively attempted to sabotage Tennent and Davies by corresponding with friends and acquaintances throughout England, Scotland and Ireland. On numerous occasions Davies and Tennent discovered to their horror that Robert Cross had written to powerful British benefactors decrying the College of New Jersey as a partisan New Side institution. Cross also sent a copy of Tennent's infamous 1740 sermon *The Danger of an Unconverted Ministry* to both the prominent London Dissenter Samuel Chandler and Lord Minto, a Scottish MP and active supporter of colonial causes.[17] He did so in order to cast Davies and Tennent as schismatics, undermining the Protesant interest in America through the promotion of disunity. In the sermon Tennent compared his Old Side rivals to New Testament Pharisees and the money-changers cast out of the Temple by Jesus.[18] Ultimately these attempts at sabotage did little to hinder the progress of the New Jersey campaign in Britain, although it is possible that they may have affected the eventual outcome of the Irish mission. Unfortunately, as Davies's journal is the only record we have of the campaign, Tennent's time spent alone in Ireland remains a mystery.

Perhaps the greatest indication that Tennent's Irish campaign was not as fruitful as nineteenth-century scholars assumed lies in the records of the General Synod of Ulster. The laity did not appear to share their clergy's enthusiasm for the charity, a fact reflected in the few proceeds raised on its behalf in the years following Tennent's departure. When the General Synod reconvened in Antrim during the summer of 1755, they were met with little good news regarding collections for the college. It was reported that there had been 'very little done by the Pbyes in the affair of the Charity to the Colledge [*sic*] in N. Jersey, as appointed at last Synod'.[19] The assembly therefore had no choice but to renew their orders and to plead with 'the several Minrs to represent it [the fund] in the warmest manner to their Congregations & to pay their Collections ... before the first of Nov. next'.[20] Apparently, the laity at the time did not recognize the utility or benefit of establishing a new college across the ocean or failed to get suitably excited about the training of ministers. This lack of enthusiasm was not remedied by the renewed efforts of the synod, and the following year the recommencement of war between Britain and France in North America provided them with a convenient excuse to abandon the campaign:

> The affair of the recommendation in favour of N. Jersey, considering the present situation of affairs in that part of the world, is put off till next Synod: and as some Bn. have made contributions for that purpose the Synod is well pleased with them.[21]

The assembly never again discussed the topic. The 'situation of affairs' that signalled the end of the Princeton campaign would soon dominate the front pages of Irish journals for nearly a decade, including those of the only newspaper then printed in Ulster, the *Belfast News-Letter*, and would transform the way Ulster Presbyterians imagined North America, and their province's relationship with it. Tennent's trip to Ireland also had an unintended consequence that would alter the complexion of American Presbyterianism. In a strange turn of events, the bitterly divisive exercise of European fundraising provided an opportunity for Presbyterian reconciliation and the reunification of the synods. Over the course of his brief stay in Ulster, Tennent witnessed the financial success of the Irish Presbyterian Widows' Fund, an operation jointly run by the General Synod and the New Light Presbytery of Antrim. Tennent had also paid a visit to the annual meeting of the Antrim Presbytery. He therefore saw both sides of a compromise between two groups for the mutual financial benefit of each. Tennent, who had mellowed on his stance on the Old Side since the publication of *The Dangers of an Unconverted Ministry* might have recognized that such a scheme could also alleviate the financial difficulties experienced by the two American synods.[22] While Tennent witnessed the bridge-building capabilities of financial reform while on campaign in Ireland, his rival, Francis Alison, was laying the groundwork for the creation of a similar scheme in Philadelphia.

American collections after the war: Charles Beatty and the Corporation for the Relief of poor and distressed Presbyterian ministers, 1760–2

In the summer of 1760, after a period of thirty-one years, the Reverend Charles Beatty returned to Ireland on a mission from the Presbyterian Synod of Philadelphia and New York. He had last seen the country of his birth at the age of fourteen when he sailed along with his widowed mother and thousands of others during the great wave of emigration that crested in the wake of the Irish famine of 1729.[23] The American synod entrusted Beatty with the task of raising European donations to benefit a recently charted Ministers' fund modelled after the Scottish scheme established in 1743. The Quaker and Anglican parties that dominated Pennsylvanian politics feared that a chartered widow's fund both legitimized the recently reunited Presbyterian Synod and, through the accumulation of wealth, would soon enable it to spread its influence throughout the colony. The scheme therefore suffered from a lack of domestic support as the Presbyterians did not have equal access to many of the colonial patronage networks open to other groups and charitable institutions. Much, then, depended upon the success of Beatty's European mission. Before the fund could become viable, he would have to raise capital and convince British and Irish donors to give generously.[24] On 24 June 1760 Beatty presented a memorial, prepared by a special committee of the American Church, before the assembled ministers of the General Synod of Ulster at their annual meeting in Lurgan. His Irish colleagues received him as a privileged guest and bestowed upon him membership in their body, an honour last granted to Gilbert Tennent six years before.[25] His memorial – prepared primarily by Francis Alison – was received and a Sabbath's day collection was promptly organized. From 1760 to 1762 Irish congregations raised approximately £427 12s 5½d, the majority of which was donated by ordinary Ulster congregants in 'exit collections' – so called because they were taken up at the end of the service – on designated Sabbath days, particularly on 21 April 1761.[26] Of this total, £120 had come from Dublin's wealthy Usher's Quay congregation after a visit from Beatty himself in the summer of 1760.[27] At first glance, this amount may not seem like much, but it was quite impressive given the economic climate in Ulster at the time. The early 1760s constituted a period of dearth, with the linen trade only just recovering from interruptions caused by the war. Also, a lack of specie continued to dog the kingdom.

The American campaign pamphlet was successful partly because its authors made the foreign seem local to Irish audiences, effectively shrinking the Atlantic and connecting two disparate communities in the minds of potential donors. Irish Presbyterian participation in the campaign also illustrates their community's willingness to identify with their co-religionists across the Atlantic, as well as their view of the empire itself as a Protestant entity. It was an expression of solidarity and of an emerging Atlantic identity. This identity may have been built upon foundations established domestically in the first decades of the eighteenth century. From 1707 onwards the General Synod agreed that each presbytery should raise funds to support weak congregations on the outskirts of Ulster Presbyterian society, in places such as Dundalk and even Galway. By 1710 the synod worked out a formula whereby each presbytery became responsible for a new or faltering congregation. Support for these so-called 'frontier congregations' instilled a sense of responsibility and community concern for those on the fringes of Presbyterian settlement. This same obligation may have underpinned the act of giving to ministers and congregations in need on a more distant frontier.

Beatty's memorial was read aloud before collections were made as well as printed in the *News-Letter*. The authors employed what can be described as a 'scattergun approach' throughout the document in which they highlighted the many different problems afflicting frontier Presbyterians that could be relieved by Irish donations. They hoped that this would increase the likelihood that Irish audiences would receive their appeal favourably. They first outlined the religious merit of giving, claiming that 'Charity is a most exalted grace: it is highly beneficial to mankind' and that those who participated in charitable endeavours would 'receive an ample reward in the great day of recompence'. They further stated, 'Great, unspeakably great, shall be their reward in heaven.' Beatty also shamed Irish Presbyterians with the assertion that their brethren in Scotland had already made a collection, thereby giving the project an aura of authenticity. His memorials to the Church of Scotland and the General Synod of Ulster illuminated the danger posed by a lack of Presbyterian ministers on the frontier: 'The most promising settlement of Presbyterians may, in a few years or months, be intirely possessed by Moravians, or any other society, however heretical, if they call themselves Christians.'[28] The prominence of heterodox and Pietist sects in the middle colonies had been broadcast to Irish readers before. In his anti-emmigration tract *America Dissected* James MacSparran warned potential immigrants against the 'Danger to the souls of Poor People that remove [to America], from the multifarious wicked and pestilent Heresies that prevail in those Parts.'[29] The memorialists made it clear that the charity was crucial to the security of the empire by asserting that frontier society was slowly sliding into barbarity because of a lack of Christian instruction and through contact with 'surrounding barbarians'. This de-evolution undermined the civilizing (i.e., Protestant) mission that supposedly underpinned Britain's imperial commitment.

Both of the Presbyterian campaigns to visit Britain and Ireland at mid-century framed Atlantic Presbyterianism within a familial metaphor in which the colonial church was a 'sister' institution to the General Synod of Ulster and both churches were 'daughters' of the Kirk. Tennent and Beatty employed a language of supplication in which the defenceless child begged its powerful but distant family for protection. Often this metaphor was couched alongside pleas to a common ancestry and religion. The College of New Jersey's appeal stated:

> The Inhabitants of the Infant Colonies, dependent upon this Seminary [College of New Jersey], unable to relieve themselves, are constrained to solicit and implore the Assistance of others. And to whom shall they look, but to their tender and powerful *Parent*? – To move her Compassion, they plead their *Relation* as Children, as Fellow-Subjects, as Christian and Protestant Brethren with her Sons that still enjoy the Advantages of residing in their native Country – They plead the deplorable Circumstances of the Church, and Exigences [*sic*] of the State, for Want of such an Institution bro't to Maturity – And they beg Leave modestly to intimate their *Importance* to their Mother-Country.[30]

The New Jersey delegation's later application to the General Assembly in Edinburgh utilized the same metaphor. It read, 'The young daughter of the Church of Scotland, helpless and exposed in this foreign Land, Cries to her tender and powerful mother for relief.'[31] These cries were accompanied by those of individual ministers and congregations, 'famishing for Want of the sincere milk of the word'.[32] Beatty's later printed memorial to the General Assembly also referred to the Synod of Philadelphia and New York as an 'infant church' and a 'daughter' of the Kirk that was 'in great distress, amidst a vast wilderness'.[33] His Irish campaign literature utilized the same familial metaphor but also referred to the General Synod as a 'sister' to the American church.[34]

Perhaps the most affecting section of the memorial detailed the misery visited upon the frontier settlements as a result of Native American raids during the previous decade. The memorialists claimed, 'An Indian war broke forth; a savage, barbarous enemy, prompted by the perfidious French, like prowling wolves, fell on the peaceful habitations of their frontier-inhabitants, and time after time plundered and robbed, murdered and scalped, without regard to age or sex.' The assertion that Native Americans had been goaded to act by the 'perfidious French' resonated with Ulster Protestants at a point when the threat of French invasion and an accompanying Catholic rising were very real. By the time of the collection in the spring of 1762, their fears were partially realized in the form of Thurot's failed landing of 1760. The landing reminded Irish Presbyterians that their island remained Britain's vulnerable underbelly during periods of war with France.

Such passages also recalled images from the 1641 Catholic rebellion, an event ingrained in the communal memory of Irish Protestants. The memorial gave graphic accounts of individual instances of Native American violence, each mirroring an episode in John Temple's *The Irish rebellion*. This was especially clear in one poignant description from Beatty's memorial, perhaps styled on the well-circulated accounts that emerged after the massacre of surrendered British forces at Fort William-Henry in 1757:

> The innocent babes, torn from their mothers breasts, were dashed against the trees, or buried alive in the presence of their almost distracted parents; while the unhappy parents durst not vent one groan, or drop a single tear, over their slaughtered little ones, much less find fault, lest they should have shared in the same dreadful fate.

As documented in the last chapter, the *News-Letter* printed gory details similar to this from the New York frontier in October 1757. This segment also bore striking similarity to James Stevenson's account, reprinted by Temple, of the death of his baby daughter, Isabel. In his deposition Stevenson recounted how he had met a band of rebels on the road in Letrim who asked a member of his party who the child belonged to. The man replied, '*it was a* Scottish-Mans *Child*', whereupon the rebels '*took the Child by the Heels, and run and beat the Brains of it out against a Tree*' while the father was forced to watch.[35] Similarly, tales of children being buried alive by the rebels are found in Temple's text. In one instance, an English child who was the sole member of his family who had survived hanging '*put out the Hand and cryed Mammy, Mammy, when without Mercy they* [Rebels] *Buried him alive*'.[36]

That American campaigners used imagery that bore such striking similarity to Irish sources should not be surprising. Beatty and the three men designated by the synod to write the memorial were all born in Ireland. Beatty, Robert Cross and Francis Alison – probably the primary author of tract – were raised within Presbyterian communities, in Ulster. Gilbert Tennent left the island with his mother and father at a very young age but grew up in the Irish milieu of his father's congregation in Neshiminey. It is probable that they had absorbed stories from Irish

Protestant martyrological tradition during their youth and adapted, perhaps subconsciously, these narratives to suit the colonial environment. The gruesome stories made famous by John Temple had become stock scenarios, so ubiquitous in the Protestant memory that they could be easily recalled and employed in descriptions of other non-specific instances of massacre. Here, American Indians were swapped for Irish Catholics as the principal antagonists. The image of children dashed against rocks is also found in the Bible, specifically in Psalm 137.9. Biblical literacy, along with the Presbyterian tendency to think of their community as a new, suffering, Israel, influenced the way in which atrocity narratives from 1641 and the American frontier were both sculpted and understood. Whether the similarity between the 1641 and 1760 narratives was intended or accidental, these tales probably provoked an emotional response, and perhaps the impulse to give, in Irish Protestants.

However stylized the above depictions of frontier massacres may have been, the 1760 campaign went to great lengths to establish that its accounts of Indian atrocity were indeed accurate. That widespread interest in the war informed the public's willingness to give towards Beatty's mission is evident in the attention they paid to Beatty's military credentials. From Dublin in the summer of 1760 he wrote: 'not to the disadvantage of my cause: my military appointments have been of great advantage, and given me access to many persons'.[37] The military appointments to which he was referring were held early in the war. He served as a chaplain on Benjamin Franklin's 1756 expedition to protect the northern Pennsylvania frontier. Later that year, he received a commission from Lieutenant Governor Robert Hunter Morris to serve as a chaplain on another western campaign under the command of Colonel William Clapham.[38] Alison and Tennent accentuated Beatty's direct experience of the war in their memorial to the people of Ireland. They made a point of mentioning that the men on the expeditions in which Beatty was involved had 'exposed themselves to the inclemency of a severe winter, and to all the dangerous incursions of the Indians, till they built forts for the defence of the frontiers'.[39] The memorial asked readers not to misconstrue mention of his wartime record as bragging. Beatty had a reason to refer to it:

> not out of vain glory, or as pretending to any distinguished merit, but that the reader might know he does not speak from hearsay, does not restate vague uncertain stories, but narrates undoubted facts; facts no less true than melancholy, of which he has access to the most certain information, or was himself the mournful spectator.[40]

The Philadelphia memorial was read and circulated in Ulster at a point when coverage of American Indian conflict in the local press was at its height as a result of the Cherokee War in the Carolinas. Public interest in this particular conflict was high because the most recent mass migration of Irish Presbyterians to the New World in the early 1750s had gone through the port of Charleston. Not only did these tales of atrocity seem to recall similar instances of Catholic violence in the Ulster Presbyterian past, they also resonated within Presbyterian communities that had recently witnessed mass migration to North America and for whom the possibility of emigration had become an established life strategy. They could cast those who had left before the war – their former friends, neighbours and family members – as victims of Indian raids. It was this sense of imagined community from which the memorialists hoped to foster and benefit.

The committee devised two different drafts of their memorial to be circulated in Scotland and Ireland. These drafts were nearly identical except for a few slight variations in the Irish edition. The Irish memorial begins with a reminder that Pennsylvania had been 'peopled from England, Ireland, and Scotland', thus establishing the British background of the victims before narrowing in on their religious and ethnic heritage.[41] The preface to the Scottish edition does not mention Ireland. Another disparity between the two drafts is found in the paragraph that followed the graphic settler victimization narratives. The Scottish edition reads, 'As the frontier counties of Pennsylvania and Virginia were mostly settled by people of the Presbyterian persuasion, their ministers have felt the blow severely.'[42] The same sentence was repeated in the Irish memorial but with one crucial addition: 'from Ireland' now followed the word 'persuasion' so that the Irish appeal stated that the Pennsylvania and Virginia frontiers 'were mostly settled by people of the Presbyterian persuasion from Ireland'.[43] This small difference was important because it underscored the ethno-religious kinship between Irish and American Presbyterians. Furthermore, the trustees claimed that the fund deserved 'the charity of the ministers and people of Ireland' because the 'greatest part of [the suffering American ministers] are their brethren by the ties of nature in the most literal sense'.[44]

Further testimony of the charity's popularity can be ascertained from Beatty's reception in Dublin. Advertisements for his charity in the Dublin papers were not as extensive as the complete memorial printed in the *News-Letter*, but they, nevertheless, conveyed the same sense of urgency and focused on similar themes. The desolation of the frontier at the hands of the 'Indian Savages' was mentioned, as was colonial inability to deal with the extent of the tragedy without help from

Britain: 'In these Provinces, as much as could be expected hath been done to forward this good design [in America], but its extensive Nature renders [colonial] Endeavours insufficient.'[45] Again, the papers pleaded for those who 'wish for the Hapiness of many Natives of this Kingdom settled in those Parts of America, to contribute towards [the charity's] support'. In total, Beatty's visit to Dublin resulted in the collection of £120, the majority of which came after his visit to Usher's Quay and the other Presbyterian congregations throughout the capital.

In Pennsylvania, the Irish leg of Beatty's campaign and the Synod of Philadelphia and New York's use of the money he raised became hot topics in local politics. The Presbyterian Fund became a major point of contention among Anglicans and Quakers supporting the Pennsylvania Assembly position during the heated election debates of 1764. Ethnic and religious tensions intensified in the months leading to the election following the Paxton Massacres in Lancaster County (perpetrated largely by local Scots Irish settlers) and the subsequent march on Philadelphia by disgruntled western Presbyterians.[46] In October 1764, the *London Chronicle* published a letter from Philadelphia, dated 22 August, detailing Quaker complacency and negligence during the recent Indian wars.[47] A pro-Assembly pamphlet accusing Francis Alison, the primary organizer of the Widow's Fund, of wilfully misleading both the charity's domestic and foreign benefactors appeared in response to the *Chronicle Letter*.[48] The young Philadelphia Anglican Isaac Hunt in his virulently anti-Presbyterian pamphlet of 1764, *A Looking-Glass for Presbyterians*, hurled a similar accusation at the organizers of the charity. Hunt imagined the moment when Charles Beatty first addressed the General Synod of Ulster at their annual meeting at Lurgan in June 1760:

this very Deputy [Beatty] of theirs [the Presbyterians] carried Home [to Ireland] with him a Parcel of Squirrel Scalps; and when he had in *Ireland*, work'd up the Passions of his Audience by dismal and melancholy Relations of murder'd *Ministers* in the back Woods to a proper Degree of Fermentation; produc'd these as Proofs, declaring they were the Skins of their Heads that were barbarously and cruelly torn off by the wild *Indians*. In consequence, I say, of this mournful Detail, the People were extremely charitable; never once dreaming that three fourths of their Donations wou'd never be applied to the Uses for which they were given.[49]

The success of Beatty's European campaign and the political leverage that such a large injection of funds provided Philadelphia Presbyterians intensified ethno-religious rivalry throughout the colony. Beatty and the trustees of the Corporation for the Relief of Poor and Distressed Ministers had always been upfront about where the money raised was going. In a way, however, Hunt was right. The Philadelphia Synod had blended shocking imagery with familial appeals in order to provoke sympathy among Irish audiences. This they did consciously and to great effect.

Irish Presbyterian charity in the eighteenth century: the culture of collection

The General Synod of Ulster appointed far fewer collections for foreign charities than contemporary churches in Britain. This is not by any fault of the body itself. Few campaigns bothered to present supplications before the Synod. In fact Tennent and Beatty were the only two international agents to petition the synod for aid in the second half of the eighteenth century. The General Assembly of the Church of Scotland, by contrast, heard numerous appeals for aid annually. Some of these appeals were quite high profile and exotic. In 1759, for instance, the Assembly heard a petition from Christian Lewis Finne, minister of the Reformed Church of Silesia, and personal chaplain to Frederick II of Prussia, to rebuild Berlin following the recent Russian invasion.[50] Foreign campaigns, especially for the benefit of Calvinist or Dissenting initiatives, recognized that their cause was likely to receive a sympathetic hearing in Edinburgh. Scotland was known as a great centre of learning thanks to the international reputation of the universities at Glasgow and Edinburgh. All of these factors made it a magnet for Protestant charity. Ireland, by contrast, was seen as a backward, Catholic and economically underdeveloped country on the fringe of Europe. It was no wonder, then, that few continental Protestant institutions sent delegations there. Many of them would have been unaware that the Synod even existed. The colonial churches sent emissaries to the General Synod only because American Presbyterianism was largely an offshoot of its Irish counterpart.

Collection for international causes in Scotland and Ireland brought the larger world into the meeting house and allowed congregants to connect with the grand historical narratives of the day through the act of giving. In Scotland, congregants heard appeals throughout the year from multiple charities originating from across Europe and America. In Ireland, a synod-wide foreign collection was rare and, when it did happen, the proceeds went towards American causes. The rarity of international collection in Ireland may have made those campaigns that did make the effort into a novelty or a community event. The presence of a foreign tour must have been exciting. For a moment at least, the larger world that people had read about in newspapers had crashed into the province. A sermon preached by a man who had been at Fort Duquesne and seen Indian war firsthand would have been an event worth attending.

Each actor in the charitable exchange – supplicant and benefactor – came to the encounter with their own expectations as to what they wanted to get out of the deal.[51] Campaigners employed every tactic that they thought might convince their audience to part with their money. Likewise, patrons expected something in return for their generosity. No doubt contributors donated to the American schemes out of a genuine urge to help the less fortunate.[52] Ulster Presbyterians certainly contributed to the Beatty campaign in order to relieve the suffering of their kinfolk in America. Yet there is also a public or voyeuristic face of charitable donation in which the act of giving allows the patron to broadcast their social status and generosity.[53] The records of the Tennent and Beatty campaigns in Ireland provide us only with lump totals of donations given from a particular location and thus do not reveal what portion of their proceeds came from individual donations. Morgan Edwards's campaign literature for the College of Rhode Island, however, does indicate who gave money and where. Edwards published lists of donations for several reasons. He explained that he had done so 'partly for the Honour of the Benefactors, and partly to satisfy them and the College of the Fidelity of their humble Servant, by whom the Money hath been collected'.[54] The list included the names of the Atlantic merchants Thomas Gregg and Waddell Cunningham, who jointly donated £2 2s, and the Rev. Thomas Drennan, the father of the United Irishman William Drennan, who contributed £1 1s towards the school. This subscription list not only advertised the generosity of the donor, it may also have enticed benefactors to give greater amounts to the campaign to bolster their public image. Edwards certainly hoped this would be the case when he devised the lists as a way to secure funds.[55]

Given this study's focus on transatlantic charity, it might be easy to forget that the overwhelming majority of money donated in the Presbyterian churches of Ulster went towards domestic causes. The main objective of a Sabbath collection was domestic poor relief. Traditionally, money for charitable causes was raised through collection, most substantially at bi-annual communion services, at the door of the meeting house or the entry to kirkyard upon the conclusion of the Sunday sermon. Money from these 'exit collections' was either kept by the congregation or delivered to the session for local dispensation or, in the case of congregations belonging to the General Synod, it was deposited into the central general fund. Individual congregations often submitted the names of the 'deserving poor' to the session. This list contained the names of those moral people whose circumstance prevented them from earning a living – including widows, the mentally or physically impaired and the elderly. It was then up to the session, comprised of lay elders and the local minister, to approve the list. Some churches developed alternative financial arrangements to cover the costs of caring for their poorer members. Carnmoney, for example, invested £100 that had been donated to the congregation by a Mr John Shaw upon his death in 1714 towards poor relief. In 1715, the congregation lent Shaw's money to Colonel Clotworthy Upton of Templepatrick at 6 per cent interest. This interest was paid biannually and then dispersed to the poor within the congregation. In 1753 the loan was repaid and subsequently reinvested for the same purpose.[56] Surviving evidence suggests that Carnmoney was unusual in this method of charity. Most congregations seemed to rely on the immediate donations of their members for the support of the poor.

Congregations were more willing to give towards collections for a specific cause or person and not an ill-defined objective such as 'poor relief'. The largest collection of 1720 in Armagh, totalling £3 15s 6d, was gathered for a new meeting house door.[57] In 1759 the congregation of Ballymoney raised an unusually large amount, 8s, towards assisting a man named Anthony 'whose house was burned & [who had] lost the most of his Efforts'.[58] It was rare for Ballymoney's normal Sabbath collection to exceed this amount, save during fastday and seasonal communion collections. Similarly, the largest of the eight collections recorded in the Glascar session book in the autumn of 1762 was 8s for the benefit of 'a young student'.[59] Sometimes domestic charity intersected with the larger historical narratives of the day and gave Ulster Presbyterians a window into the world beyond their shores. For example, on several occasions in the first quarter of the century Irish congregations raised money to pay ransoms for local sailors held by the French and Turks.[60] The Synod also took up a collection to assist the Huguenots of Dublin in the construction of a new meeting house.[61]

It was into this world of local charity, where close relationships between those who gave and those who received mattered, and where intimacy with the object of charity – whether it be an individual or a cause – determined the extent to which people were willing to give, that Beatty's American campaign thrived. It was able to do so, in part, because the American supplicants made the foreign seem local to Irish audiences, effectively shrinking the Atlantic and connecting two disparate communities in the minds of potential donors. Irish Presbyterian participation in the campaign also illustrates their community's affinity with their Scots Irish brethren across the Atlantic.

The Ulster economy and American fundraising

In order to determine whether American charity drives succeed in Ireland we must first come to a basic understanding of the ability and willingness to give to international appeals. Unlike most English benefactors, the majority of those who contributed to Beatty's charity in the north of Ireland did so 'out of their deep poverty'.[62] Partially owing to trade disruption caused by war, the 1750s and early 1760s were an unstable period in the economic history of Ireland. The late 1750s in Ireland witnessed severe dearth and banking crisis.[63] The Linen trade suffered as a result of the disruption caused by war. Irish linen exports to North America dropped from £13,000 in Irish currency for the period 1748–52, to about £10,000 in the years 1753–7.[64]

To make matters worse, Ireland, like the American Colonies, suffered from an acute shortage of specie in the eighteenth century.[65] Many eighteenth-century Irish polemicists arguing for greater economic autonomy for their island certainly would have agreed with such a statement. Across the century, observers complained of a lack of specie in the Kingdom. In 1721 the Irish Parliament threw out the heads of bills that would have established a national Bank of Ireland. Parliamentary opposition arose to such a move on the grounds that a bank was an attack on the traditional privileges of the landed gentry, that it would be an avenue for scheming men to become rich at the expense of the Kingdom, and that it would further subjugate the Irish economy to the whims of British financiers.[66] Opponents argued that it would also lead to the export of silver and gold from the kingdom, leaving the country even more strapped for cash.[67] Critics of the passenger trade in the north claimed that Protestant migrants hurt the Irish economy by draining it of coin. Migrants, they argued, converted their assets to gold and silver coin in order to make their wealth transportable and useable in their new home.[68] In Ulster the currency drought may have been less severe than in other parts of the kingdom because linen transactions were conducted in coin. Money 'percolated' throughout the province as a result.[69] A lack of native money did not necessarily impede the development of a cash system in Ireland. Evidence suggests that the shortage of Irish coin led to a ready circulation of foreign currency – particularly Spanish and Portuguese gold and silver – throughout the Ulster countryside.[70] However, the scarcity of cash in eighteenth-century Ireland leaves the historian of international charity with some pressing, though ultimately unanswerable questions. What is the material significance of coin as an object in a primarily credit economy? What then is the significance of giving it away?

There were many demands on family earnings in Presbyterian communities. Presbyterians had to pay towards the support of their church and community. Congregations pooled their money and resources together to maintain their meeting house and provide their minister with an adequate stipend. Congregations often failed to provide a full stipend, forcing their ministers to petition the Synod for relief. The people of Diremond, near Omagh, had difficulty cobbling together a stipend in 1717. One congregant found a compromise and was able to pay his portion in corn instead of coin.[71] On top of this, Dissenters were compelled by law to support a church to which they did not belong. One of the major grievances that contributed to Presbyterian migration – tithes to the Church of Ireland – was a strain on the resources of Dissenters throughout the kingdom. As was the case in Britain, parishioners were expected to contribute a tenth of their labour towards the upkeep of the established church. In Ulster, the Jacobean 'tything table' that was confirmed by law in 1695 set monetary payments on goods and services. By the eighteenth century monetary payment had largely eclipsed tithes in kind.[72]

Rents throughout the north skyrocketed in this period owing to the spread and success of the linen industry, particularly in the 'linen triangle' of east Ulster. Rents per statutory acre on eight Ulster estates studied by Peter Roebuck rose substantially during the years 1750 and 1769, in some cases more than doubling, as was the case on the Sandwich estate in County Armagh.[73] This development was detrimental to the interst of the tenant as it would first appear. W. H. Crawford has shown that the expiration of leases allowed many sub-tenants the opportunity to take out a lease at a better rate directly from the landlord himself.[74] Nevertheless, most families were hit with the burdens of ever more expensive grain and the depression in the linen industry during the late 1750s.

Weaving families required a large pool of labour to ensure prosperity. The entire household contributed towards the weaving and flax production in order to turn a profit.[75] Women were crucial to the production of linen, aiding in the planting, harvesting and spinning of flax.[76] Arthur

Young recalled upon his visit to Armagh that women were employed in some form or another at every stage of linen production. He noted that, 'In spinning a woman will do 5 or 6 hanks a week, and get 30s, for it by hire, as wages for half a year; a girl of 12 years old, three halfpence or two-pence a day.'[77] Female labour was also instrumental in the pulling, rippling, drying and beating of flaxseed. Of the £6 6s 4d expended on the preparation of flax to be made into textiles in the county, calculations on Young's data reveal that the labour of women and children constituted *at least* £1 6s 10d of the total.[78] The centrality of women to the family or cottage industry of linen production should not be underestimated. Nor should their purchasing power or stake in the familial consumption and expenditure that resulted from it.[79] For a majority of the rural Presbyterian population, the choice to give to a particular cause and the size of a donation were more than probably family, rather than an individual's, decisions. Donation to the American campaigns of the 1750s and 60s reflected the imperial concerns of both Presbyterian men and women. In other words, charitable giving was a personal sacrifice entered into as consciously by the women of a household as by their husbands, brothers and sons.

The congregations of Armagh were early and enthusiastic contributors to Beatty's fund. The secretary of the General Synod evidently was shocked by the diligence and success of the collection in the county. He wrote that it 'appeared that in the Presbytery of Armagh consisting of eight Congregations only' a total of £51 3s 8½d had been amassed.[80] This represented just under one-eighth of the total collected. Within three years the minister of one of the eight Armagh congregations, Rev. George Henry of Narrow-water, had himself sailed for America.[81] The ink on the Treaty of Paris was hardly dry before his departure.

Despite the lull in trade caused by the threat of French privateers, many Ulster ports became more integrated into the Atlantic system during the 1750s. Nowhere was this more evident than in Derry. The city became more integrated into the triangular linen trade between the American colonies, Ulster and Lancashire in the 1750s and 1760s. This was due in part to local improving landlords and the number and the prominence of Derrymen in the Philadelphia merchant community.[82] Both Derry's American and English export markets relied heavily on flax imported from the mid-Atlantic colonies. The arrival of the flax fleet in November also heralded the annual migration of Protestants who – particularly in peacetime – flooded into the empty hulls of ships returning to Delaware ports. Like the industry upon which it was dependent, the passenger trade also expanded in Derry during the 1750s and 1760s.

If anything, the evolution of the city as a major Atlantic port made those involved in the local linen industry, or those contemplating migration, all the more aware of American events, especially when war jeopardized trade. In 1781, a traveller from Dublin noted that migration to America from the countryside surrounding Limavady and Coleraine had spurred 'cordiality to the American Cause [of Independence]'.[83] He further claimed that 'when communication is again open with America ... numbers will go off'.[84] Probably earlier international conflicts and hostilities in America stimulated similar attachments in the weaving districts surrounding Derry. This imperial sympathy probably translated into financial support for the charity drives of 1754 and 1760–2. From the burst in migration that followed the end of hostilities in 1763, it is clear that many would-be migrants in these areas had waited until a more favourable moment before leaving for America. This was certainly the case in Monaghan, where Thomas Clark had been in negotiation with the authorities in New York over land on Lake George as early as 1763. The Cahans exodus occurred only when both the voyage was safe and the frontier was pacified.

Derry and its hinterland provided nearly a quarter of the total donations to Beatty's campaign and over a third of the total amount collected in Ulster. Congregations within the Presbytery of Londonderry collected £47 for the cause, while those under the administration of Letterkenny amassed an impressive £57. Letterkenny's returns are all the more remarkable when one considers that the Presbytery continued to receive aid from the Synod as one of the 'weak' or 'frontier' presbyteries. Not surprisingly, however, Beatty's mission met with the most success in the Presbyterian heartland of the northeast. The Presbytery of Bangor amassed £77 for the charity, Drumore £30, Route £28 5s 11d, and Templepatrick £16 19s 5½d. Like Armagh, Bangor would soon thereafter see one of it ministers leave his congregation for a new life in the colonies. Rev. William Rea remitted his charge over the Kirkdonald congregation in May 1765. His wife later petitioned the Synod for her proportion of the Widows' Fund in 1775, a year after the issue of emigration had forced the body to consider what to do with the money paid into the fund by those who subsequently left Ireland.[85] Other ministers in the northwest were clearly contemplating a move. At the meeting of the General Synod in 1769, the assembled ministers heard 'A declaration of two Derry Ministers saying that they can not live comfortably in Ireland and are therefore leaving for America'.[86]

In contrast, the southwest of Ulster was also a region where the Beatty campaign failed to garner support. Neither the Presbytery of Monaghan nor the Presbytery of Tyrone raised money towards the American charity. Many reasons probably contributed to this, including the relative lack of coin and the comparatively small populations of Dissenters. A large proportion of Monaghan Presbyterians were non-subscribers. Their donations, therefore, would not have been sent to the General Synod.

We can now return to the issue of whether the £427 12s 5½d raised by the Beatty campaign constituted a success. At the time of Beatty's arrival, Ulster congregations were expected to pay into two funds for the benefit of the church as a whole. The money paid into these funds often did not include provisions for local poor relief or ministerial stipends. Since the establishment of the Synod in the previous century, congregations pooled their resources into a general fund, which contributed towards, among other things, poor relief, property maintenance and, periodically, ministerial upkeep. From 1707 onwards the fund was regulated and augmented with a 'subscription fund' for the benefit and support of 'weak' or 'frontier' congregations on the edge of Protestant settlement. Each Presbytery, as we have seen, was then partnered with poor and emerging congregations to which they were expected to provide annual monetary aid.[87]

The next major shake-up of Irish Presbyterian church finance occurred in 1750 when the General Synod and the Presbytery of Antrim came together to found a ministerial widows' scheme on the model established by the Church of Scotland five years earlier. The two Irish churches pooled their resources for the mutual benefit of their clergy and 'to support the Credit of the dissenting interest in general'.[88] If the scheme were to be a success, the two synods needed to establish an endowment by raising a large sum of investment capital. Both bodies began taking up subscriptions immediately and appointed collections on its behalf the following year.

The strain put on many congregations by their support of these two funds during this period of economic uncertainty was difficult to bear. At the 1759 meeting of the General Synod it emerged that a congregation at Broughshane, in the Presbyterian heartland of Ballymena, County Antrim, 'was not willing to pay fund money to any Cogn, but to such as they thought proper'. The Synod quashed Broughshane's objections in a separate committee. The congregation was forced to pay their annual share to the subscription fund, amounting to £1 10s, and was ordered to 'use diligence, in raising the arrear of the fund money, & to bring it to the Genl Synod with the Annual Fund'. This episode was part of a long-running dispute between the Synod of Ballymena and the Presbyteries of Derry and Strabane, on one side, and the Presbytery of Letterkenny, on the other. In 1754, the 'weak' congregations of Rye, who were under the jurisdiction of the Presbytery of Letterkenny, complained to the Synod that they could not support a minister on the money transmitted to them by their partnered Presbyteries. The Synod entreated Derry and Strabane to act on the matter. Two years later, nothing had been done and in 1758 allegations emerged that a Mr White of the congregation of Broughshane had collected money for the supplication fund but then applied it to other purposes.[89] In 1760 the congregations of Moira supplicated the Synod for financial assistance to cover the expenses accrued during a lawsuit they were involved in against local Seceders over the control of property rights to a meeting house. A year later, many congregations that had been asked to provide assistance to Moira, County Down, at the previous session had not done so and were then instructed by the Synod to act quickly.[90]

Popular support for Beatty's charity mirrored, and sometimes exceeded, the collections made on behalf of the General Synod's own widows' fund. The total amount donated to the Irish Widows' Fund by the five Dublin congregations after a Sabbath collection in 1754 was just over £168.[91] Beatty's collection after visiting Dublin and preaching before the Usher's Quay congregation came to £120.[92] It is difficult to piece together an accurate picture of the totals gathered in the different regions of Ulster for the Irish Widows' Fund, but limited evidence suggests that it raised similar amounts to Beatty's campaign. In 1754 the Irish fund stood at about £2,122 after three years of fundraising. A decade later it had increased to £6,179.[93] It is unclear how exactly this growth occurred. The bulk of these sums came from the 40s annual subscription paid into it by ministers. Private donations probably contributed towards the increase. Public donations on collection days were low as far as we can ascertain from the minutes of the General Synod.

The same difficulties that plagued Tennent's earlier collection apparently also afflicted the Irish Widows' Fund. Many ministers were lax in promoting the scheme to their congregations and some sessions initially refused to take up collections for its benefit at all.[94] The Synod agreed to punish ministers who failed to campaign on the Irish fund's behalf. In 1752 the Synod agreed to an overture in which every minister within its bounds was read a letter on behalf of the charity asking each man to 'use such prudent methods as may appear to him most effectual for raising such a Collection, & that an attempt be made in each Congregation for this purpose'.[95] Those who refused to adhere to these procedures faced exclusion from the scheme. A few years later, the Synod agreed again to attempt collections for the fund. At the annual meeting of the Synod at

Lurgan in June 1758, an interlocutor passed an overture that a collection be made within the bounds of both the Synod and the Presbytery of Antrim. For those ministers who continued to ignore the Synod's request to petition their congregations on behalf of the fund, the committee decided upon a new penalty. Non-compliance now resulted in the deduction of a guinea from the minister's annual share of the *regium donum*. Even then, there were those who were slow to act.

The minutes of the General Synod reveal that, over the five-year period between 1759 and 1764, collections appointed by the General Synod and the Presbytery of Antrim netted approximately £236 for the Irish Widows' Fund. The initial pull in 1759, when ministers could reasonably have been assumed to be more vigorous in presenting the collection and congregations more willing to give to a fresh initiative, was about £128. Over the next four years annual totals ranged from £34 in 1760 to £6 in 1763. The £236 total for domestic collections over five years was significantly lower than the £430 collected contemporaneously for Beatty in Ireland between 1760 and 1762.

Overall the Corporation for the Relief of Poor Presbyterian Ministers received £4,384 10s 9d worth of donations as a result of Charles Beatty's European fundraising tour. Irish contributions totalling £427 12s 5½d constituted roughly 10 per cent of this overall sum. What might at first look like a small amount, especially to those familiar with the world of contemporary London charities, was actually quite an achievement, one not matched by any of the other American charities that operated in mid-eighteenth-century Ireland. Beatty's success, in the immediate aftermath of the largest economic downturn in Ireland during the second half of the eighteenth century, illustrates how emotionally attached Ulster Presbyterians had become to their colonial brethren over the course of the Seven Years War. They demonstrated their empathy in the most concrete manner possible: through the donation of cash. The emotional attachment and bonds of kinship (real and imagined) that underpinned this gesture formed the foundation upon which northern Presbyterian attitudes towards the imperial crisis of the 1760s and 1770s were based.

Between 1760 and 1762, ordinary Presbyterians across the province demonstrated their sympathy and compassion for their beleaguered kinfolk on the other side of the ocean in the most concrete way possible: through charitable donation. We cannot ascertain exactly what Irish benefactors thought they were doing by giving to Beatty's charity. Many might have contributed out of concern for those that they had seen sail to America before the war. Others might have done so with the understanding that their money would help expand the borders of Christendom through the funding of missionary endeavours among the Native Peoples of the North American interior. Some may have simply wanted to see the families of colonial ministers cared for through the establishment of a widows' fund. Whatever reason underpinned donation, Beatty made clear that Irish donations would help 'spread the gospel of peace through the dark places of the earth, that have been long the habitations of cruelty'.[96]

Postscript: John Moore's Return and Reflections on America, 1763

This study ends where it began, with the young Irishman, John Moore, staring into the American woods. Three years on, the sense of wonderment that he had experienced on the road to Ticonderoga had long since left him as he settled into the routine of a new life. By 1763 Moore and his sister had left the New York frontier and found themselves living with relatives in Philadelphia. On 13 September of that year he returned to his journal to record further observations about America, its people, and the long war then in the process of winding down. Reflecting on the backcountry that he had come to know personally, Moore had now accepted that those woods that had once so affected him in fact were not empty. Perhaps owing to his direct experience working with British infantry regiments and their Indian allies in the north, Moore had developed strong opinions about the treatment of the native peoples of America by the imperial authorities. 'We seem to have got too much of the Spanish spirit towards the Indians', he wrote, 'kill them, kill them, they are vile barbarious [*sic*] savage brutes, is the cry of many.'[1] This attitude, he concluded, was not befitting a free and Christian people. Moore claimed that Britain's misguided Indian policy was to blame for the recent war. He explained:

> With respect to our conduct to the Indians, the whole English nation and people are highly to blame in their scandalous neglect of civilizing and converting them to Christianity. Even for political reasons they ought to have done it. The present and most cruel and barbarious [*sic*] war which they are now carrying on against us is a dreadful instance of our neglect. I can't help looking on it as a just judgement from Heaven upon us for our sinful neglect.[2]

135

Moore's observations mirror those made by the soldier author of the 'Americus' letter to Henry Joy printed in the *Belfast News-Letter* in the summer of 1760.[3] It appears that both men's direct experiences of American Indian culture and the blatant injustices of European policy regarding land rights had led to a more nuanced view of the causes of the recent war. Their understanding of the conflict, to some extent, ran contrary to the reigning narratives and justifications for the war. The British on both sides of the ocean were certainly no saints. In their 'sinful neglect' the British had ignored their duty to spread the gospel among the nations of North America. Colonial authorities, duplicitous traders and settlers, and London investors all had favoured personal gain at the expense of the Indians. If anything, Britons could turn to God's recent deliverance in the light of such grave sins for proof of his love for his chosen people – his new Protestant Israel. Britain's abysmal war record until 1759, however, demonstrated the need for the peoples of the empire to hold true to their end of his covenant if they wished to continue in his favour. John Moore's thoughts on the plight of the continent's original inhabitants, while still coloured by the cultural chauvinism that underpinned Britain's imperial 'mission' in America, did not exclude their humanity.

Moore's reflections reveal that European perceptions of Native Americans were often more nuanced than the one-dimensional coverage of the Indian wars in contemporary newspaper coverage suggests. The fact that Moore returned home, as did thousands of the migrants and soldiers – including 'Americus', reminds us that contrary views of the American Indian did circulate in mid-eighteenth-century Ireland. Later Irish Patriot recognition of the failures of the freshly established United States to live up to the promise of its revolutionary rhetoric regarding slavery and the treatment of Native Americans was, therefore, not without precedent. Contrary to Moore's observations, however, the dominant image of Native Americans presented to most Ulster Presbyterians at mid-century was that of the skulking, remorseless killer – driven to commit acts of wanton violence by French/Catholic agents. Newspaper accounts, fast day sermons and American campaigners made it very clear that the victims of Indian violence were Irish immigrants.

Historians often subsume the Atlantic or imperial experience of both the Ulster Scots and the Scots Irish of colonial North America within the methodological framework of a Scottish Atlantic. The pioneering work of Ned Landsman and T. M. Devine in particular has exposed the social, economic and religious networks radiating outwards from Edinburgh and Glasgow across the Irish Sea and Atlantic

Ocean.[4] By offering Scotland as the metropole of the imperial subculture of transatlantic Presbyterianism, Landsman and Devine challenged Anglo-centric perceptions of Britain's place at the centre of the Atlantic empire. These studies, however, by virtue of their scope and emphasis on the overarching Scottish character of Atlantic Presbyterianism, have overlooked Ulster Scots' engagement and understanding of the empire on the back of mass migration to the colonies. The mid-Atlantic and Southern colonies were deeply embedded in the world-view of Ulster Presbyterians, perhaps more so than was the case in Scotland. Where eighteenth-century Scottish congregants routinely received Sabbath-day appeals from institutions across Europe and the empire, the only international appeals heard by Ulster Scots under the bounds of the General Synod of Ulster came exclusively from their American brethren. The Atlantic experience of these people differed substantially from the cosmopolitan world of Lowland Scotland. How Ulster Scots, or those 'hybrid people', as Devine refers to them, made sense of British imperial expansion deserves deeper investigation in its own right, outside the framework of Scottish Atlanticism.[5] This book, I hope, has come some way in recovering Ulster Presbyterian engagement with the first British Empire at its height.

From 1754 to 1763, Irish Presbyterians came to understand British imperial expansion within the context of perceived religious conflict and mass migration into their province. Thousands of their kin had settled on the fringes of European settlement and had therefore borne the brunt of the American Indian raids following Braddock's defeat along the banks of the Monongahela in 1754. The gruesome reality of frontier warfare was reinforced in the 142 stories of murder, mutilation and kidnapping printed in the *Belfast News-Letter* throughout the war. These tales of settler victimization at the hands of Indians – often presented to be pawns of the Catholic French – resonated within Presbyterian communities whose relationship with their Catholic neighbours was often coloured by the memory of seventeenth-century atrocities. The recalibration of European alliances prior to the official declaration of war in 1756 meant that Britain (and therefore Ireland as well) was now a member of a largely Protestant coalition of powers. French aggression in North America and the opening of hostilities in India could therefore be interpreted within the context of an eschatological battle between Protestant and Catholic nations. By adhering to national fasts following British defeats and joining in public celebrations for overseas victories, Irish Protestants shared in the highs and lows of the war alongside their countrymen and women across the empire. Like their fellow subjects on the other side of the ocean, Irish Presbyterians discovered their 'Britishness' as a consequence of Britain's struggle for imperial supremacy in the 1750s and 60s.

Ulster Presbyterians came to embrace British imperial expansion in the era of the Seven Years' War because they self-identified with the plight of their colonial brethren across the Atlantic. Presbyterian concern for the security and stability on the empire's western frontiers was based upon the knowledge that the American backcountry was settled, in large part, by people of their ethnicity and religion. The suffering of their colonial brethren recalled episodes from Irish history that remained central to the identity of Irish Protestants. Ulster Scots therefore embedded tales of frontier atrocity with an added layer of meaning based upon their own seventeenth-century 'settler experience'. Historians of the Scots Irish Diaspora, with the exception of R. J. Dickson in his 1966 work, *Ulster Emigration to Colonial America*, have focused primarily on how Irish immigration had transformed American society and culture on the eve of the Revolution.[6] They have largely overlooked the social ramifications of mass emigration within the communities who, throughout the eighteenth century, supplied passengers to fill the empty holds of the American flax fleet before its annual return journey to Delaware ports. Similarly, recent historians focusing on mass politicization and the emergence of Irish republicanism in the 1780s and 1790s have ignored the topic of popular imperialism at midcentury. In 1763, few in Ireland focused on the debts resulting from nearly a decade of global conflict that ultimately resulted in later squabbles over national sovereignty in both North America and Ireland. With peace concluded and Britain victorious, Ulster Presbyterians looked to their enlarged empire with optimism and pride.

Appendices

Appendix 1　Shipping advertisements and accounts of American Indian violence published in the *Belfast News-Letter* (14 August 1764). Image courtesy of the Linen Hall Library, Belfast.

We were hopeful our troubles were in some measure over; but, to our surprise, the Indians came Friday last, about seven miles from me, and took one Day's wife and four children. Next morning, about sun-rise, four families going to the fort with horses loaded, the Indians waylaid them, and killed and captured twenty one. (*Extract of a Letter from Virginia, June 8, 1764*)

[T]he Indians being often heard yelling and hallowing, in their frightful manner, among the hills and through the settlements, dispersed in small parties of two or three together; that they had fired at several of our people ... That the country was evacuated entirely (excepting two or three families) ... (*Philadelphia, June* 21)

Appendix 2 'A PLAN of the Town and Harbour of *LOUISBOURG* in the Island of *Cape Breton', Faulkner's Dublin Journal* (17 June 1758). Image courtesy of the National Library of Ireland.

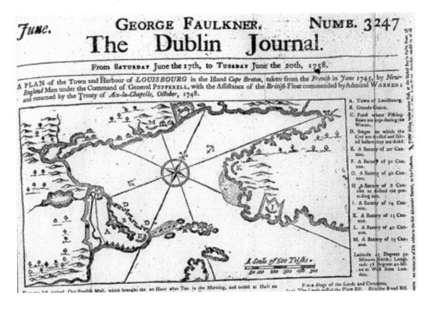

Appendix 3   'A PLAN of *QUEBEC* the Capital of Canada,
or *New France*, in *America'*, *Faulkner's Dublin Journal*
(30 October 1759). Image courtesy of the National Library
of Ireland.

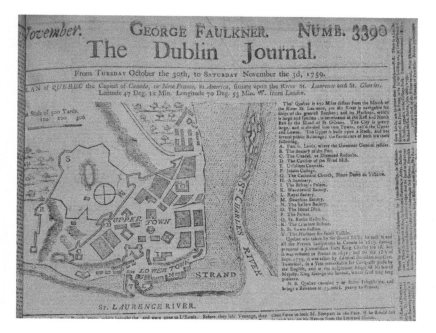

Appendix 4   'ACCURATE and CORRECT MAP of *NORTH AMERICA*, the Seat of the present Actions against the French', *Faulkner's Dublin Journal* (26 August 1755). Image courtesy of the National Library of Ireland.

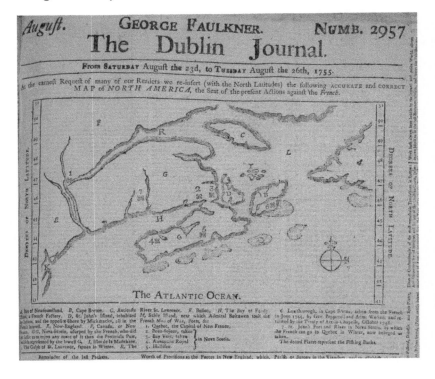

Appendix 5 'The Order of Battle [Braddock's Field]', *Faulkner's Dublin Journal* (2 September 1755). Image courtesy of the National Library of Ireland.

Appendix 6 'A PLAN of the Battle fought *September 7*, between the *English Army* under General Johnson, and the *French* under General Dishkau', *Faulkner's Dublin Journal* (2 December 1755). Image courtesy of the National Library of Ireland.

Notes

Introduction: John Moore's Crossing, 1760

1. Journal of John Moore of Carrickfergus, 1760–1770, PRONI, Malcolm Papers, D/3165/2/p. 4.
2. Ibid.
3. Ibid., p. 9.
4. Ibid., p. 15.
5. Roderick Frazier Nash, *Wilderness and the American Mind*, 4th edn (New Haven: Yale University Press, 2001), pp. 23–43.
6. The 'Walking Purchase' occurred when John and Thomas Penn produced a land deed from the 1680s that they called into effect in 1737. The deed promised the Pennsylvanian proprietors an amount of land along the junction of the Delaware and Lehigh rivers that was equivalent to a day and half's walk. The deed was either a forgery or was a treaty that had never been ratified. See James H. Merrell, *Into the American Woods: Negotiators on the Pennsylvania Frontier* (New York: W. W. Norton, 1999), p. 24.
7. For a synopsis of population density in America and Indian demographics see Daniel K. Richter, *Looking East from Indian Country: A Native History of Early America* (Cambridge, MA: Harvard University Press, 2001), pp. 1–10.
8. Steven C. Harper, 'Delaware and Pennsylvanians after the Walking Purchase', in William A. Pencak and Daniel K. Richter (eds), *Friends and Enemies in Penn's Woods: Indians, Colonists, and the Racial Construction of Pennsylvania* (University Park, PA: The Pennsylvania State University Press, 2004), pp. 167–79.
9. Bernard Bailyn, *Voyagers to the West: Emigration from Britain to America on the Eve of the Revolution* (London: I. B. Tauris, 1987), pp. 36–7.
10. The size and ethno-religious makeup of Irish migration to Colonial America are highly contentious issues. Nineteenth- and twentieth-century scholars of the Scots Irish, such as Wayland Dunaway, marginalized the Catholic element of the Ulster exodus. In reaction to such ethnic trumphalism, scholars including Michael O'Brian and Audrey Lockhart examined the Catholic and southern contribution to eighteenth-century Irish migration. In 1988, Kerby Miller concluded that perhaps as many as one in four Irish migrants to America between the years 1700 and 1776 were Catholic. The overwhelming consensus is that eighteenth-century Irish migration to North America was largely Presbyterian in nature. According to Miller, Presbyterians constituted as much as two-thirds or three-fourths of the total number of migrants. See Wayland F. Dunaway, *The Scotch-Irish of Colonial Pennsylvania* (London: Archon Books, 1944), p. 41; Michael Joseph O'Brien, *A Hidden Phase of American History: Ireland's Part in America's Struggle for Liberty* (New York: Dodd, Mead & Co., 1919); Audrey Lockhart, *Some Aspects of Emigration from Ireland to the North American Colonies between 1660 and 1775* (New York: Arno Press, 1976); Kerby A. Miller, *Emigrants and Exiles: Ireland and the Irish Exodus to North America* (Oxford: Oxford University Press,, 1985), p. 137.

In his seminal study on Ulster Migration in the eighteenth century, R. J. Dickson relied upon tonnage statistics for ships advertised in the *Belfast News-Letter* to arrive at a total number 250,000 Ulster emigrants to America in the colonial period (1601–1776): R. J. Dickson, *Ulster Emigration to Colonial America, 1718–1775* (London: Routledge & Kegan Paul, 1966), pp. 229–37. Subsequent scholars doubt Dickson's statistics, sometimes minimizing the number of Ulster migrants over the period to as few as 60,000. Using figures from the tonnage data in available shipping advertisements, Marrianne Wokeck estimates that as few as 51,676 people left from ALL Irish ports (northern and southern) for America between 1730 and 1774: Marriane Wokeck, *Trade in Strangers: The Beginnings of Mass Migration to North America* (University Park, PA: Pennsylvania State University Press, 1999), pp. 172–3. Kerby A. Miller and Líam Kennedy have recently revived Dickson's intitial total claiming that those who questioned his tonnage data failed to take into consideration ship captains' reasons for lying to colonial authorities about the number of passengers they were freighting (captains under-counted passengers on their vessels in order to avoid colonial tariffs). Also, Miller and Kennedy argue that these minimal tallies failed to take into account the vast numbers of clandestine voyages that were not advertised in Irish newspapers. They conclude that Dickson's 250,000 total was a suitable estimate and that the overall total might have exceeded this number. I agree with Kennedy and Miller and therefore use their estimate of 250,000 emigrants throughout this thesis. For an overview of the migration debate see Kerby A. Miller and Líam Kennedy, 'Appendix 2: Irish Migration and Demography, 1659–1831', in Kerby A. Miller, Arnold Schrier, Bruce D. Boling and David N. Doyle (eds), *Irish Immigrants in the Land of Canaan: Letters and Memoirs from Colonial and Revolutionary America, 1675–1815* (Oxford: Oxford University Press, 2003), pp. 656–78.

11. Bailyn, *Voyagers to the West*, p. 26; Stephen Conway, *War, State, and Society in Mid-Eighteenth-Century Britain and Ireland* (Oxford: Oxford University Press, 2006), pp. 92–3.

12. David Noel Doyle, *Ireland, Irishmen, and Revolutionary America, 1760–1820* (Dublin: Mercier Press, 1981), p. 52.

13. David Noel Doyle, 'Scots Irish or Scotch-Irish', in J. J. Lee and Marion R. Casey (eds), *Making the Irish American: History and Heritage of the Irish in the United States* (New York: New York University Press, 2006), pp. 151–70 (163).

14. For more on this controversy see: O'Brien, *Hidden Phase of American History*; and Kerby A. Miller, 'Ulster Presbyterians and the "Two Traditions" in Ireland and America', in Lee and Casey (eds), *Making the Irish American*, pp. 258–70.

15. Patrick Griffin, *The People with No Name: Ireland's Ulster Scots, America's Scots Irish, and the Creation of a British Atlantic World, 1689–1764* (Princeton: Princeton University Press, 2001).

16. Doyle, 'Scots Irish or Scotch-Irish', pp. 151–2.

17. The reasons for this are partially owing to my source base, which includes a large body of Presbyterian church records from archives in both Philadelphia and Belfast.

18. Griffin, *People with No Name*, p. 7.

19. Following the publication of *The People with No Name*, many historians have built upon Griffin's argument about Scots Irish cultural adaptability in America. Often these studies seek to counter the essentialism of 'Scots

Irish myth' of an unchanging quasi-racial identity in modern America. See: Warren R. Hofstra, 'Introduction: From the North of Ireland to North America: The Scots-Irish and the Migration Experience', in Warren R. Hofstra (ed.), *Ulster to America: The Scots-Irish Migration Experience, 1680–1830* (Knoxville: University of Tennessee Press, 2012), pp. xi–xxvii; and David W. Miller, 'Searching for a New World: The Background and Baggage of Scots-Irish Immigrants', in Hofstra (ed.), *Ulster to America*, pp. 1–24.

20. Vincent Morley, *Irish Opinion and the American Revolution, 1760–1783* (Cambridge: Cambridge University Press, 2002).

21. Padhraig Higgins, *A Nation of Politicians: Gender, Patriotism, and Political Culture in Late Eighteenth-Century Ireland* (Madison: University of Wisconsin Press, 2010); Martyn J. Powell, *The Politics of Consumption in Eighteenth-Century Ireland* (Basingstoke: Palgrave Macmillan, 2005), pp. 47–50; see also R. B. McDowell, *Ireland in the Age of Imperialism and Revolution, 1760–1801* (Oxford: Oxford University Press, 1979), pp. 252–5.

22. Timothy Breen notes the same process at work in America during the imperial crisis of the 1760s. He points out a similar example of British manufactureres pandering to anti-metropolitan political trends in the colony. The piece in question is a teapot held in the Wallace Gallery in Colonial Williamsburg, which was made in the English Midlands and sold in the colonies. It was emblazoned with the slogan 'No Stamp Act'. See T. H. Breen, *The Marketplace of Revolution: How Consumer Politics Shaped American Independence* (Oxford: Oxford University Press, 2004), pp. xi–xii.

23. For contemporary Anglo-Irish understandings of the term see Joep Th. Leersen, 'Anglo-Irish Patriotism and Its European Context: Notes towards a Reassessment', *Eighteenth-Century Ireland: Iris an dá chultúr* 3 (1988), pp. 7–24.

24. Quoted in Higgins, *Nation of Politicians*, p. 105.

25. For more on the conception of the empire as a 'greater Britain' see Eliga H. Gould, *The Persistence of Empire: British Political Culture in the Age of the American Revolution* (Chapel Hill: University of North Carolina Press, 2000), pp. 66–9, 212–14. For the existence of a unifying imperial identity see also P. J. Marshall, *The Making and Unmaking of Empires: Britain, India, and America c. 1750–1783* (Oxford: Oxford University Press, 2005), p. 160.

26. Ian McBride, 'The School of Virtue: Francis Hutcheson, Irish Presbyterians and the Scottish Enlightenment', in D. G. Boyce, R. Eccleshall and V. Geoghegan (eds), *Political Thought in Ireland since the Seventeenth Century* (London: Routledge, 1993), pp. 73–99 (74). For the Scottish Atlantic and evangelical networks principally in the nineteenth century see David W. Miller, 'Religious Commotions in the Scottish Diaspora: A Transatlantic Perspective on "Evangelicalism" in a Mainline Denomination', in David A. Wilson and Mark G. Spencer (eds), *Ulster Presbyterians in the Atlantic World: Religion, Politics and Identity* (Dublin: Four Courts Press, 2006), pp. 22–38.

27. For more on the influence of the Scottish universities in Ulster and America see Mark G. Spencer, '"Stupid Irish teagues" and the Encouragement of Enlightenment: Ulster Presbyterian Students of Moral Philosophy in Glasgow University, 1730–1795', in Wilson and Spencer (eds), *Ulster Presbyterians in the Atlantic World*, pp. 50–61.

28. Nancy J. Curtin, *The United Irishmen: Popular Politics in Ulster and Dublin, 1791–1798* (Oxford: Oxford University Press, 1994), pp. 18–19; Ian McBride,

Scripture Politics: Ulster Presbyterianism and Irish Radicalism in the Late Eighteenth Century (Oxford: Oxford University Press, 1998), pp. 114–16.

1 Atlantic Migration and North America in the Irish Presbyterian Imagination

1. Graeme Kirkham, 'Ulster Emigration to North America, 1680–1720', in H. Tyler Blethen and Curtis W. Wood, Jr. (eds), *Ulster and North America: Transatlantic Perspectives on the Scotch-Irish* (Tuscaloosa: The University of Alabama Press, 1997), pp. 76–97 (84); R. J. Dickson, *Ulster Emigration to Colonial America, 1718–1775* (London: Routledge & Kegan Paul, 1966), p. 65.
2. For Ulster Presbyterian indenture in the colonies see James Leyburn, *The Scotch-Irish: A Social History* (Chapel Hill: University of North Carolina Press, 1962), pp. 174–9; Patrick Griffin, *People with No Name: Ireland's Ulster Scots, America's Scots Irish, and the Creation of a British Atlantic World, 1689–1764* (Princeton: Princeton University Press, 2001), pp. 93–4, 159–61.
3. Griffin, *People with No Name*, p. 95.
4. Ibid., pp. 159–60.
5. Leyburn, *The Scotch-Irish*, p. 174.
6. Michael Billig coined the term 'banal nationalism' to describe the ways in which the display of mundane national symbols, such as flags on public buildings, reinforce the sense of national belonging in the observer. Like Billig's 'banal nationalism', the ephemera of the Atlantic passenger trade created a sense of belonging to an imperial community among mid-eighteenth-century Ulster Presbyterians. See Michael Billig, *Banal Nationalism* (London: Sage Publications, 1995), p. 6.
7. For more on emigrant letters see Trevor Parkhill, 'Philadelphia Here I Come: A Study of the Letters of Ulster Immigrants in Pennsylvania, 1750–1875', in Blethen and Wood (eds), *Ulster and North America*, pp. 118–33; E. R. R. Green, 'Ulster Emigrants' Letters', in E. R. R. Green (ed.), *Essays in Scotch-Irish History* (London: Routledge & Kegan Paul, 1969), pp. 87–103; Kerby A. Miller, *Emigrants and Exiles: Ireland and the Irish Exodus to North America* (Oxford: Oxford University Press, 1985); A. C. Davies, '"As Good a Country as Any Man Needs to Dwell in"; Letters from a Scotch-Irish Immigrant in Pennsylvania, 1766, 1767, and 1784', *Pennsylvania History* 50.4 (1983), pp. 313–22.
8. *Pennsylvania Gazette* (27 October 1737).
9. Ibid.
10. Letter from John Denison, Pennsylvania, to Samuel Denison, Dromore, County Down, 1789, PRONI, John Denison Papers, T/2294/1.
11. Letter from John Dunlop, Philadelphia, to [Robert Rutherford], 12 May 1789, PRONI, Dunlop, Rutherford and Delap Papers, T/1336/1/18.
12. Journal of Captain Alexander Chesney, born 12 September 1755, died 1843, PRONI, Wilson-Chesney Family Pedigree, T/1095/3/1–3.
13. PRONI, Journal of John Moore, D/3165/2, pp. 1–2.
14. Dickson, *Ulster Emigration*, p. 29; Wayland F. Dunaway, *The Scotch-Irish of Colonial Pennsylvania* (London: Archon Books, 1944), p. 34; Griffin, *People with No Name*, pp. 65–71.

15. Conrad Gill, *The Rise of the Irish Linen Industry* (Oxford: Oxford University Press, 1925), p. 341.
16. This was probably the second migration for many who sailed from Irish ports to America in 1717–20. Recent research suggests that perhaps as many as 41,000 Scots settled in Ulster in the 1690s. Many of the early Ulster migrants to America were familiar with migration as a life strategy because of their previous journey from Scotland to Ulster. The mobility of the Scots migrants of the 1690s therefore laid the groundwork for future migrations. See Patrick Fitzgerald, '"Black '97": Reconsidering Scottish Migration to Ireland in the Seventeenth Century and the Scotch Irish in America', in William Kelly and John Young (eds), *Ulster and Scotland, 1600–2000: History, Language and Identity* (Dublin: Four Courts Press, 2004), pp. 71–84 (79).
17. James Kelly, 'Harvests and Hardship: Famine and Scarcity in Ireland in the Late 1720s', *Studia Hibernica* 26 (1991–2), pp. 65–105.
18. Dickson, *Ulster Emigration*, pp. 25–6.
19. Hugh Boulter, *Letters Written by his Excellency Hugh Boulter, D. D. Lord Primate of All Ireland* (Dublin: 1770), pp. 230–1.
20. For more on the relationship between Presbyterians and the Irish state see Ian McBride, 'Presbyterians in the Penal Era', *Bullán: A Journal of Irish Studies* 1.2 (Autumn 1994), pp. 73–99 (73–86).
21. All historians agree that Irish emigration to America was the product of a complex cocktail consisting of religious persecution, optimistic expectation and poverty. Scholars differ, however, on the degree to which any of these factors outweigh the others. Patrick Griffin emphasizes the importance of religious grievances within Ulster Presbyterian communities, and a sense of their existing on the cultural peripheries of the British world led thousands to migrate in the 1720s, *People with No Name*, pp. 37–64. Graeme Kirkham and Marianne Wokeck both stress the importance of economic hardship in animating mass migration. See Kirkham, 'Ulster Emigration', p. 85; Marraine S. Wokeck, *Trade in Strangers: The Beginnings of Mass Migration to North America* (University Park, PA: Pennsylvania State University Press, 1999), pp. 191–4.
22. E. R. R. Green, 'The "Strange Humours" That Drove the Scotch-Irish to America, 1729', *WMQ* 3rd series, 7 (1955), pp. 113–23 (118).
23. 'A Brief Representation of some of the causes, why protestant Dissenters are inclined To Remove from Ireland to America, [1728]', National Library of Scotland, Wodrow MSS, Oct. XLV, p. 216.
24. Dickson, *Ulster Emmigration*, p. 38.
25. Ibid., p. 39.
26. Archbishop William King to William Wake, Archbishop of Canterbury, 2 June 1719, in William King, *A Great Archbishop of Dublin, William King D. D. 1650–1729*, ed. Charles Simeon King (London: Longmans, Green, and Co., 1906), p. 302.
27. For more on the official response to the migration of 1727–9 see Patrick Walsh, 'The Differing Motivations for Preventing Transatlantic Emigration: A Case Study from West Ulster, 1718–1729', in Shane Alcobia-Murphy, Joanna Archibold, John Gibney and Carole Jones (eds), *Beyond the Anchoring Grounds: More Cross-currents in Irish and Scottish Studies* (Belfast: Cló Ollscoil na Banríona, 2005), pp. 324–30.

28. Dickson, *Ulster Emigration*, p. 34.

29. Petition by the masters of nine ships lying in the Port of Belfast, to George Macartney, Collector of the Port of Belfast, 19 April 1736, PRONI, Mussenden Papers, D/354/508.

30. Ibid.

31. John Stewart's letter is reproduced in the following format: John Stewart, 'Obstructions to Irish Immigration to Pennsylvania, 1736', *PMHB* 21.4 (1897), pp. 485–7.

32. Ibid., p. 485.

33. Ibid., p. 486.

34. Ibid.

35. Ibid. Commentators often blamed optimistic accounts from shipmasters for giving the people false accounts of the new world. See Green, '"Strange Humours"', p. 118.

36. Jonathan Swift, *A Letter from the Revd. J.S.D.S.P.D. to a Country Gentleman in the North of Ireland* [Signed A. North. Reprinted from no. 19 of *The Intelligencer*] ([Dublin?], 1736), pp. 6–8. Swift's pamphlet resulted in a furious reply from at least one American author who noted the absurdity of Swift's claim that colonial officials could possibly police the correspondence of thousands of migrants and hundreds of sailors. See [Roscommon], *To the Author of those Intelligencers printed at Dublin* (New York, 1733).

37. Swift, *Letter from the Revd. J.S.D.S.P.D.*, p. 7.

38. Quoted in Leyburn, *The Scotch-Irish*, pp. 191–2.

39. Kerby A. Miller, Arnold Schrier, Bruce D. Boling and David N. Doyle (eds), *Irish Immigrants in the Land of Canaan: Letters and Memoirs from Colonial and Revolutionary America, 1675–1815* (Oxford: Oxford University Press, 2003), p. 30.

40. *Historical Collections Relative to the Town of Belfast: from the Earliest Period to the Union with Great Britain* (Belfast, 1817), p. 114.

41. Arthur Young, *A Tour in Ireland; with General Observations on the Present State of that Kindgom: made in the Years 1776,1777, and 1778* (London, 1780), pp. 108, 111, 125, 143.

42. William Drennan to Dr. William Bruce, March [no date] 1783, PRONI, Drennan Bruce Letters, D/553/1.

43. Ibid.

44. William Drennan to Martha McTier, 13 December 1777, in David Alfred Chart (ed.), *The Drennan Letters. Being a Selection from the Correspondence ... between William Drennan, M.D., and His Brother-in-Law and Sister, Samuel and Martha McTier, during the Years 1776–1819* (Belfast: 1931), pp. 3–4. Irish professional emigration from the middling-sorts occurred throughout the century. Contributing factors to this type of migration, especially in the south, largely existed independently from the social stimuli that caused the main waves of Ulster Migration. Dublin architect Samuel Cardy is one example of such a migrant. He moved to Charleston, South Carolina, in 1752, where he was entrusted with the task of designing the state house, as it was later known, and St. Michael's Episcopal church. See Kenneth Severns, 'Emigration and Provincialism: Samuel Cardy's Architectural Career in the Atlantic World', *Eighteenth-Century Ireland: Iris an dá chultúr* 5 (1990), pp. 21–36.

45. Dickson, *Ulster Emigration*, p. 199.

46. Ibid., pp. 196–200.
47. Miller, Schrier, Boling and Doyle (eds), *Irish Immigrants in the Land of Canaan*, p. 28.
48. Cahans Session minutes, 15 April 1756, PRONI, Cahans Session Book, 1751–8, CR/3/25B/1, p. 67.
49. [Anonymous], *The Answer to Shawn ouge a Glanea. To which are Added, II. The Yorkshie Conflict. III. The Phoenix of Ulster. IV. The Rambling Journeyman* (Monaghan, 178[9?]), pp. 5–7.
50. [Anonymous], *An Answer to the Phoenix of Ulster* (Monaghan, 1789), p. 6.
51. For more on Clark's ministry in Ireland and the Cahans exodus see James H. Murnane and Peadar Murnane, *At the Ford of the Birches: The History of Ballybay, It's People and Vicinity* (Monaghan: R & S Printers, 1999), pp. 174–92.
52. Tyler H. Blethen and Curtis W. Wood Jr., *From Ulster to Carolina: The Migration of the Scotch-Irish to Southwestern North Carolina* (Raleigh: North Carolina Department of Cultural Resources and Office of Archives and History, 1998), p. 18.
53. Blethen and Wood, *From Ulster to Carolina*, p. 43. For more on North Carolina as a destination for Irish immigrants earlier in the century see John Raymond Shute, 'The Irish in North Carolina', *Journal of the Royal Society of Antiquaries of Ireland* 2, Series 7 (1932), pp. 116–19.
54. Dobbs was the first of three major agents investigated by R. J. Dickson in his *Ulster Emigration to Colonial America*, pp. 128–34. For more information on the life and career of Arthur Dobbs see: Robert M. Calhoon, 'Dobbs, Arthur (1689–1765)', *Oxford Dictionary of National Biography* (Oxford: Oxford University Press, 2004); Desmond Clarke, *Arthur Dobbs, Esquire, 1689–1765: Surveyor-General of Ireland, Prospector and Governor of North Carolina* (London: Bodley Head, 1957).
55. Dickson, *Ulster Emigration*, p. 130.
56. Marianne S. Wokeck, 'Searching for Land: The Role of New Castle, Delaware, 1720s– 1770s', in Warren R. Hofstra (ed.), *Ulster to America: The Scots-Irish Migration Experience, 1680–1830* (Knoxville: University of Tennessee Press, 2012), pp. 51–76.
57. Mary M. Schweitzer, *Custom and Contract: Household, Government, and the Economy in Colonial Pennsylvania* (New York: Columbia University Press, 1987), p. 217.
58. PHSI, MSS Books of Rev. William Caldwell, 1772–8.
59. [Joseph Pollock], *The Letters of Owen Roe O'Nial* (Dublin, 1779), pp. 42, 24.
60. It is difficult to tell when Drennan received this gift. It might have been as late as 1815 when the tree fell in a storm and pieces of it were sold as souvenirs.
61. William Drennan, undated poem, Commonplace Book of Wm. Drennan, PRONI, D/531/8/16.
62. See Kevin Kenny, *Peaceable Kingdom Lost: The Paxton Boys and the Destruction of William Penn's Holy Experiment* (Oxford: Oxford University Press, 2009).
63. 'Extract of a Message from the Governor to the Assembly of Philadelphia', *BNL*, 18 March 1755; 'The SPEECH of his Excellency WILLIAM FRANKLIN, Esq; Captain General, Governor, and Commander in Chief of the Province of New-Jersey … ' *BNL*, 16 November 1764; 'To the Honourable James

Hamilton ... The humble address and a remonstrance of the Protestant Ministers of the several denominations ... ', *BNL*, 13 October 1761.

64. *BNL*, 13 December 1754.
65. Ibid.
66. Orr, Dunlope and Glenholme to Red. James Macky, 5 December 1768, HSP, Letterbook, Orr, Dunlope, and Glenholme, 1767–1769, AM.111.
67. Ibid.
68. Waddell Cuningham to Thomas Greg, 20 September 1756, in Thomas Truxes (ed.), *Letterbook of Greg & Cunningham, 1756–57: Merchants of New York and Belfast* (Oxford: Oxford University Press, 2001), p. 208.
69. Peter Roebuck, 'The Lives Lease System and Emigration from Ulster: An Example from Montgomery County, Pennsylvania', *Directory of Irish Family Research* 18 (1995), pp. 75–7.
70. For more on James MacSparran see Kerby A. Miller, 'James MacSparran's *America Dissected* (1753): Eighteenth-Century Emigration and Constructions of "Irishness"', *History Ireland* 11.4 (Winter 2003), pp. 17–22.
71. Quoted in Miller, 'James MacSparran's *America Dissected*', p. 18.
72. Ibid.
73. Quoted in Wilkins Updike, *History of the Episcopal Church in Narragansett, Rhode Island* (New York: Henry M. Onderdonk, 1847), p. 530.
74. Ibid.
75. William Smith to Richard Peters, 18 October 1763, quoted in P. J. Marshall, *The Making and Unmaking of Empires: Britain, India, and America c. 1750–1783* (Oxford: Oxford University Press, 2005), p. 28.
76. *BNL*, 13 May 1763.
77. Ibid.
78. Ibid.
79. Ibid.
80. Ibid.
81. Ian McBride, *Eighteenth-Century Ireland: The Isle of Slaves* (Dublin, 2009), p. 352.
82. Terence Denham, '"Hibernia officina militum"': Irish Recruitment to the British Regular Army, 1660–1815', *Irish Sword: The Journal of the Military History Society of Ireland* 20.80 (Winter 1996), pp. 148–66 (156–8).
83. Stephen Conway, *The British Isles and the War of American Independence* (Oxford: Oxford University Press, 2000), pp. 28–9.
84. Quoted in Thomas Bartlett, 'Army and Society in Eighteenth-Century Ireland', in W. A. Maguire (ed.), *Kings in Conflict: The Revolutionary War in Ireland and Its Aftermath, 1689–1750* (Belfast: Ulster Museum, 1990), pp. 173–82 (180).
85. For Protestant enlistment in the Irish home establishment see Bartlett, 'Army and Society', pp. 175, 178–80; Eoin Magennis, 'Politics and Government in Ireland during the Seven Years War, 1756–63', PhD thesis (Queen's University Belfast, 1996), pp. 29–37; Stephen Conway, *War, State, and Society in Mid-Eighteenth-Century Britain and Ireland* (Oxford: Oxford University Press, 2006), p. 62; L. M. Cullen, 'The Irish Diaspora of the Seventeenth and Eighteenth Centuries', in Nicholas Canny (ed.), *Europeans on the Move: Studies on European Migration, 1500–1800* (Oxford: Oxford University Press, 1994), pp. 113–49 (125, 139–40).

86. Neal Garnham, 'Ireland's Protestant Militia 1715–76: A Military Assessment', *Irish Sword: The Journal of the Military History Society of Ireland* 20.80 (Winter 1996), pp. 131–6.
87. Ibid., p. 133.
88. Ibid., pp. 133–4.
89. Magennis, 'Politics and Government', p. 32.
90. Ibid., p. 35.
91. Stephen Brumwell, *Redcoats: The British Soldier and War in the Americas, 1755–1763* (Cambridge: Cambridge University Press, 2002), pp. 73–4.
92. Ibid., p. 74.
93. Paul E. Kopperman, 'The British High Command and Soldiers' Wives in America, 1755–1783', *Journal of the Society for Army Historical Research* 60.241 (Spring 1982), pp. 14–34 (26–7).
94. *BNL*, 1 March 1757.
95. Ibid.
96. A. J. H. Richardson, 'Busby, Thomas', in *The Dictionary of Canadian Biography* IV, pp. 115–16. It is unclear what Busby's religious background was. He was certainly a Protestant and joined the first Anglican congregation in Montreal under the stewardship of Rev. David Charbrand Delisle. This may have been because Delisle was the sole Protestant minister in the city at the time. Busby's family later helped towards the establishment of Presbyterian building on St. Gabriel Street. See Rev. Robert Campbell, *A History of the Scotch Presbyterian Church St. Gabriel Street, Montreal* (Montreal: W. Drysdale, 1887), pp. 120–1.
97. Brumwell, *Redcoats*, pp. 297–8.
98. See Thomas M. Truxes, *Irish-American Trade, 1660–1783* (Cambridge: Cambridge University Press, 1988), pp. 212–30.

2   The Press, Associational Culture and Popular Imperialism in Ulster, 1750–64

1. Hugh Mongomery, Pederborn Camp, to Ms Montgomery of Greyabbey and Catherine Hall of Strangford, 9 August 1759, PRONI, Perceval-Maxwell Papers, D/906/283/A1–A3.
2. Francis Joy was a prominent Presbyterian of Huguenot ancestry who was connected to the Sovereign of the Town of Belfast through marriage. He founded the *Belfast News-Letter*, Ireland's oldest continuingly printed newspaper, in September 1737. The paper was printed bi-weekly and sold for one penny an issue through the middle of the century. In the 1740s Joy passed ownership over to his two sons, Henry and Robert Joy.
3. Bob Harris, *Politics and the Rise of the Press: Britain and France, 1620–1800* (London: Routledge, 1996), pp. 1–2; Eliga H. Gould, *The Persistence of Empire: British Political Culture in the Age of the American Revolution* (Chapel Hill: University of North Carolina Press, 2000), p. xxxiv. For many historians, the idea of the press as an 'active force' in history has become so overpowering as to negate concerns over reception. Padhraig Higgins, for example, claimed that 'the idea that newspapers shaped public opinion is axiomatic among historians': *A Nation of Politicians: Gender, Patriotism, and Political Culture*

in Late Eighteenth-Century Ireland (Madison: University of Wisconsin Press, 2010), p. 31.

4. John Caldwell, 'Particulars of the History of a North Country Irish Family', PRONI, Caldwell Papers, T/3541/5/3/73.

5. Ibid., p. 202.

6. See David Dickson, *Old World Colony: Cork and South Munster, 1630–1830* (Cork: Cork University Press, 2005), p. 360; Ian McBride, *Eighteenth-Century Ireland: The Isle of Slaves* (Dublin: Gil and Macmillan, 2009), pp. 381–4; Beandán MacSuibhne, 'Politicization and Paramilitarism: North-West and South-West Ulster, *c.* 1772–98', in Thomas Bartlett, David Dickson, Dáire Keogh and Kevin Whelan (eds), *1798: A Bicentenary Perspective* (Dublin: Four Courts Press, 2003), pp. 243–78 (258–9).

7. Linda Colley, *Captives: Britain, Empire and the World, 1600–1850* (London: Jonathan Cape, 2002), pp. 173–4. For more information about images of the Native American in eighteenth-century Britain see Troy O. Bickham, *Savages within the Empire: Representations of American Indians in Eighteenth-Century Britain* (Oxford: Oxford University Press, 2005).

8. *FDJ*, 31 May 1755.

9. Irish products shipped to America rose from 10 per cent of the country's total exports before 1756 to roughly 16 per cent in the decade before American Independence. Thomas M. Truxes, *Irish-American Trade, 1660–1783* (Cambridge: Cambridge University Press, 1988), p. 38.

10. Arthur Young, *A Tour in Ireland; with General Observations on the Present State of that Kindgom: made in the Years 1776,1777, and 1778* (London, 1780), p. 103.

11. John Greene and Elizabeth McCrum, '"Small Clothers": The Evolution of Men's Nether Garments as Evidenced in *The Belfast Newsletter* Index 1737–1800', *Eighteenth-Century Ireland: Iris an dá chultúr* 5 (1990), pp. 153–71 (164).

12. For the imperial dimension of British Patriotism during the Seven Years War see P. J. Marshall, 'A Nation Defined by Empire, 1755–1776', in Alexander Grant and Keith J. Stringer (eds), *Uniting the Kingdom? The Making of British History* (London: Routledge, 1995), pp. 208–22. For more on the relationship between national identity and the press see Kathleen Wilson, *Sense of the People: Politics, Culture and Imperialism in England, 1715–1785* (Cambridge: Cambridge University Press, 1995).

13. David Hayton has warned against the assumption that Ulster Presbyterians subscribed to a 'British' identity before the 1760s. In a review of Patrick Griffin's *People with No Name*, Hayton questioned if there was evidence to suggest that such an identity existed in the early eighteenth century. See D. W. Hayton, 'Review: *People with No Name: Ireland's Ulster Scots, America's Scots Irish, and the Creation of a British Atlantic World* by Patrick Griffin', *Eighteenth Century Ireland: Iris an dá chultúr* 19 (2004), pp. 232–5. Gerald Newman and Katheen Wilson have both emphasized the early importance of imperial expansion and the Seven Years War to the emergence of English national-ism. See Gerald Newman, *The Rise of English Nationalism: A Cultural History, 1740–1830*, 2nd edn (Basingstoke: MacMillan, now Palgrave Macmillan, 1997), pp. 67, 74–5; and Kathleen Wilson, *The Island Race: Englishness, Empire and Gender in the Eighteenth Century* (London: Routledge, 2003), pp. 1–28.

14. Normally, the foreign news section of the newspaper was restricted to the front page. But during periods of international tension in 1755–6 or 1759

the section sometimes poured over to the third page. Some of this may have been because of a wartime dip in foreign trade.

15. Troy O. Bickham, *Making News: The American Revolution as Seen through the British Press* (Dekalb: Northern Illinois University Press, 2009), pp. 19–20.

16. Benedict Anderson, *Imagined Communities: Reflections on the Origin and Spread of Nationalism* (London: Verso, 1983), p. 33.

17. *BNL*, 13 February 1760.

18. Interestingly, given his belief in the 'fictive' character of news periodicals, Anderson did not endeavour to broach the topic of the subjectivity of regional presses and the biases of individual editors. *Imagined Communities* was an attempt to document the formation of national consciousness among large groups of people over the course of five hundred years. The scope of the project restricted Anderson's focus to the construction of monolithic, abstract structures and institutions such as the 'press' and not the varying degrees in which sub- or supra-national community consciousness was expressed in, and moulded by, regional newspapers.

19. Wilson, *Island Race*, pp. 31–4.

20. Robert Munter in *The History of the Irish Newspaper, 1685–1760* (Cambridge: Cambridge University Press, 1967), pp. 96–7.

21. By successful I mean that they survived longer than five years. The other paper was the *Limerick Journal* (title changed to the *Munster Journal* in 1744), founded in 1739 and printed until 1777. For more on the development of a newspaper press in Belfast in the eighteenth and nineteenth centuries see A. Albert Campbell, *Belfast Newspapers, Past and Present* (Belfast: W. & G. Baird, 1921).

22. Survival rates for provincial papers increased from 1750 onwards. The Bagnell publishers of Cork maintained the *Cork Evening Post* from 1755 to at least 1774. For more on newspapers in Munster and Leinster with an emphasis on the second half of the century see Máire Kennedy, 'Eighteenth-Century Newspaper Publishing in Munster and South Leinster', *Journal of the Cork Historical and Archaeological Society* 103 (1998), pp. 67–88.

23. J. R. R. Adams, *The Printed Word and the Common Man, Popular Culture in Ulster 1700–1900* (Belfast: Institute of Irish Studies, The Queen's University Belfast, 1987), pp. 9–12. For the reading habits of later eighteenth-century Ulster Presbyterians and the centrality of the Bible to their identity see Andrew R. Holmes, *The Shaping of Ulster Presbyterian Belief and Practice 1770–1840* (Oxford: Oxford University Press, 2006), pp. 273–5.

24. Bickham, *Making News*, p. 24.

25. *BNL*, 15 November 1794.

26. Based on totals calculated by Munter in *History of the Irish Newspaper*, p. 86.

27. Ibid., pp. 86–9.

28. The collections were entitled *The Public Gazetteer. Containing the Most remarkable Occurences of the Present War. And A Collection of other Foreign and Domestic Intelligence, with some Original Pieces in Prose and Verse; and several; agreeable Essays, &c. from the London Chronicle, Lloyd's Evenng-Post, and other English Papers.*

29. Munter stated that this was possible. See *History of the Irish Newspaper*, p. 89.

30. Ibid.

31. The 1841 census indicates that Ulster was the most literate province in Ireland. This was largely because of the large Presbyterian population. See Niall Ó Ciosáin, *Print and Popular Culture in Ireland, 1750–1850*

(Basingstoke: Macmillan, now Palgrave Macmillan, 1997), p. 38. Catholics, however, did engage with the burgeoning newspaper and periodical press in the eighteenth century. See Raymond Gillespie, *Reading Ireland: Print, Reading and Social Change in Early Modern Ireland* (Manchester: Manchester University Press, 2005), pp. 39–41.

32. For more on the transformation of Belfast after 1750 see the epilogue in Raymond Gillespie, *Early Belfast: The Origins and Growth of an Ulster Town to 1750* (Belfast: Ulster Historical Foundation, 2007), pp. 167–74.

33. Colonial news regarding provincial politics, e.g., from the *New York Mercury* was first printed in the *News-Letter* on 16 October 1764 before being picked up by the *Dublin Journal* on 27 October.

34. See Nini Rodgers, *Ireland, Slavery and Anti-Slavery: 1612–1865* (Basingstoke: Palgrave MacMillan, 2007), pp. 145–58.

35. For the partnership of Greg and Cunningham see Thomas Truxes (ed.), *The Letterbook of Greg & Cunningham* (Oxford: Oxford University Press, 2001).

36. Both the Dublin and Belfast papers routinely advertised available leases. The *News-Letter*, however, publicized locally available land as opposed to the *Dublin Journal*, whose circulation throughout the country provided the paper with numerous advertisers eager to utilize the Dublin press in lieu of a local paper to attract desirable tenants.

37. *BNL*, 11 March 1762; *BNL*, 20 June 1764; *BNL*, 9 March 1764.

38. *BNL*, 13 May 1763.

39. Ibid.

40. Vincent Morley, *Irish Opinion and the American Revolution, 1760–1783* (Cambridge: Cambridge University Press, 2002), p. 83.

41. A letter from Belfast regarding the Hearts of Oak disturbances and published in the *Dublin Journal* referred to a journal from Newry. If this publication existed, or if it were anything more than simply a news-sheet, it is likely that it had a very limited print run and probably folded within a fairly short period after its initial printing. *FDJ*, 8 March 1760.

42. *BNL*, 6 April 1756.

43. Quoted in David Dickson, *Arctic Ireland: The Extraordinary Story of the Great Frost and Forgotten Famine of 1740–41* (Belfast: White Row Press, 1997), p. 18.

44. *BNL*, 18 August 1761.

45. *BNL*, 14 April 1761.

46. *BNL*, 3 January 1764.

47. J. C. D. Clark, *The Language of Liberty, 1660–1832: Political Discourse and Social Dynamics in the Anglo-American World* (Cambridge: Cambridge University Press, 1994), pp. 277–8.

48. For accounts published in the *Belfast Journal*, relative to the present state of America see *Historical Collections Relative to the Town of Belfast: from the Earliest Period to the Union with Great Britain* (Belfast, 1817), p. 118.

49. Ibid., p. 110.

50. *BNL*, 14 September 1759.

51. On 1 March 1757, e.g., the Joys received word from a Philadelphian ship captain of several French prizes taken by the *Winchelsea* man of war in the North Atlantic.

52. See: Robert Darnton, 'Readers Respond to Rousseau: The Fabrication of Romantic Sensitivity', *The Great Cat Massacre and Other Episodes in French*

Cultural History (London: Allen Lane, 1984), pp. 215–56; and Lisa Jardine and Anthony Grafton, 'How Gabriel Harvey Read His Livy', *Past & Present* 129 (November 1990), pp. 30–78.

53. John Feather, 'The Power of Print: Word and Image in Eighteenth-Century England', in Jeremy Black (ed.), *Culture and Society in Britain, 1660–1800* (Manchester: Manchester University Press, 1997), pp. 51–68 (61).

54. Roger Chartier, 'General Introduction: Print Culture', in Alain Boureau, Roger Chartier, Marie-Elisabeth Ducreux, Christian Jouhaud, Paul Saenger and Catherine Velay-Vallantin (eds), *The Culture of Print: Power and the Uses of Print in Early Modern Europe*, trans. Lydia G. Cochrane (Cambridge: Polity, 1989), pp. 1–10 (2–3).

55. For more on the birth of the coffee house and its eventual spread throughout the three kingdoms see Brian Cowan, *The Social Life of Coffee: The Emergence of the British Coffee House* (New Haven: Yale University Press, 2005). See also Woodruff D. Smith, 'From Coffee House to Parlour: The Consumption of Coffee, Tea and Sugar in North-Western Europe in the Seventeenth and Eighteenth Centuries', in Jordan Goodman, Paul E. Lovejoy and Andrew Sherratt (eds), *Consuming Habits: Drugs in History and Anthropology* (London: Routledge, 1995), pp. 148–64.

56. For more on the development of the alehouse see Peter Clark, *The English Alehouse: A Social History, 1200–1830* (London: Longman, 1983).

57. R. W. M. Strain, *Belfast and Its Charitable Society: A Story of Urban Social Development* (Oxford: Oxford University Press, 1961), p. 17.

58. Ibid., p. 19.

59. MacSuibhne, 'Politicization and Paramilitarism', p. 248.

60. For the price of the *News-Letter* see: Hugh Oram, *The Newspaper Book: A History of Newspapers in Ireland, 1649–1983* (Dublin: MO Press, 1983), pp. 31–2; Robert Munter, 'A Hand-list of Irish Newspapers, 1685–1750', *Cambridge Bibliographical Monograph* 4 (London: Bowes & Bowes, 1960), p. 29.

61. Higgins, *Nation of Politicians*, p. 31; Munter, 'Hand-list of Irish Newspapers', p. 15.

62. [Anonymous], *A Description of the English and French Territories, in North America* (Dublin, 1756), p. 1. More examples of Dublin pamphlets on American geography and demographics include two editions of John Brickell's *The Natural History of North-Carolina* (Dublin, 1737, 1744); Richard Falconer, *The Voyages, Dangerous Adventures, and Miraculous Escapes of Capt. Richard Falconer, Containing, The Laws, Customs, and Manners of the Indians in America* (Dublin, 1752); Robert Rogers, *A Concise Account of North America: Containing a Description of the Several British Colonies on that Continent* (Dublin, 1769).

63. [Anonymous], *Description of the English and French Territories*, p. 1

64. George Faulkner's *Dublin Journal* epitomized the complicated character of mid-century patriot Dublin. It enjoyed a long print run stretching back to 1724, and by the 1750s had established itself as one of the foremost bi-weekly journals in Dublin. It was the leading publication of the opposition patriots throughout the middle decades of the century until it was joined in 1763 by the *Freemen's Journal*. Both were sympathetic to the cause of Catholic emancipation. Aside from the patriot bias that manifested primarily in letters, the *Dublin Journal* was in many ways a typical Dublin

paper reflecting the culture and outlook of the city. It catered largely to the city's Protestant professional and artisan classes, the majority of whom belonged to the Church of Ireland. It printed the same news from the London packets carried by most other Irish and British provincial papers and contained accounts of parliamentary gossip and proceedings found in its competitors.

65. An overview of maps published in British monthly magazines between 1754 and 1765 shows that North American topics constituted 15 per cent of those printed in the *Universal Magazine*, 40 per cent of the *Scots Magazine*, 21 per cent of the *London Magazine* and 26 per cent of the *Gentleman's Magazine*. See David C. Jolly, *Maps in British Periodicals: Part I, Major Monthlies before 1800* (Brookline, MA: David C. Jolly, 1990), pp. 567–71, 105–29, 174–8, 192–204). These statistics makes Faulkner's inclusion of exclusively American maps in the *Dublin Journal* during the same period all the more strange. He probably had ready access to maps of other locations but opted not to print them. Why this would be the case, especially when lulls in American news were often accompanied by an upsurge in European coverage and vice-versa, has yet to be ascertained.

66. William J. Smyth, *Map-making, Landscapes and Memory: A Geography of Colonial and Early Modern Ireland c.1530–1750* (Notre Dame: Field Day, 2006), p. 25; Berhard Klein, *Maps and the Writing of Space in Early Modern England and Ireland* (London: Palgrave, now Basingstoke: Palgrave Macmillan, 2000), pp. 171–85; J. Brian Harley, 'Maps, Knowledge and Power', in Denis Cosgrove and Stephen Daniels (eds), *The Iconography of Landscape* (Cambridge: Cambridge University Press, 1988), pp. 277–312, and 'Deconstructing the Map', in Trevor Barnes and James Duncan (eds), *Writing Worlds: Discourse, Text and Metaphor in the Representation of Landscape* (London: Routledge, 1992), pp. 231–47; Simon Ryan, 'Inscribing the Emptiness: Cartography, Exploration and the Construction of Australia', in Chris Tifflin and Alan Lawson (eds), *De-Scribing Empire: Post-colonialism and Textuality* (New York: Routledge, 1994), pp. 115–30.

67. Martin Brückner, *The Geographic Revolution in Early America: Maps, Literacy, and National Identity* (Chapel Hill, NC: University of North Carolina Press, 2006), pp. 3–4, 6–7.

68. For the print explosion of American topics in Britain during the Seven Years War see Colley, *Captives*, pp. 172–86.

69. Gould, *Persistence of Empire*, pp. xxxiv, 212–14. For 'Greater Britain' see also: David Armitage, 'Greater Britain: A Useful Category of Analysis?' *American Historical Review* 104.2 (April 1999), pp. 427–45; and J. G. A. Pocock, 'British History: A Plea for a New Subject', *Journal of Modern History* 47.4 (December 1975), pp. 601–21.

70. David Armitage, *The Ideological Origins of the British Empire* (Cambridge: Cambridge University Press, 2000), p. 173. This definition of empire was complicated by the annexation of large non-Protestant populations into the British Empire in Canada and the Indian subcontinent in the aftermath of the Seven Years War. See P. J. Marshall, *The Making and Unmaking of Empires: Britain, India, and America c. 1750–1783* (Oxford: Oxford University Press, 2005), pp. 6–7, 182–206.

71. *Pue's Daily Occurrences*, 1 August 1761.

72. *BNL*, 20 February 1759.
73. *BNL*, 13 February 1760.
74. For the economic impact and costs of the Seven Years War, see: Nancy F. Koehn, *The Power of Commerce: Economy and Governance in the First British Empire* (Ithaca, NY: Cornell University Press, 1994), pp. 3–18; and Larry Neal, 'Interpreting Power and Profit in Economic History: A Case Study of the Seven Years' War', *Journal of Economic History* 37 (1977), pp. 20–35.
75. *BNL*, 18 April 1755. The pamphlet was a reprint of Henry Macculloch's, *A Miscellaneous Essay concerning the courses pursued by Great Britain in the affairs of her Colonies, &c.* (London, 1755).
76. *BNL*, 18 April 1755.
77. Ibid.
78. For the role of the press in the development of nationalism and the construction of national identities see Anderson, *Imagined Communities*, ch. 2.
79. S. J. Connolly, *Divided Kingdom: Ireland 1630–1800* (Oxford: Oxford University Press, 2008), pp. 345–83.
80. *FDJ*, 19 August 1755. See Appendix 2.
81. *FDJ*, 19 August 1755.
82. See Appendix 3.
83. Wolfe's contribution to the battle had not yet been established. In consequence, the Plains of Abraham were not included on the map.
84. *Dublin Courier*, 16 January 1760; *Public Gazetteer*, 23 December 1758; *Pue's Daily Occurences*, 1 August 1761.
85. See Appendix 4.
86. See Appendix 3.
87. *FDJ*, 30 August 1755. See Appendix 5.
88. *FDJ*, 2 December 1755. See Appendix 6.
89. *BNL*, 29 November, 1754.
90. Ibid.
91. *BNL*, 17 December 1754.
92. Ibid.
93. Ibid.
94. *BNL*, 13 December 1765.
95. Ibid.
96. *BNL*, 11 March 1762.
97. Ports along the Delaware River were the favoured destinations for Presbyterian migrants for a number of reasons including the initial availability of land in Philadelphia's hinterland and Pennsylvania's famed charter guaranteeing freedom of conscience. The American flaxseed fleet that fed the Irish linen industry also serviced passenger traffic (particularly of indentured servants) on the return journey. For a general introduction see: R. J. Dickson, *Ulster Emigration to Colonial America, 1718–1775* (London: Routledge & Kegan Paul, 1966); and Truxes, *Irish-American Trade*, pp. 127–46, 170–211.
98. Philadelphia and other Delaware ports held a near monopoly over the emigrant trade during the late 1750s and early 1760s. McNutt was ultimately unable to tempt potential passengers away from that with which they had become familiar. For more information on McNutt's devious attempts to settle Irish migrants in Nova Scotia see Dickson, *Ulster Emigration*, pp. 134–52.

99. For an excellent synopsis of the 'Kingdom or Colony' debate in Irish history see Joe Cleary, '"Misplaced Ideas" Colonialism, Location, and Dislocation in Irish Studies', in Clare Carroll and Patricia King (eds), *Ireland and Postcolonial Theory* (Notre Dame: University of Notre Dame Press, 2003), pp. 16–45. For Irish participation in empire-building see Thomas Bartlett, '"What Ish My Nation?": Themes in Irish History: 1550–1850', in Thomas Bartlett, Chris Curtain, Riana O'Dwyer and Gearoid O'Tuathaigh (eds), *Irish Studies: A General Introduction* (Dublin: Gil and Macmillan, 1988), pp. 44–59; Hiram Morgan, 'An Unwelcome Heritage: Ireland's Role in British Empire-Building', *History of European Ideas* 19.4–6 (July 1994), pp. 619–25.

100. For commemorative festivals see James Kelly, '"The Glorious and Immortal Memory": Commemoration and Protestant Identity in Ireland, 1660–1800', *Proceedings of the Royal Irish Academy* 94 C.2 (1994), pp. 25–52; Jacqueline Hill, 'National Festivals, the State and "Protestant Ascendancy" in Ireland, 1790–1829', *Irish Historical Studies* 24.93 (May 1984), pp. 30–51.

101. Kelly, '"Glorious and Immortal Memory"', p. 42.

102. *BNL*, 21 November 1755.

103. *BNL*, 7 September 1756.

104. *BNL*, 20 February 1756.

105. *BNL*, 20 February, 8 June 1756.

106. *BNL*, 20 April 1756.

107. David Waldstriecher, *In the Midst of Perpetual Fetes: The Making of American Nationalism* (Chapel Hill: University of North Carolina Press, 1997).

108. Ibid., pp. 51–2.

109. Martyn J. Powell, 'Political Toasting in Eighteenth-Century Ireland', *History: The Journal of the Historical Associaion* 91.304 (October 2006), pp. 508–29 (509–10).

110. 'Success to our American Forces' was number eight in the list of toasts drunk by the Down Patriots on 23 April 1756: *BNL*, 30 April 1756.

111. *BNL*, 18 April 1755.

112. *BNL*, 14 and 21 November, and 26 December 1755.

113. *BNL*, 24 September 1756.

114. *BNL*, 29 June 1756.

115. *BNL*, 26 April and 5 August 1757.

116. *BNL*, 5 August 1757.

117. *BNL*, 6 February 1759.

118. Ibid.

119. *BNL*, 2 July 1762.

120. *FDJ*, 10 August 1762.

121. Martyn J. Powell, *The Politics of Consumption in Eighteenth-Century Ireland* (Basingstoke: Palgrave Macmillan, 2005), pp. 1–7, 28–33, 172–97.

3 He Never Wants for Suitable Instruments: The Seven Years War as a War of Religion

1. *BNL*, 1 June 1756.

2. *BNL*, 8 March 1757.

3. John Scott, Philadelphia, to Daniel Mussenden, 7 July 1755, PRONI, Mussenden Papers D/354/1030.
4. Matthew Leslie, '"Copy of a letter from Major Leslie to a respectable merchant of Philadelphia" July 30, 1755', in Paul E. Kopperman, *Braddock at the Monongahela* (Pittsburgh: University of Pittsburgh Press, 1977), pp. 204–5.
5. Ibid.
6. Ibid.
7. The behaviour of Irish troops in the battle became a major issue in Dublin following a claim made in the London press that the Irish regiments had become confused and had left their officers – Colonels Gage and Burton – to die on the battlefield. The reports further claimed that 'Had the Irish Regiments done their Duty General Braddock would have gained a complete Victory'. George Faulkner countered by asserting that most Irishmen were not permitted to serve in the army and that those regiments, while based in Ireland, were largely raised in England and Scotland. *FDJ*, 6 September 1755.
8. Quoted in Gerald Newman, *The Rise of English Nationalism: A Cultural History, 1740–1830*, 2nd edn (Basingstoke: MacMillan, now Palgrave Macmillan, 1997), p. 75.
9. Samuel Blacker to Sir Archibald Acheson, 27 January 1762, PRONI, Gosford Papers, D1606/1/1/36.
10. Samuel Davies, *Religion and Patriotism the constituents of a Good Soldier. A Sermon preached to Captain Overton's Independent Company of Volunteers, raised in Hanover County, Virginia, August 17, 1755* (Philadelphia, 1755), p. 18.
11. *BNL*, 6 April 1756.
12. For more on the life and writings of James Bryson see Thomas Witherow, *Historical and Literary Memorials of Presbyterianism in Ireland (1731–1800)* (London and Belfast: William Mullan and Sons, 1880), pp. 141–4.
13. James Bryson, 'Sermon for the Fast, 5 May 1763', Queen's University Belfast, Special Collections, Antrim Presbytery Collection, MSS Bryson Sermons, Volume 1.
14. Ibid.
15. Ibid.
16. J. G. Simms, 'The Irish on the Continent, 1691–1800', in T. M. Moody and W. E. Vaughan (eds), *A New History of Ireland: IV, Eighteenth-Century Ireland* (Oxford: Clarendon Press, 1986), pp. 629–53 (637).
17. William Bruce, Dublin, to Hugh Hamilton, Killyleagh, 29 May 1755, PRONI, Bruce Correspondence, T/3041/1/C18.
18. *BNL*, 22 April 1755.
19. Ibid.
20. *BNL*, 6 April 1756.
21. John Brady, *Catholics and Catholicism in the Eighteenth-Century Press* (Maynooth: Catholic Record Society of Ireland, 1965), p. 319.
22. John Russell, 4th Duke of Bedford, to William Pitt, 29 August 1758, NA (PRO), SP 30/8/19, p.18.
23. *FDJ*, 9 November 1759.
24. Ibid.
25. See: John F. Berens, '"Good News from a Far Country": A Note on Divine Providence and the Stamp Act Crisis', *Church History* 45.3 (September 1976),

pp. 308–15; and Berens, *Providence & Patriotism in Early America, 1640–1815* (Charlottesville: University Press of Virginia, 1978), pp. 1–13.

26. For more on the diffusion of Enlightenment thought in Ireland see Geraldine Sheridan, 'Irish Periodicals and the Dissemination of French Enlightenment Writings in the Eighteenth Century', in Thomas Bartlett, David Dickson, Dáire Keogh and Kevin Whelan (eds), *1798: A Bicentenary Perspective* (Dublin: Four Courts Press, 2003), pp. 28–51; Sheridan, 'Irish Literary Review Magazines and Enlightenment France, 1730–1790', in Graham Gargett and Geraldine Sheridan (eds), *Ireland and the French Enlightenment,1700–1800* (Basingstoke: Macmillan, now Palgrave Macmillan, 1999), pp. 21–46; Máire Kennedy, 'The Distribution of a Locally-Produced French Periodical in Provincial Ireland: The *Magazin à la mode, 1777–1778*', *Eighteenth-Century Ireland* 9 (1994), pp. 83–98.

27. For providence as an explanation for worldly events see: Richard B. Sher, 'Witherspoon's *Dominion of Providence* and the Scottish Jeremiad Tradition', in Richard B. Sher and Jeffrey R. Smitten (eds), *Scotland and America in the Age of the Enlightenment* (Edinburgh: Edinburgh University Press, 1990), pp. 46–64 (50); Tony Claydon and Ian McBride, 'The Trials of the Chosen Peoples: Recent Interpretations of Protestantism and National Identity in Britain and Ireland', in Tony Claydon and Ian McBride (eds), *Protestantism and National Identity: Britain and Ireland, c.1650–c.1850* (Cambridge: Cambridge University Press, 1998), pp. 1–29 (9–15). For how the Great Awakening and the Seven Years War transformed providential thinking in America see Berens, *Providence & Patriotism in Early America*, pp. 32–50.

28. Andrew R. Holmes, *The Shaping of Ulster Presbyterian Belief and Practice 1770–1840* (Oxford: Oxford University Press, 2006), pp. 78–88 (quotation 80).

29. R. S. Tosh, 'An Examination of the Origin and Development of Irish Presbyterian Worship', PhD thesis (Queen's University Belfast, 1983), p. 361.

30. Meeting of the Ballybay session, 15 April 1755, PRONI, Cahans Session Book, 1751–58, CR/3/25B/1/pg. 41.

31. *BNL*, 9 January 1761; 26 January 1762.

32. The sermon is not listed in Witherow's *Historical and Literary Memorials of Presbyterianism in Ireland*.

33. [Presbyterian Historical Society of Ireland], *A History of Congregations in the Presbyterian Church in Ireland, 1610–1982* (Belfast: Presbyterian Historical Society of Ireland, 1982), pp. 322–4.

34. *BNL*, 11 June 1756.

35. *BNL*, 10 February 1757.

36. For more on the reception of the Lisbon earthquake in Britain see: Robert G. Ingram, '"The Trembling Earth Is God's Herald": Earthquakes, Religion and Public Life in Britain during the 1750s', in Theodore E. D. Braun and John B. Radner (eds), *The Lisbon Earthquake of 1755: Representations and Reactions* (Oxford: Voltaire Foundation, 2005), pp. 97–115; and Robert Webster, 'The Lisbon Earthquake: John and Charles Wesley Reconsidered', in Braun and Radner (eds), *Lisbon Earthquake*, pp. 116–26.

37. For the reactions of the philosophes to the earthquake see: Theodore E. D. Braun, 'Voltaire and Le Franc de Pompignan: Poetic Reactions to the Lisbon Earthquake', in Braun and Radner (eds), *Lisbon Earthquake*, pp. 145–55; and Jeff Loveland, 'Guéneau de Montbeillard, the *Collection académique* and the

Great Lisbon Earthquake', in Braun and Radner (eds), *Lisbon Earthquake*, pp. 191–207.

38. Brady, *Catholics and Catholicism in the Eighteenth-Century Press*, p. 88.

39. Ibid., p. 89.

40. *BNL*, 9, 13, 16 January 1756; *Dublin Inteligencer*, 17 June 1756.

41. *FDJ*, 22 November 1755.

42. *BNL*, 10 February 1757.

43. *BNL*, 30 January 1756. The author is identified as 'E.L.' and the letter is dated 7 January, from Mansfield.

44. *BNL*, 30 January 1756.

45. Ibid.

46. *BNL*, 2 January 1756.

47. *Pue's Daily Occurences*, 28 July 1759.

48. *BNL*, 16 October 1759.

49. *FDJ*, 20 October 1759.

50. *BNL*, 17 October 1760.

51. Thomas Vance, *A Thanksgiving Sermon for the Late Successes of his Majesty's Arms Preached at Ussher's-Quay, November 29, 1759* (Dublin, 1760), p. 22.

52. *BNL*, 3 February 1756. Another example of a 'Protestant Wind' was the gale that spirited William's troops to England while simultaneously keeping James II's fleet bottled-up in the Thames Estuary.

53. *BNL*, 28 October 1760.

54. William Fletcher, *A Sermon Preached in St. Andrew's, Dublin; Before the Honourable House of Commons: On Thursday, Nov. 29, 1759; Being the Day appointed for a General Thanksgiving* (Dublin, 1759), p. 11.

55. Ibid.

56. Ibid., p. 6.

57. Ibid., p. 11.

58. Ibid.

59. Tosh, 'Origin and Development of Irish Presbyterian Worship', p. 361.

60. Vance, *Thanksgiving Sermon*, p. 15. This sermon, while printed in Dublin, was advertised for sale in Belfast (*BNL*, 8 January 1760).

61. Ibid., p. 24.

62. William Boulton, *A Sermon Preached in the Baptist Meeting House in Swift's-Alley, Nov. 9th. 1760. On the Death of His late and most Excellent Majesty, George II* (Dublin, 1760), p. 15.

63. Ibid., p. 14.

64. *FDJ*, 15 April 1758.

65. Ibid.

66. Ibid.

67. Arthur Dobbs, Brunswick, to Dr. Alexander McAuley, 19 February 1761, PRONI, Dobbs Papers, D/162/78.

68. *Dublin Gazette*, 2 February 1760.

69. *BNL*, 1 March 1757.

70. For the *King of Prussia* and Irish migration see *BNL*, 31 May and 13 September 1759.

71. See David Bell, *The Cult of the Nation in France, Inventing Nationalism* (Cambridge, MA: Harvard University Press, 2001), esp. ch. 3.

72. *FDJ*, 27 October 1759; *BNL*, 26 January 1760.

73. For more on Thurot's landing see: Alan J. Guy, 'The Irish Military Establishment, 1660–1776', in Thomas Bartlett and Keith Jeffery (eds), *A Military History of Ireland* (Cambridge: Cambridge University Press, 1996), pp. 211–30 (226–8); and T. Percy Armstrong, 'Thurot at Carickfergus, 1760', *Notes and Queries* 175 (July–December 1938), pp. 261, 317, 353. For Belfast merchant John Black's account of the landing see David Kennedy, 'Thurot's Landing at Carrickfergus', *Irish Sword: The Journal of the Military History Society of Ireland* 6.24 (Summer 1964), pp. 149–53.

74. Guy, 'Irish Military Establishment', p. 227. The number of prisoners listed in *BNL*, on 7 March 1760, differs slightly from Gay's total of 231.

75. *Dublin Courier*, 12 June 1761.

76. *BNL*, 24 January 1764.

77. Ibid.

78. Sean Murphy, 'The Dublin Anti-Union Riot of 3 December 1759', in Gerard O'Brien (ed.), *Parliament, Politics and People: Essays in Eighteenth-Century Irish History* (Dublin: Irish Academic Press, 1989), pp. 49–68 (53).

79. Duke of Bedford to William Pitt, 25 December 1759, NA(PRO), State Papers, SP 63/416, f. 260.

80. Ibid.

81. *FDJ*, 16 May 1761.

4 Sorrowful Spectators: Ulster Presbyterian Opinion and American Frontier Atrocity

1. Louis Antoine de Bougainville, *Adventure in the Wilderness: The American Journals of Louis Antoine de Bougainville, 1756–1760*, trans. and ed. Edward P. Hamilton (Norman: University of Oklahoma Press, 1964), 29 August 1757, p. 179.

2. De Bougainville was involved in several French frontier campaigns, including the offensive against Fort Oswego in 1756 and the notorious siege of Fort William Henry in 1757. Despite receiving a wound in battle in 1758, he aided in the defence of Quebec and was present at its fall in 1759.

3. Francis Alison, Sermon delivered in July 1755 and again in 1776, PHS (Phila.) Francis Alison Papers, 1743–1871, RG 294/1/1.

4. See especially Luke Gibbons, '"The Return of the Native": The United Irishmen, Culture and Colonialism', in Thomas Bartlett, David Dickson, Dáire Keogh and Kevin Whelan (eds), *1798: A Bicentenary Perspective* (Dublin: Four Courts Press, 2003), pp. 52–74.

5. [Joseph Pollock], *The Letters of Owen Roe O'Nial* (Dublin, 1779), p. 20.

6. Gibbons, '"Return of the Native"', p. 74.

7. For more on the American Indian and the Scottish Enlightenment see Troy O. Bickham, *Savages within the Empire: Representations of American Indians in Eighteenth-Century Britain* (Oxford: Oxford University Press, 2005), pp. 171–209.

8. Robert Burton [Nathaniel Crouch], *The English Empire in America: or a View of the dominions of the Crown of England* (Dublin, 1735), pp. 81–3.

9. Linda Colley, *Captives: Britain, Empire and the World, 1600–1850* (London: Jonathan Cape, 2002), p. 174.

10. One in five books about American topics published in Britain between 1640 and 1760 were printed in the 1750s. See Richard A. Simmons, 'Americana in British Books, 1621–1760', in Karen Ordahl Kupperman (ed.), *America in European Consciousness 1493–1750* (Chapel Hill: University of North Carolina Press, 1995), pp. 361–87.
11. Colley, *Captives*, p. 177.
12. Peter Silver, *Our Savage Neighbors: How Indian War Transformed Early America* (New York: W. W. Norton, 2008), pp. xiv–xx.
13. The link between barbarity, Native Americans and Catholicism in *BNL* reporting was commonly made in regards to Acadian loyalty and Quebec's support of continued violence against colonials in New England and Nova Scotia in 1756: *BNL*, 23 January 1756.
14. Bickham, *Savages within the Empire*, pp. 225–7.
15. *BNL*, 26 August 1760.
16. Ibid.
17. 'David Lindsey, near Desertmartin, County Londonderry, to Thomas or Andrew Fleming, "Pennsillvena," 19 March 1758', in Kerby A. Miller, Arnold Schrier, Bruce D. Boling and David N. Doyle (eds), *Irish Immigrants in the Land of Canaan: Letters and Memoirs from Colonial and Revolutionary America, 1675–1815* (Oxford: Oxford University Press, 2003), pp. 28–9.
18. Ibid.
19. 'Waddell Cunningham to John McCamon & sons, Newry, 17 June 1756', in Thomas Truxes (ed.), *Letterbook of Greg & Cunningham, 1756–57: Merchants of New York and Belfast* (Oxford: Oxford University Press, 2001), p. 154.
20. Ibid.
21. *BNL*, 17 October 1755. The three spikes in Native American violence corresponded with lulls in news from the European campaigns.
22. *BNL*, 26 February 1762.
23. For background information see R. J. Dickson, *Ulster Emigration to Colonial America, 1718–1775* (London: Routledge & Kegan Paul, 1966), pp. 128–34.
24. *BNL*, 4 June 1763. In 1765 Dobbs succeeded in convincing the British government to establish the Church of England as the official church of North Carolina: Miller et al. (eds), *Irish Immigrants in the Land of Canaan*, p. 519, footnote 34.
25. *BNL*, 28 September 1764.
26. For more about Native American violence being an affront to European masculinity see Krista Camenzind, 'Violence, Race, and the Paxton Boys', in William A. Pencak and Daniel K. Richter (eds), *Friends and Enemies in Penn's Woods: Indians, Colonists, and the Racial Construction of Pennsylvania* (University Park, PA: Pennsylvania State University Press, 2004), pp. 201–20 (206–7).
27. *BNL*, 24 December 1754.
28. *BNL*, 27 January 1756.
29. *BNL*, 29 June 1764.
30. *BNL*, 21 October 1757.
31. Ibid.
32. *BNL*, 9 March 1764.
33. *BNL*, 24 December 1754.
34. Ibid.

35. *BNL*, 25 March 1759.

36. Frederick John Belcher to Robert Wilmot, 4 September 1762, PRONI, Wilmot Papers, T/30/9/4369. For more on the experience of soldier captives among American Indians see Stephen Brumwell, *Redcoats: The British Soldier and War in the Americas, 1755–1763* (Cambridge: Cambridge University Press, 2002), pp. 168–79.

37. *BNL*, 4 December 1759.

38. *BNL*, 2 January 1756.

39. Ibid.; *BNL*, 13 August 1763.

40. *BNL*, 19 January 1759.

41. *BNL*, 6 December, 1757.

42. Ibid.

43. Ibid.

44. *BNL*, 14 November 1755, 28 October 1760.

45. For more information on William Johnson as a land agent in Ulster see Dickson, *Ulster Emigration*, p. 54.

46. *BNL*, 15 April 1763.

47. *BNL*, 30 March 1764.

48. John Black Sr. to John Black Jr. and James Black, 2 August 1766, PRONI, Black Family Letter, D/719/78. I am grateful to Dr. Ian McBride for alerting me to this quote.

49. Kerby A. Miller, *Emigrants and Exiles: Ireland and the Irish Exodus to North America* (Oxford: Oxford University Press, 1985), pp. 38–9; Ian McBride, *Eighteenth-Century Ireland: The Isle of Slaves* (Dublin: Gil and Macmillan, 2009), p. 104.

50. Edward Willes, *The Letters of Lord Chief Baron Edward Willes to the Earl of Warwick, 1757–62: An Account of Ireland in the Mid-Eighteenth Century*, ed. James Kelly (Aberystwyth: Boethius, 1990), p. 52.

51. Andrew Stewart, Killymoon, to James Stewart, 8 July 1763, PRONI, Wilmot Papers, T3019/4631.

52. Jonathan Swift, *A Modest Proposal For Preventing the Children of Poor People From being a Burthen to Parents and Country, &c* (London, 1730), p. 10. For cannibalism as an imperialist trope see Peter Hulme, 'Introduction: The Cannibal Scene', in Francis Barker, Peter Hulme and Margaret Iversen (eds), *Cannibalism and the Colonial World* (Cambridge: Cambridge University Press, 1998), pp. 1–38; Hulme, *Colonial Encounters: Europe and the Native Caribbean, 1492–1797* (London and New York: Routledge, 1986).

53. For debates about Ireland and postcolonial theory and Ireland as a colony see Clare Carroll, 'Introduction: The Nation and Postcolonial Theory', in Clare Carroll and Patricia King (eds), *Ireland and Postcolonial Theory* (Notre Dame: University of Notre Dame Press, 2003), pp. 1–15.

54. McBride, *Eighteenth-Century Ireland*, p. 100.

55. Jill Lepore, *New York Burning: Liberty, Slavery, and Conspiracy in Eighteenth-Century Manhattan* (New York: Alfred A. Knopf, 2005), p. 51.

56. Ibid. See also Gordon S. Wood, 'Conspiracy and the Paranoid Style: Causality and Deceit in the Eighteenth Century', *WMQ*, 3rd series, 39.3 (July 1982), pp. 401–41.

57. James Kelly, '"We were all to have been massacred": Irish Protestants and the Experience of Rebellion', in Thomas Bartlett, David Dickson, Dáire Keogh

and Kevin Whelan (eds), *1798: A Bicentenary Perspective* (Dublin: Four Courts, 2003), pp. 313–16. For Protestant paranoia and fear of the Catholic threat see also S. J. Connolly, *Religion, Law, and Power: The Making of Protestant Ireland* (Oxford: Clarendon Press, 1992), pp. 233–4, 249–62.

58. Eoin Magennis, 'Politics and Government in Ireland during the Seven Years War, 1756–63', PhD thesis (Queen's University Belfast, 1996), p. 40.

59. McBride, *Eighteenth-Century Ireland*, p. 241. Eoin Magennis points out that the Lord Chancellor and Lord Limerick pursued the trial as a matter of routine rather than out of an actual belief that O'Reilly had dealings with the French: 'Politics and Government in Ireland', p. 40.

60. George Whitefield, *A short address to persons of all denominations, occasioned by the alarm of an intended invasion*, quoted in P. J. Marshall, 'A Nation Defined by Empire, 1755–1776', in Alexander Grant and Keith J. Stringer (eds), *Uniting the Kingdom? The Making of British History* (London: Routledge, 1995), pp. 208–22 (217).

61. [Anonymous], *An Alarm to the Unprejudiced and Well-Minded Protestants of Ireland: Or Seasonable Queries upon the Rise, Danger and Tendency of the Whiteboys* (Cork, 1762), pp. 10, 13–14, 18. For a resurgence in Protestant fears regarding Catholics in the early 1760s see David Dickson, *New Foundations: Ireland 1660–1800*, 2nd edn (Dublin: Irish Academic Press, 2000), pp. 147–8.

62. *FDJ*, 16 April 1763.

63. For the Whiteboys see James S. Donnelly, 'The Whiteboy Movement, 1761–5', *Irish Historical Studies* 21.81 (March 1978), pp. 20–54; and Thomas P. Power, *Land, Politics and Society in Eighteenth-Century Tipperary* (Oxford: Oxford University Press, 1993), pp. 178–88.

64. Quoted in Donnelly, 'Whiteboy Movement', p. 21. Donnelly claims that Fant was not of sound mind.

65. Quoted in Donnelly, 'Whiteboy Movement', p. 43.

66. *BNL*, 3 February 1758.

67. Ibid.

68. There is a large body of work devoted to early modern English comparisons between American Indians and Irish Catholics. For how British imperial policy towards Native Americans was influenced by previous colonial ventures in Ireland see: James Muldoon, 'The Indian as Irishman', *Essex Institute Historical Collections* 3 (1975), pp. 267–89; and Muldoon, *Identity on the Medieval Irish Frontier: Degenerate Englishmen, Wild Irishmen, Middle Nations* (Gainsville: University of Florida Press, 2003). Both Gaelic Irish and American Indian societies were conceptualized as barbarous foils to English society. See Nicholas Canny, 'The Permissive Frontier: The Problem of Social Control in English Settlements in Ireland and Virginia, 1550–1650', in K. R. Andrews, N. P. Canny and P. E. H. Hair (eds), *The Westward Enterprise: English Activities in Ireland, the Atlantic, and America 1480–1650* (Liverpool: University of Liverpool Press, 1978), pp. 17–44 (32–4). For an ethno-cultural comparison between Gaelic Highlanders and the Algonquins and Iroquois see Margaret Connell Szasz, *Scottish Highlanders and Native Americans: Indigenous Education in the Eighteenth-Century Atlantic World* (Norman: University of Oklahoma Press, 2007), pp. 15–42.

69. See Burton, *English Empire in America*; Robert Russell, *Seven Sermons* (Belfast: 1750).

70. Burton, *English Empire in America*, pp. 81, 83.

71. Ian McBride, 'Introduction: Memory and National Identity in Modern Ireland', in Ian McBride (ed.), *History and Memory in Modern Ireland* (Cambridge: Cambridge University Press, 2001), pp. 1–42 (2).

72. For a detailed analysis of the emergence of a national Protestant calendar see David Cressy, *Bonfires and Bells: National Memory and the Protestant Calendar in Elizabethan and Stuart England* (London: Weidenfeld and Nicolson, 1989).

73. Cressy, *Bonfires and Bells*, p. 206.

74. Toby C. Barnard, 'The Uses of 23 October 1641 and Irish Protestant Celebrations', *English Historical Review* 106.421 (October 1991), pp. 889–920.

75. Samuel Bruce, Sermon 23 October 1742 (preached subsequently on 23 October 1761, 1765), National Library of Ireland, Samuel Bruce Sermons, 90/903.p.14.

76. Quoted in Cressy, *Bonfires and Bells*, p. 196.

77. The continued persecution of the Huguenots was a topic of interest in Belfast pamphlets in the 1750s. In 1753, James Magee sold a pamphlet by Antoine Court entitled *An Historical memorial of the Most remarkable Proceedings against Protestants in France, from the Year 1744 to 1751*: BNL, 27 March 1753.

78. For a brief discussion of how these groups contributed to the Protestant interest in Ireland see Toby C. Barnard, 'Protestantism, Ethnicity and Irish Identities, 1660–1760', in Tony Claydon and Ian McBride (eds), *Protestantism and National Identity: Britain and Ireland, c.1650–c.1850* (Cambridge: Cambridge University Press, 1998), pp. 206–35 (210–11). For Huguenots see: Raymond Pierre Hylton, 'The Less-favoured Refuge: Ireland's Nonconformist Huguenots at the Turn of the Eighteenth Century', in Kevin Herlihy (ed.), *The Religion of Irish Dissent, 1650–1800* (Dublin: Four Courts Press, 1996), pp. 83–99; Grace Lawless Lee, *The Huguenot Settlements in Ireland* (London: Longmans, 1936). For Limerick Palatines see Vivien Hick, '"As nearly related as possible": Solidarity amongst the Irish Palatines', in Kevin Herlihy (ed.), *The Irish Dissenting Tradition, 1650–1750* (Dublin: Four Courts Press, 1995), pp. 11–125.

79. Editions of the *BNL* in which Palatine migration is mentioned: 8 February 1754, 11 February 1755, 18 June 1755, 19 November 1755, 17 July 1761, 11 September 1764; Huguenots mentioned: 5 November 1754, 23 November 1764.

80. *BNL*, 1 November 1754.

81. Eirwen Nicholson, 'Eighteenth-Century Foxe: Evidence for the Impact of the *Acts and Monuments* in the "Long" Eighteenth Century', in David Loades (ed.), *John Foxe and the English Reformation* (Aldershot, UK: Scolar Press, 1997), pp. 143–57.

82. Sir John Temple, *The Irish rebellion: or, a history of the general rebellion raised ... together with the barbarous cruelties and bloody massacres ensured thereupon* (Dublin, 1716), p. 73.

83. Toby C. Barnard, '1641: A Bibliographic Essay', in Brian Mac Cuarta (ed.), *Ulster 1641: Aspects of the Rising* (Belfast: The Institute of Irish Studies, The Queen's University of Belfast, 1993), pp. 173–86 (178–9).

84. One such pirated edition was published in Boston on the eve of the Seven Years War: [Anonymous], *Popish Cruelty displayed: being a full and true Account Of the Bloody and Hellish Massacre in Ireland ... in 1641* (Boston, 1753). Such pamphlets may have helped an American audience contextualize the Indian violence to come in the following years within the larger paradigm of international Protestant victimization.

85. Ibid., p. 179.
86. Thomas P. Power, 'Publishing and Sectarian Tension in South Munster in the 1760s', *Eighteenth Century Ireland: Iris an dá chultúr* 19 (2004), pp. 75–110 (80–4).
87. [Charles Smith], *The Antient and Present State of the County of Down. Containing a Chorological Description, with the Natural and Civil History of the Same* (Dublin, 1744), pp. 12, 35, 76, 81, 85–6, 92–3, 106–7, 111–12.
88. John Wesley, *The Journal of John Wesley, a Selection*, ed. Elisabeth Jay (Oxford: Oxford University Press, 1987), Friday, 14 August 1747, p. 103.
89. Wesley, *Journal*, 15 April 1758, pp. 142–3.
90. Brutus Search and Humphrey Search, *Essays, Historical, Political and Moral; Being a Proper Supplement to Bararariana. Vol. II* (Dublin, 1774?), pp. 117–18.
91. Ibid., pp. 128–30.
92. *BNL*, 5 November 1754.
93. *BNL*, 2 March 1764.
94. *BNL*, 6 December 1763; *FDJ*, 19 November 1763.
95. *BNL*, 24 July 1764. See also *BNL*, 24 October 1758, for an example of Acadian treachery and scalp taking.
96. *BNL*, 14 August 1764.
97. *BNL*, 30 January 1759.
98. Ibid.
99. *BNL*, 9 February 1759.
100. Ibid.
101. English authors first used the image of the French monarch as a 'Christian Turk' to attack French foreign policy during the reign of Louis XIV. These writers argued that Louis's alleged support of the Turkish invasion of Austria in 1683 proved that the 'universal monarchy' that he sought to establish was anti-Christian – and not simply anti-Protestant – in character. See Tony Claydon, *Europe and the Making of England, 1660–1760* (Cambridge: Cambridge University Press, 2007), pp. 172–83.
102. *DC*, 31 August 1761.
103. *FDJ*, 21 January 1755.
104. The seventh edition of the pamphlet was published and sold in Dublin in 1766.
105. *DC*, 25 January 1760.
106. *BNL*, 5 August 1763.
107. Roy Foster, *Modern Ireland, 1600–1972* (London: Allen Lane, 1988), p. 86.
108. American historian and political commentator, Arthur Schlesinger Jr., used the phrase, perhaps also coining it, in his 1968 examination of American violence in the aftermath of the Kennedy and King assassinations. He argued that the escalation of violent crime throughout the decade was due, in part, to the gradual acceptance of 'anonymous violence' in the media. 'Movies and television', Schlesinger claimed in a statement that still resonates in the arguments of social conservatives in the US culture wars today, 'have developed a pornography of violence far more demoralizing than the pornography of sex which still seizes the primary attention of the guardians of civic virtue' (*Violence: America in the Sixties* (New York: Signet Books, 1968), p. 53).
109. See especially Carolyn J. Dean, 'Empathy, Suffering, and Holocaust "Pornography"', *The Fragility of Empathy after the Holocaust* (Ithaca, NY: Cornell University Press, 2004), pp. 16–42.

110. Camenzind, 'Violence, Race, and the Paxton Boys', pp. 205–6.
111. Karen Halttunen, 'Humanitarianism and the Pornography of Pain in Anglo-American Culture', *American History Review* 100.2 (April 1995), pp. 303–34 (304). Halttunen did not take into consideration the pervasiveness of victimization narratives in mid- to late eighteenth-century periodicals. She asserted that depictions of pain became pornographic as the eighteenth century gave way to the nineteenth because at that point both reading and punishment became largely private affairs.
112. James Kelly, *Gallows Speeches from Eighteenth-Century Ireland* (Dublin: Four Courts Press, 2001); Brian Henry, *Dublin Hanged: Crime, Law Enforcement and Punishment in Late Eighteenth-Century Dublin* (Dublin: Irish Academic Press, 1994), pp. 16–36.
113. Neal Garnham, 'How Violent Was Eighteenth-Century Ireland?' *Irish Historical Studies* 30 (1996–7), pp. 377–92; S. J. Connolly, 'Violence and Order in the Eighteenth-Century', in Patrick O'Flanagan, Paul Ferguson and Kevin Whelan (eds), *Rural Ireland 1600–1900: Modernisation and Change* (Cork: Cork University Press, 1987), pp. 42–61.
114. Francis Hutcheson, *A System of Moral Philosophy in Three Books; ... Volume 1* (London: 1755), p. 19.
115. Adam Smith, *The Theory of Moral Sentiments* (London, 1759), p. 4.
116. Ibid., p. 5. Smith did not mean to conflate sympathy with self-love. He later claimed that 'tho' sympathy is very properly said to arise from an imaginary change of situations with the person principally concerned, yet this imaginary change is not supposed to happen to me in my own person and character, but in that of the person with whom I sympathize' (496). Just because one can only develop sympathy for others by imagining the sensation of the sufferer's pain does not mean that one imagines him/herself in the sufferer's position.
117. Edmund Burke, *A Philosophical Enquiry Into the Origin of the Sublime and Beautiful* (London, 1757), p. 24.

5 'An Infant Sister Church, in Great Distress, Amidst a Great Wilderness': American Presbyterian Fundraising in Ireland, 1752–63

1. Between 1749 and 1775 fourteen American colleges sent agents to the British Isles to solicit funds totalling £24,063 (of which £21,513 was netted after expenses were covered). These funds went towards new buildings, teachers' salaries and student aid. But perhaps most importantly they were used to establish endowments. On the eve of the revolution the liquid assets of these schools roughly totalled the net profit made from European fundraising tours. Beverly McAnear, 'The Raising of Funds by the Colonial Colleges', *Mississippi Valley Historical Review* 38.4 (March 1952), pp. 591–612 (606–7). See also McAnear, 'College Founding in the American Colonies, 1745–1775', *Mississippi Valley Historical Review* 42.1 (June 1955), pp. 24–44.
2. For British support of American charities see: Jacob M. Price, 'Who Cared about the Colonies: The Impact of the Thirteen Colonies on British Society and Politics, circa 1714–1775', in Bernard Bailyn and Philip D. Morgan (eds), *Strangers within the Realm: Cultural Margins of the First British Empire* (Chapel

Hill: University of North Carolina Press, 1991), pp. 395–436; P. J. Marshall, 'Who Cared about the Thirteen Colonies? Some Evidence from Philanthropy', *Journal of Imperial and Commonwealth History* 27.2 (May 1999), pp. 53–67.

3. The overall total collected by Smith in Dublin amounted to £15 13s: William Smith, *The Collection Books of Provost Smith*, intro. Jasper Yeates Brinton and Neda M. Westlake (Philadelphia: University of Pennsylvania Press, 1964), p. 43. For more on the New York and Phialdelphia delegation to Ireland see David C. Humphrey, *From King's College to Columbia, 1746–1800* (New York: Columbia University Press, 1976), p. 132.

4. Copy of Morgan Edwards's Commission to Europe, Brown University Archives, Rhode Island College Miscellaneous Papers, 1763 to 1804, Series 1. Correspondence and documents, 1763 to 1769, Box 1 / Folder I:29 (1). For the background of the campaign and its success in Ireland see: Walter C. Bronson, *The History of Brown University, 1764–1914* (Providence, Rhode Island: Brown University Press, 1914), pp. 38–9; and Reuben Aldridge Guild, *Early History of Brown University, including the Life, Times, and Correspondence of President Manning. 1756–1791* (Providence: Snow & Farnham, 1896), pp. 11–15.

5. For more about the Rhode Island delegation and their experiences in Europe see Samson Occom, *The Collected Writings of Samson Occom, Mohegan: Leadership and Literature in Eighteenth-Century Native America*, ed. Joanna Brooks, foreword Robert Warrior (Oxford: Oxford University Press, 2006), pp. 19–20, 76–85, 264–74. For Occom and Whitaker in Ireland see: Frederick Chase, *A History of Dartmouth College and the Town of Hanover New Hampshire*, vol. 1 (Cambridge: Cambridge University Press, 1891), p. 59; and Leon Burr Richardson, *History of Dartmouth College*, Vol. 1 (Hanover, New Hampshire: Dartmouth College Publications, 1932), p. 63.

6. Morgan Edwards, to James Manning, London, England, 26 April 1768, Brown University Archives, Rhode Island College miscellaneous papers, 1763 to 1804, Series 1. Correspondence and documents, 1763 to 1769, Box 1 / Folder I:33

7. For Tennent's life and education see the introduction in Milton J. Coulter, *Gilbert Tennent, Son of Thunder: A Case Study of Continental Pietism's Impact on the First Great Awakening in the Middle Colonies* (New York: Greenwood Press, 1986). For the Davies and Tennent campaign in Britain see: Craig Gilborn, 'The Reverend Samuel Davies in Great Britain', *Winterthur Portfolio* 8 (1973), pp. 45–62; and Samuel Davies, *The Reverend Samuel Davies Abroad: The Diary of a Journey to England and Scotland, 1753–55*, ed. George William Pilcher (London: University of Illinois Press, 1967).

8. *RGSU*, vol. 2, p. 385; R. J. Dickson, *Ulster Emigration to Colonial America, 1718–1775* (London: Routledge & Kegan Paul, 1966), pp. 19–54.

9. Elizabeth Nybakken, 'New Light on the Old Side: Irish Influences on Colonial Presbyterianism', *Journal of American History* 68 (1982), pp. 813–32 (814). Griffin, *People with No Name*, pp. 115 and 146. Lack of clergy would later become a major setback for American Presbyterian churches as they saw multitudes of potential initiates flock to the pulpits of evangelical Baptist and Methodist preachers and circuit riders like Francis Ashbury. See Nathan O. Hatch, *The Democratization of American Christianity* (New Haven: Yale University Press, 1988).

10. William Peartree Smith, *A General Account of the Rise and State of the College Lately Established in the Province of New-Jersey, in America; And the End and Design of its Institution* ... (London, 1754), p. 6.
11. *RGSU*, 2:385.
12. John Maclean, *History of the College of New Jersey, From its Origin in 1746 to the Commencement of 1854* (Philadelphia: J. B. Lippincott & Co., 1877), p. 152; Richard Webster, *A History of the Presbyterian Church in America, From its Origin to the Year 1760* (Philadelphia: Joseph M. Wilson, 1857), p. 261; Charles Augustus Briggs, *American Presbyterianism, its Origin and Early History, together with an appendix of letters and documents, many of which have recently been discovered* (New York: Charles Scribner's Sons, 1885), p. 309.
13. For more on these statistics see Webster, *History of the Presbyterian Church in America*, p. 261.
14. The Dublin credit crisis of 1754–5 occurred following rumours that local merchant Robert Dillon's Rotterdam partners were insolvent. L. M. Cullen, 'Economic Development, 1691–1750', in T. W. Moody and W. E. Vaughan (eds), *A New History of Ireland, Vol. IV, Eighteenth-Century Ireland, 1691–1800* (Oxford: Clarendon Press, 1986), pp. 123–58 (154).
15. Reuben Aldridge Guild, a librarian at Brown University pointed out in 1897 that the details of the 1754/55 campaign were lost due to the calamities that befell Princeton in the late eighteenth century. See Maclean, *History of the College of New Jersey*, pp. 153–4.
16. *Minutes of the Presbyterian Church in America, 1706–1788*, ed. Guy Soulliard Klett (Philadelphia: Presbyterian Historical Society, 1976), pp. 298–9.
17. Davies, *Samuel Davies Abroad*, pp. 75–6, 96.
18. Gilbert Tennent, *The Danger of An Unconverted Ministry, Considered in a Sermon on Mark VI. 34. Preached at Nottingham, in Pennsylvania, March 8. Anno 1739, 40* (Philadelphia, 1740), pp. 25–6.
19. *RGSU*, 2:392.
20. Ibid.
21. Ibid., 2:398.
22. For Tennent's moderation and spirit of reconciliation adopted later in life see Janet F. Fishburn, 'Gilbert Tennent, Established "Dissenter"', *Church History* 63.1 (March 1994), pp. 31–49.
23. Charles Beatty, *Journals of Charles Beatty, 1762–1769*, ed. Guy Soulliard Klett (University Park, Pennsylvania: The Pennsylvania State University Press, 1962), p. xiv.
24. For more on the founding of the Presbyterian Widows Fund see John Baird, *Horn of Plenty: The Story of the Presbyterian Ministers' Fund* (Wheaton, Illinois: Tyndale House, 1982), pp. 1–34; Mackie, *Facile Princeps: The Story of the Beginning of Life Insurance in America* (Lancaster, Pennsylvania: Lancaster Press, 1956); Burton Alva Konkle, *A History of the Presbyterian Ministers' Fund, 1712–1928: The Oldest Life Insurance Company in the World*, HSP, MSS Presbyterian Ministers' Fund, AM.77, pp. 1–37; Carey Majewicz, *Collection 3101: Presbyterian Ministers' Fund Records*, HSP collection finding aid (2009), pp. 2–5. For ethno-religious politics spurred by changing colonial demographics and the Great Awakening see: Ned C. Landsman, 'Roots, Routes, and Rootedness: Diversity, Migration, and Toleration in Mid-Atlantic Pluralism', *Early American Studies* 2.2 (Fall 2004), pp. 267–309 (294–306);

and Alan Tully, *Forming American Politics: Ideals, Interests, and Institutions in Colonial New York and Pennsylvania* (Baltimore: The Johns Hopkins University Press, 1994), pp. 164–202, 241–9, 303–10, 391–413. The political anxieties in Pennsylvania that followed the founding and rapid expansion of the Presbyterian fund and the reunification of the synods came to the surface during the 1763 pamphlet debates over the Paxton Massacres. See: Peter A. Butzin, 'Politics, Presbyterians, and the Paxton Riots, 1763–64', *Journal of Presbyterian History* 51 (1973), pp. 70–84; and Benjamin Bankhurst, 'A Looking-Glass for Presbyterians: Recasting a Prejudice in Late Colonial Pennsylvania', *PMHB* 133.4 (October 2009), pp. 317–48.

25. *RGSU*, 2:436.

26. The Synod of Philadelphia and New York's letter of thanks to the General Synod of Ulster listed the total earned in Ireland as being £413. This did not account for the late delivery of Templepatrick's returns totalling £16 19s 5½d in 1762. *RGSU*, 2:455.

27. 'Address to the Very Rev'd & Honoured The General Synod in the North of Ireland … in General Synod', *RGSU* 2:467.

28. Charles Beatty [Francis Alison, Gilbert Tennent and Robert Cross], *The Memorial and Representation of Mr. Charles Beatty, minister at Nishaminy, in name and behalf of the Synod of York [sic] and Philadelphia, and of the corporation for the relief of poor and distressed Presbyterian ministers in the province of Pensylvania* (Edinburgh, 1761), p. 2; *BNL*, 14 April 1761.

29. Quoted in Kerby A. Miller, 'James MacSparran's *America Dissected* (1753): Eighteenth-Century Emigration and Constructions of "Irishness"', *History Ireland* 11.4 (Winter 2003), pp. 17–22 (18).

30. Smith, *General Account*, p. 7.

31. Maclean, *History of the College of New Jersey*, Appendix XXIX, p. ciii.

32. Ibid.

33. Charles Beatty, *Memorial and Representation of Mr. Charles Beatty*, p. 4.

34. *BNL*, 14 April 1761.

35. Sir John Temple, *The Irish rebellion: or, a history of the general rebellion raised … together with the barbarous cruelties and bloody massacres ensured thereupon* (Dublin, 1716), p. 93

36. Ibid., p. 90.

37. Quoted in W. R. Allison, *Record of the Family of Charles Beatty, who emigrated from Ireland to America in 1729* (Steubenville, Ohio, 1873), p. 18.

38. Popular tradition has it that Beatty also accompanied Colonel John Armstrong's expedition that ended in the destruction of the Delaware town of Kittanning. Guy Klett claims that this would have been impossible because Beatty was noted as present at a meeting of the Presbytery of Abington at approximately the same time. For Beatty's military career see Beatty, *Journals*, pp. xvi–xviii.

39. *BNL*, 14 April 1761.

40. Ibid.

41. Ibid.

42. Beatty, *Memorial and Representation of Mr. Charles Beatty*, p. 2.

43. *BNL*, 14 April 1761.

44. This sentence is also different in the Scottish edition, which reminds readers that many of those suffering on the frontier were 'descended of Scottish parents': Beatty, *Memorial and Representation of Mr. Charles Beatty*, p. 4.

45. *FDJ*, 15 July 1760.

46. In December 1763 a largely Scots Irish mob formed in Lancaster County, Pennsylvania, to exact revenge, as they saw it, on a group of local Conestoga Indians, who they accused of assisting the raids committed on western settlements during the previous summer. In January their leaders met a delegation from the capital that included Benjamin Franklin on the outskirts of the city and agreed to disband if their concerns were aired before the legislature. See: Brooke Hindle, 'The March of the Paxton Boys', *WMQ*, 3rd series, 3.4 (October 1946), pp. 461–86; John R. Dunbar's introduction to *The Paxton Papers* (The Hague: Martinus Nijhoff, 1957), pp. 3–51; Peter Silver, *Our Savage Neighbors: How Indian War Transformed Early America* (New York: W. W. Norton, 2008), pp. 177–90; Hubertis M. Cummings, 'The Paxton Killings', *Journal of Presbyterian History* 44.4 (1966), pp. 219–43; James Kirby Martin, 'The Return of the Paxton Boys and the Historical State of the Pennsylvania Frontier, 1764–1774', *Pennsylvania History* 38.2 (April 1971), pp. 117–33; Alden T. Vaughan, 'Frontier Banditti and the Indians: The Paxton Boy's Legacy, 1763–1775', *Pennsylvania History* 51.1 (1984), pp. 1–29; Krista Camenzind, 'Violence, Race, and the Paxton Boys', in William A. Pencak and Daniel K. Richter (eds), *Friends and Enemies in Penn's Woods: Indians, Colonists, and the Racial Construction of Pennsylvania* (University Park, Pennsylvania: Pennsylvania State University Press, 2004), pp. 201–20; George W. Franz, *Paxton: A Study of Community Structure and Mobility in the Colonial Pennsylvania Backcountry* (New York: Garland, 1989), p. 7; and Richard Beeman, *The Varieties of Political Experience in Eighteenth-Century America* (Philadelphia: University of Pennsylvania Press, 2004), pp. 241–2.

The *News-Letter* provided limited coverage of the event, despite the publication of a lengthy letter written by Benjamin Franklin on the matter in the April 1764 edition of the *Gentleman's Magazine*. The Joys routinely reprinted excerpts from the *Gentleman's Magazine*. The *News-Letter* focused on the bad character of the rioters and settler victimization. See: Sylvanus Urban [David Henry] (ed.), *The Gentleman's Magazine, and Historical Chronicle* 34 (London, 1764), pp. 173–8; *BNL*, 13 July 1764 and 2 March 1764.

47. *London Chronicle*, 20 October 1764.

48. [A Lover of Truth], *An Address to the Rev. Dr. Alison, the Rev. Mr. Ewing, &c. Being a Vindication of the Quakers* (Philadelphia, 1765), p. 8.

49. Issac Hunt, *A Looking-Glass for Presbyterians*, combined edn (Philadelphia, 1764), p. 18.

50. 'The Petition of Mr. Christian Lewis Finne, Chaplain of the King of Prussia & Minister of the reformed Church at Silesia, formerly at Breslaw', National Archives of Scotland, Papers of the General Assembly of the Church of Scotland, Main Series, CH1/2/100 – 1758–1759.

51. For the 'interaction system of poor relief' see Marco H. D. van Leeuwen, 'Logic of Charity: Poor Relief in Preindustrial Europe', *Journal of Interdisciplinary History* 24.4 (Spring 1994), pp. 589–613; Colin Jones, 'Some Recent Trends in the History of Charity', in Martin Daunton (ed.), *Charity, Self-Interest and Welfare in the English Past* (London: University College London Press, 1996), pp. 51–63.

52. For strategies of supplication see: Andrew, T. Donna, 'On Reading Charity Sermons: Eighteenth-Century Anglican Solicitation and Exhortation', *Journal of Ecclesiastical History* 43.4 (October 1992), pp. 581–91; and Bronwyn Croxson, 'The Public and Private Faces of Eighteenth-Century London Dispensary Charity', *Medical History* 41.2 (April 1997), pp. 127–49 (131, 139–41).

53. For more on the 'public face' of eighteenth-century charity, see Croxson, 'Public and Private Faces'.

54. Morgan Edwards, *A List of Persons in IRELAND, who have contributed towards endowing the College in Rhode-Island Government* (Dublin [?], 1767), p. 1.

55. Morgan Edwards, to James Manning, London, England, 26 April 1768, Brown University Archives, Rhode Island College miscellaneous papers, 1763 to 1804, Series 1. Correspondence and documents, 1763 to 1769, Box 1 / Folder I:33

56. See Robert H. Bonar, *Nigh on Three and a Half Centuries: A History of Carnmoney Presbyterian Church* (Belfast, 2004), pp. 302–3.

57. Armagh Collections 1720, PHSI, Armagh Session Minutes, 1707–1729.

58. Poor Accounts, 21 October 1759, PRONI, Ballymoney Presbyterian Church Register, Accounts of the Poor Money, 4 August 1751 to 13 December 1759, CR3/1B/1.

59. Glascar session poor accounts 1762, PHSI, Glascar Session Minutes, 1760–1818.

60. *Minutes of the General Synod of Ulster*, 1:49 and 60.

61. Ibid., 237, 241, 296, 331–2.

62. James Seaton Reid, *History of the Presbyterian Church in Ireland: Comprising the Civil History of the Province of Ulster, from the Accession of James the First*, vol. 3 (London: Whittaker, 1853), pp. 324–5.

63. R. C. Nash, 'Irish Atlantic Trade in the Seventeenth and Eighteenth Centuries', *WMQ*, 3rd series, 42.3 (July 1985), pp. 329–56 (332); L. M. Cullen, 'The Irish Economy in the Eighteenth Century', in L. M. Cullen (ed.), *The Formation of the Irish Economy* (Cork: Mercier Press, 1969), pp. 9–21 (14); Graeme Kirkham, 'Economic Diversification in a Marginal Economy: A Case Study', in Peter Roebuck (ed.), *Plantation to Partition: Essays in Ulster History in Honour of J. L. McCracken* (Belfast: Blackstaff, 1981), pp. 64–81 (64–5). Cullen, 'Economic Development, 1691–1750', p. 154. For more on the credit failures of the 1750s see Marie-Louise Legg, 'Money and Reputations: The Effects of the Banking Crises of 1755 and 1760', *Eighteenth-Century Ireland: Iris an dá chultúr* 11 (1996), pp. 74–87. For dearth and riots in Ulster in the late 1750s see: Eoin Magennis, 'In Search of the "Moral Economy": Food Scarcity in 1756–57 and the Crowd', in Peter Jupp and Eoin Magennis (eds), *Crowds in Ireland, c.1720–1920* (Basingstoke: Macmillan, now Palgrave Macmillan, 2000), pp. 189–211; William Edward Hartpole Leckey, *History of Ireland in the Eighteenth Century*, New Edition, vol. 1 (London: Longmans, Green, and Co., 1892), p. 468; Reid, *History of the Presbyterian Church*, p. 323, footnote 72; *FDJ*, 23 April 1757.

64. Nash, 'Irish Atlantic Trade in the Seventeenth and Eighteenth Centuries', p. 332.

65. William F. Hixson, *Triumph of the Bankers: Money and Banking in the Eighteenth and Nineteenth Centuries* (Westport, CT: Praeger, 1993), p. 46.

66. Michael Ryder, 'The Bank of Ireland, 1721: Land, Credit and Dependency', *Historical Journal* 25.3 (September 1982), pp. 557–82; [Patriophilus Misolestes], *Objections against the general Bank in Ireland as it Stands now Circumstanciated, whether it Do's or Do's not Receive a Parliamentary Sanction, in ANSWER to a LETTER sent from a Gentleman in the City to his Friend in the Country* (Dublin, 1721), p. 3.

67. Ryder, 'Bank of Ireland', p. 574.

68. Swift made this claim in 1736 as did Henry Joy in 1772, when he claimed that one emigrant ship contained a total of £4,000 in coin. See Swift, *Intelligencer* 19, 7; and *Historical Collections Relative to the Town of Belfast: from the Earliest Period to the Union with Great Britain* (Belfast, 1817), p. 114. Arthur Young noted the effect of emigration in Armagh during his tour of the county in 1776: 'The emigration were chiefly in 1772 and 1773. Many weavers and spinners, with all their families, went. Some farmers, who sold their leases, went off with sums from 100l. to 300l. and carried many with them' (*A Tour in Ireland; with General Observations on the Present State of that Kingdom: made in the Years 1776,1777, and 1778* (London, 1780), p. 108.

69. W. H. Crawford, *The Impact of the Domestic Linen Industry in Ulster* (Belfast: Ulster Historical Foundation, 2005), p. 2.

70. W. H. Crawford, *The Handloom Weavers and the Ulster Linen Industry*, 2nd edn (Belfast: Ulster Historical Foundation, 1994), p. 10.

71. Minutes of the Presbytery of Strabane, August 1717 to 13 July 1740, PRONI CR/26/2/1, pp. 18–19.

72. See Mcbride, *Eighteenth-Century Ireland: The Isle of Slaves* (Dublin: Gil and Macmillan, 2009), pp. 322–3; and Maurice J. Bric, 'The Tithe System in Eighteenth-Century Ireland', *Proceedings of the Royal Irish Academy* 86, C, No. 7 (1986), pp. 271–88.

73. Peter Roebuck, 'Rent Movement, Proprietorial Incomes, and Agricultural Development, 1730–1830', in Peter Roebuck (ed.), *Plantation to Partition: Essays in Ulster History in Honour of J. L. McCracken* (Belfast: Blackstaff, 1981), pp. 82–101 (88). Across the country as a whole between the 1720s and the 1770s rents may have even trebled. See L. M. Cullen, *An Economic History of Ireland since 1660*, 2nd edn (London: Batsford, 1987), p. 83.

74. W. H. Crawford, 'Landlord–Tenant Relations in Ulster, 1609–1820', *Irish Economic and Social History* 2 (1975), pp. 5–21 (12–15).

75. Weaving households in rural Ulster therefore fit into a larger European phenomenon in the mid- to late eighteenth century: what Jan de Vries has called the industrious revolution. De Vries defined the concept as 'a household-based intensification of market-directed labour and/or production, related to an increased demand for market-supplied goods and services': de Vries, 'Between Purchasing Power and the World of Goods: Understanding the Household Economy in Early Modern Europe', in John Brewer and Roy Porter (eds), *Consumption and the World of Goods* (London: Routledge, 1993), pp. 85–132 (126).

76. Crawford, *Impact of the Domestic Linen Industry*, pp. 117–26.

77. Young, *Tour*, p. 103.

78. Ibid., p. 106.

79. For the family economy see Hans Medick, 'The Proto-Industrial Family Economy', in Peter Kriedte, Hans Medick and Jürgen Schlumbohm (eds), *Industrialization before Industrialization: Rural Industry in the Genesis of Capitalism*, trans. Beate Schempp (Cambridge: Cambridge University Press, 1981), pp. 38–93.

80. *RGSU*, 2:444.

81. Ibid., 475.

82. For the actions taken by local landlords such as Charles Eccles of Tyrone and Ralph Gore of Fermangh to stimulate linen production

see: Graeme E. Kirkham, '"To Pay the Rent and Lay up Riches": Economic Opportunity in Eighteenth-Century North-West Ulster', in Rosalind Mitchison and Peter Roebuck (eds), *Economy and Society in Scotland and Ireland, 1500–1939* (Edinburgh: John Donald Publishers, 1988), pp. 95–104 (97–8). For Derry merchants in Philadelphia see Thomas M. Truxes, *Irish-American Trade, 1660–1783* (Cambridge: Cambridge University Press, 1988), pp. 81–2, 118–19. Truxes claimed that 'more than any other Irish port, the overseas commerce of Derry was dominated by trade with America' (81).

83. Journal of a Tour from Dublin to the North, 4 July to 4 August, 1781, Queen's University Belfast, Library, Miscellaneous Manuscripts 1, Box 1, p.18.
84. Ibid.
85. It was decided that foreign widows receive the amount that their husband had paid into the scheme. *RGSU*, 2:566–7.
86. *RGSU*, 2:521.
87. Ibid., 136–8, 153, 185.
88. Ibid., 354.
89. Ibid., 419.
90. Ibid., 439.
91. *FDJ*, 26 January 1754.
92. *RGSU*, 2.455.
93. *RGSU*, 2:387, 481.
94. Ibid., 394.
95. Ibid., 372.
96. *BNL*, 14 April 1761.

Postscript: John Moore's Return and Reflections on America, 1763

1. Journal of John Moore of Carrickfergus, 1760–1770, PRONI, Malcolm Papers, D/3165/2/p. 79.
2. Ibid., pp. 76–7.
3. *BNL*, 26 August 1760.
4. Ned C. Landsman, *Scotland and Its First American Colony, 1683–1765* (Princeton: Princeton University Press, 1985); T. M. Devine, *Scotland's Empire, 1600–1815* (London: Allen Lane, 2003). See also Landsman's edited collection *Nation and Province in the First British Empire: Scotland and the Americas, 1600–1800* (Lewisburg, PA: Bucknell University Press, 2001).
5. Devine, *Scotland's Empire*, p. 141.
6. R. J. Dickson, *Ulster Emigration to Colonial America, 1718–1775* (London: Routledge & Kegan Paul, 1966).

Bibliography

Primary sources

Manuscripts

Belfast

Queen's University Library, Special collections
    Journal of a Tour from Dublin to the North, 1781
    MSS Bryson Sermons
Presbyterian Historical Society
    Armagh Session Minutes, 1707–29
    Bangor Presbytery Book, 1739–74
    Coleraine (New Row) Account Book, 1774–1834
    Glascar Session Minutes, 1760–1818
    MSS Books of Rev. William Caldwell, 1772–8
Public Record Office of Northern Ireland
    Ballymoney Presbyterian Church Register, Poor Accounts 1751–9
    Black Family Letters
    Bruce Correspondence
    Cahans Session Book, 1751–8
    Caldwell Papers
    Commonplace Book of William Drennan
    Denison Papers
    Dobbs Papers
    Drennan, Bruce Letters
    Drennan Papers
    Dunlop, Rutherford and Delap Papers
    Gosford Papers
    Malcolm Papers
    Minutes of the Presbytery of Strabane, 1717–40
    Mussenden Papers
    Perceval-Maxwell Papers
    Wilmot Papers
    Wilson-Chesney Family Pedigree

Dublin

National Library of Ireland
    Samuel Bruce Sermons

Edinburgh

National Archives of Scotland
National Library of Scotland
    Wodrow MSS
Papers of the General Assembly of the Church of Scotland, Main Series

177

London

National Archives, Kew (Public Record Office)
  Court of Chancery, Pleadings 1758 to 1800
  State Papers, William Pitt Correspondence
Papers of Treasury Solicitor and HM Procurator General: West New Jersey
  Society

Philadelphia

Corporation for the Relief of Poor and Distressed Ministers
  Accounts
  Minutes
Historical Society of Pennsylvania
  Letterbook, Orr, Dunlope, and Glenholme, 1767–9
  Logan Collection
  Penn MSS, Autograph Petitions
  Presbyterian Ministers' Fund: Konkle MSS
  Presbyterian Widows Fund Papers
Presbyterian Historical Society
  Francis Alison Papers
University of Pennsylvania, Archives
  William Smith Papers

Providence, Rhode Island

  Brown University Archives
  Rhode Island College Miscellaneous Papers, 1763 to 1804

Newspapers and periodicals

  Belfast News-Letter
  Dublin Courier
  Dublin Gazette
  Dublin Intelligencer
  Dublin Mercury
  Faulkner's Dublin Journal
  Gentleman's Magazine
  Lloyd's Evening Post and British Chronicle (London)
  London Chronicle
  London Gazette
  London Magazine
  New-York Mercury
  Pennsylvania Gazette
  The Public Gazetteer (Dublin)
  Pue's Daily Occurrences (Dublin)
  Royal Westminster Journal and London Political Miscellany
  St. James's Chronicle or the British Evening Post (London)
  Scots Magazine (Edinburgh)

Contemporary pamphlets and books

[Anonymous], *An Alarm to the Unprejudiced and Well-Minded Protestants of Ireland: Or Seasonable Queries upon the Rise, Danger and Tendency of the Whiteboys* (Cork, 1762).

[Anonymous], *The Answer to Shawn ouge a Glanea. To which are Added, II. The Yorkshie Conflict. III. The Phoenix of Ulster. IV. The Rambling Journeyman* (Monaghan, 178[9?]).

[Anonymous], *An Answer to the Phoenix of Ulster* (Monaghan, 1789).

[Anonymous], *A Description of the English and French Territories, in North America* (Dublin, 1756).

[Anonymous], *Popish Cruelty displayed: being a full and true Account Of the Bloody and Hellish Massacre in Ireland ... in 1641* (Boston, 1753).

Beatty, Charles, *Journals of Charles Beatty, 1762–1769*, ed. Guy Soulliard Klett (University Park, Pennsylvania: The Pennsylvania State University Press, 1962).

Beatty, Charles [Francis Alison, Gilbert Tennent and Robert Cross], *The Memorial and Representation of Mr. Charles Beatty, minister at Nishaminy, in name and behalf of the Synod of York [sic] and Philadelphia, and of the corporation for the relief of poor and distressed Presbyterian ministers in the province of Pensylvania* (Edinburgh, 1761).

Boulter, Hugh, *Letters Written by his Excellency Hugh Boulter, D. D. Lord Primate of All Ireland* (Dublin, 1770).

Boulton, William, *A Sermon Preached in the Baptist Meeting House in Swift's-Alley, Nov. 9th. 1760. On the Death of His late and most Excellent Majesty, George II* (Dublin, 1760).

Brickell, John, *The Natural History of North-Carolina* (Dublin, 1737, 1744).

Brown, John, *On Religious Liberty: A Sermon Preached at St. Paul's Cathedral, on Sunday the 6th of March, 1763 [...] To which is prefixed An Address to the principal Inhabitants of the North American Colonies, on Occasion of the Peace* (London, 1763).

Burke, Edmund, *A Philosophical Enquiry Into the Origin of the Sublime and Beautiful* (London, 1757).

Burton, Richard [Nathaniel Crouch], *The English Empire in America: or a View of the dominions of the Crown of England* (Dublin, 1735).

Davies, Samuel, *The Duties, Difficulties and Reward of the faithful Minister* (Glasgow, 1754),

Davies, Samuel, *Religion and Patriotism the Constituents of a Good Soldier. A Sermon preached to Captain Overton's Independent Company of Volunteers, raised in Hanover County, Virginia, August 17, 1755* (Philadelphia, 1755).

Davies, Samuel, *The Reverend Samuel Davies Abroad: The Diary of a Journey to England and Scotland, 1753–55*, ed. George William Pilcher (London: University of Illinois Press, 1967).

Davies, Samuel, *A Sermon preached at Henrico, 29th April 1753. And at Canongate, 26th May 1754.* (Edinburgh, 1754).

De Bougainville, Louis Antoine, *Adventure in the Wilderness: The American Journals of Louis Antoine de Bougainville, 1756–1760*, trans. and ed. Edward P. Hamilton (Norman: University of Oklahoma Press, 1964).

Dexter, Franklin Bowditch (ed.), *Extracts from the Itineraries and Other Miscellanies of Ezra Stiles, D.D., LL.D., 1755–1794, with a Selection From His Correspondence* (New Haven: Yale University Press, 1916).

Drennan, William, the Elder, *The Drennan Letters. Being a Selection from the Correspondence ... between William Drennan, M.D., and His Brother-in-Law and Sister, Samuel and Martha McTier, during the Years 1776–1819*, ed. David Alfred Chart (Belfast: 1931).

Edwards, Morgan, *A List of Persons in IRELAND, who have contributed towards endowing the College in Rhode-Island Government* ([Dublin?], 1767).

Elliot, Gilbert, Sir, Bart., *Life and Letters of Sir Gilbert Elliot, First Earl of Minto from 1751 to 1806*, 3 vols, ed. Nina Minto (Countess of Minto) (London: Longmans, Green, and Co., 1874).

Falconer, Richard, *The Voyages, Dangerous Adventures, and Miraculous Escapes of Capt. Richard Falconer, Containing, The Laws, Customs, and Manners of the Indians in America* (Dublin, 1752).

Fletcher, William, *A Sermon Preached in St. Andrew's, Dublin; Before the Honourable House of Commons: On Thursday, Nov. 29, 1759; Being the Day appointed for a General Thanksgiving* (Dublin, 1759).

Historical Collections Relative to the Town of Belfast: from the Earliest Period to the Union with Great Britain (Belfast, 1817).

[Hunt, Issac], *A Looking-Glass for Presbyterians*, combined edn (Philadelphia, 1764).

Hutcheson, Francis, *A System of Moral Philosophy in Three Books ... Volume 1* (London, 1755).

King, William, *A Great Archbishop of Dublin, William King D. D. 1650–1729*, ed. Charles Simeon King (London: Longmans, Green, and Co., 1906).

Kirkpatrick, James, *An Historical essay upon loyalty of Presbyterians in Great Britain and Ireland from the Reformation to the present year; 1713* [...] (Belfast, 1713).

[A Lover of Truth], *An Address to the Rev. Dr. Alison, the Rev. Mr. Ewing, &c. Being a Vindication of the Quakers* (Philadelphia, 1765).

McArdell, James, *His Excellency Arthur Dobbs, Esq.* (London, 1755[?]).

Macculloch, Henry, *A Miscellaneous Essay concerning the courses pursued by Great Britain in the affairs of her Colonies, &c.* (London, 1755).

[Misolestes, Patriophilus], *Objections against the general Bank in Ireland as it Stands now Circumstanciated, whether it Do's or Do's not Receive a Parliamentary Sanction, in ANSWER to a LETTER sent from a Gentleman in the City to his Friend in the Country* (Dublin, 1721).

Occom, Samson, *The Collected Writings of Samson Occom, Mohegan: Leadership and Literature in Eighteenth-Century Native America*, ed. Joanna Brooks, foreword Robert Warrior (Oxford: Oxford University Press, 2006).

[Pollock, Joseph], *The Letters of Owen Roe O'Nial* (Dublin, 1779).

Rogers, Robert, *A Concise Account of North America: Containing a Description of the Several British Colonies on that Continent* (Dublin, 1769).

[Roscommon], *To the Author of those Intelligencers printed at Dublin* (New York, 1733).

Russell, Robert, *Seven Sermons* (Belfast, 1750).

Search, Brutus, and Humphrey Search, *Essays, Historical, Political and Moral; Being a Proper Supplement to Bararariana. Vol. II* (Dublin, 1774?).

Smith, Adam, *The Theory of Moral Sentiments* (London, 1759).

[Smith, Charles], *The Antient and Present State of the County of Down. Containing a Chorological Description, with the Natural and Civil History of the Same* (Dublin, 1744).

Smith, Horace Wemyss (ed.), *Life and Correspondence of the Rev. William Smith, D. D., First Provost of the College and Academy of Philadelphia,* vol. 1 (Philadelphia: S.A. George & Co., 1879).

Smith, William, *Additional discourses and essays. Being a supplement to the first edition of discourses on several public occasions during the war in America* (London, 1762).

Smith, William, *The Collection Books of Provost Smith,* intro. Jasper Yeates Brinton and Neda M. Westlake (Philadelphia: University of Pennsylvania Press, 1964).

Smith, William, *Discourses on Public Occasions in America,* 2nd edn (London, 1762).

Smith, William Peartree, *A General Account of the Rise and State of the College Lately Established in the Province of New-Jersey, in America; And the End and Design of its Institution …* (London, 1754).

Swift, Jonathan, *A Letter from the Revd. J.S.D.S.P.D. to a Country Gentleman in the North of Ireland* [Signed A. North. Reprinted from no. 19 of *The Intelligencer*] ([Dublin?], 1736).

Swift, Jonathan, *A Modest Proposal For Preventing the Children of Poor People From being a Burthen to Parents and Country,* &c (London, 1730).

Temple, Sir John, *The Irish rebellion: or, a history of the general rebellion raised … together with the barbarous cruelties and bloody massacres ensured thereupon* (Dublin, 1716).

Tennent, Gilbert, *The Danger of An Unconverted Ministry, Considered in a Sermon on Mark VI. 34. Preached at Nottingham, in Pennsylvania, March 8. Anno 1739, 40* (Philadelphia, 1740).

Vance, Thomas, *A Thanksgiving Sermon for the Late Successes of his Majesty's Arms Preached at Ussher's-Quay, November 29, 1759* (Dublin, 1760).

Wesley, John, *The Journal of John Wesley, a Selection,* ed. Elisabeth Jay (Oxford: Oxford University Press, 1987).

Whitefield, George, *A short address to persons of all denominations, occasioned by the alarm of an intended invasion* (London, 1756).

Whitefield, George, *The two first parts of his life, with his journals, revised, corrected, and abridged, by George Whitefield, A.B. Chaplain to the Right Hon. The Countess of Huntingdon* (London, 1756).

Willes, Edward, *The Letters of Lord Chief Baron Edward Willes to the Earl of Warwick, 1757–62: An Account of Ireland in the Mid-Eighteenth Century,* ed. James Kelly (Aberystwyth: Boethius, 1990).

Young, Arthur, *A Tour in Ireland; with General Observations on the Present State of that Kindgom: made in the Years 1776, 1777, and 1778* (London, 1780).

Edited primary sources

Davies, A. C., '"As Good a Country as Any Man Needs to Dwell in"; Letters from a Scotch-Irish Immigrant in Pennsylvania, 1766, 1767, and 1784', *Pennsylvania History* 50.4 (1983), pp. 313–22.

Dunbar, John R. (ed.), *The Paxton Papers* (The Hague: Martinus Nijhoff, 1957).

Green, E. R. R., 'The "Strange Humours" That Drove the Scotch-Irish to America, 1729', *WMQ* 3rd series, 7 (1955), pp. 113–23.

Minutes of the Presbyterian Church in America, 1706–1788, ed. Guy Soulliard Klett (Philadelphia: Presbyterian Historical Society, 1976).

Stewart, John, 'Obstructions to Irish Immigration to Pennsylvania, 1736', *PMHB* 21.4 (1897), pp. 485–7.

[Synod of the Presbyterian Church (Ulster)] *Records of the Presbyterian Church of Ulster from 1691 to 1820*, 3 vols (Belfast, 1890–8).

Truxes, Thomas (ed.), *Letterbook of Greg & Cunningham, 1756–57: Merchants of New York and Belfast* (Oxford: Oxford University Press, 2001).

Secondary literature

Adams, J. R. R., *The Printed Word and the Common Man, Popular Culture in Ulster 1700–1900* (Belfast: Institute of Irish Studies, The Queen's University Belfast, 1987).

Allison, W. R., *Record of the Family of Charles Beatty, who emigrated from Ireland to America in 1729* (Steubenville, Ohio, 1873).

Anderson, Benedict, *Imagined Communities: Reflections on the Origin and Spread of Nationalism* (London: Verso, 1983).

Andrew, Donna T., 'On Reading Charity Sermons: Eighteenth-Century Anglican Solicitation and Exhortation', *Journal of Ecclesiastical History* 43.4 (October 1992), pp. 581–91.

Armitage, David, 'Greater Britain: A Useful Category of Analysis?' *American Historical Review* 104.2 (April 1999), pp. 427–45.

Armitage, David, *The Ideological Origins of the British Empire* (Cambridge: Cambridge University Press, 2000).

Armstrong, T. Percy, 'Thurot at Carickfergus, 1760', *Notes and Queries* 175 (July–December 1938), pp. 261, 317, 353.

Bailyn, Bernard, *Voyagers to the West: Emigration from Britain to America on the Eve of the Revolution* (London: I. B. Tauris, 1987).

Baird, John, *Horn of Plenty: The Story of the Presbyterian Ministers' Fund* (Wheaton, Illinois: Tyndale House, 1982).

Bankhurst, Benjamin, 'A Looking-Glass for Presbyterians: Recasting a Prejudice in Late Colonial Pennsylvania', *PMHB* 133.4 (October 2009), pp. 317–48.

Barker, Francis, Peter Hulme and Margaret Iversen (eds), *Cannibalism and the Colonial World* (Cambridge: Cambridge University Press, 1998).

Barnard, Toby C., '1641: A Bibliographic Essay', in Brian Mac Cuarta (ed.), *Ulster 1641: Aspects of the Rising* (Belfast: The Institute of Irish Studies, The Queen's University of Belfast, 1993), pp. 173–86.

Barnard, Toby C., 'Protestantism, Ethnicity and Irish Identities, 1660–1760', in Claydon and McBride (eds), *Protestantism and National Identity*, pp. 206–35.

Barnard, Toby C., 'The Uses of 23 October 1641 and Irish Protestant Celebrations', *English Historical Review* 106.421 (October 1991), pp. 889–920.

Bartlett, Thomas, 'Army and Society in Eighteenth-Century Ireland', in W. A. Maguire (ed.), *Kings in Conflict: The Revolutionary War in Ireland and Its Aftermath, 1689–1750* (Belfast: Ulster Museum, 1990), pp. 173–82.

Bartlett, Thomas, '"What Ish My Nation?": Themes in Irish History: 1550–1850', in Thomas Bartlett, Chris Curtain, Riana O'Dwyer and Gearoid O'Tuathaigh (eds), *Irish Studies: A General Introduction* (Dublin: Gil and Macmillan, 1988), pp. 44–59.

Bartlett, Thomas, David Dickson, Dáire Keogh and Kevin Whelan (eds), *1798: A Bicentenary Perspective* (Dublin: Four Courts Press, 2003).

Beeman, Richard, *The Varieties of Political Experience in Eighteenth-Century America* (Philadelphia: University of Pennsylvania Press, 2004).

Bell, David, *The Cult of the Nation in France: Inventing Nationalism* (Cambridge, MA: Harvard University Press, 2001).

Berens, John F., '"Good News from a Far Country": A Note on Divine Providence and the Stamp Act Crisis', *Church History* 45.3 (September 1976), pp. 308–15.

Berens, John F., *Providence & Patriotism in Early America, 1640–1815* (Charlottesville: University Press of Virginia, 1978).

Bickham, Troy O., *Making News: The American Revolution as Seen through the British Press* (Dekalb: Northern Illinois University Press, 2009).

Bickham, Troy O., *Savages within the Empire: Representations of American Indians in Eighteenth-Century Britain* (Oxford: Oxford University Press, 2005).

Billig, Michael, *Banal Nationalism* (London: Sage Publications, 1995).

Blethen, Tyler H., and Curtis W. Wood Jr., *From Ulster to Carolina: The Migration of the Scotch-Irish to Southwestern North Carolina* (Raleigh: North Carolina Department of Cultural Resources and Office of Archives and History, 1998).

Blethen, Tyler H., and Curtis W. Wood Jr. (eds), *Ulster and North America: Transatlantic Perspectives on the Scotch-Irish* (Tuscaloosa: The University of Alabama Press, 1997).

Bonar, Robert H., *Nigh on Three and a Half Centuries: A History of Carnmoney Presbyterian Church* (Belfast: 2004).

Brady, John, *Catholics and Catholicism in the Eighteenth-Century Press* (Maynooth: Catholic Record Society of Ireland, 1965).

Braun, Theodore E. D., 'Voltaire and Le Franc de Pompignan: Poetic Reactions to the Lisbon Earthquake', in Braun and Radner (eds), *Lisbon Earthquake*, pp. 145–55.

Braun, Theodore E. D., and John B. Radner (eds), *The Lisbon Earthquake of 1755: Representations and Reactions* (Oxford: Voltaire Foundation, 2005).

Breen, T. H., *The Marketplace of Revolution: How Consumer Politics Shaped American Independence* (Oxford: Oxford University Press, 2004).

Bric, Maurice J., 'The Tithe System in Eighteenth-Century Ireland', *Proceedings of the Royal Irish Academy* 86, C, No. 7 (1986), 271–88.

Briggs, Charles Augustus, *American Presbyterianism, its Origin and Early History, together with an appendix of letters and documents, many of which have recently been discovered* (New York: Charles Scribner's Sons, 1885).

Bronson, Walter C., *The History of Brown University, 1764–1914* (Providence, Rhode Island: Brown University Press, 1914).

Brückner, Martin, *The Geographic Revolution in Early America: Maps, Literacy, and National Identity* (Chapel Hill, NC: University of North Carolina Press, 2006).

Brumwell, Stephen, *Redcoats: The British Soldier and War in the Americas, 1755–1763* (Cambridge: Cambridge University Press, 2002).

Butzin, Peter A., 'Politics, Presbyterians, and the Paxton Riots, 1763–64', *Journal of Presbyterian History* 51 (1973), pp. 70–84.

Calhoun, Craig (ed.), *Habermas and the Public Sphere* (Cambridge: Cambridge University Press, 1992).

Calhoon, Robert M., 'Dobbs, Arthur (1689–1765)', *Oxford Dictionary of National Biography* (Oxford: Oxford University Press, 2004).

Camenzind, Krista, 'Violence, Race, and the Paxton Boys', in Pencak and Richter (eds), *Friends and Enemies in Penn's Woods*, pp. 201–20.

Campbell, A. Albert, *Belfast Newspapers, Past and Present* (Belfast: W. & G. Baird, 1921).

Campbell, Rev. Robert, *A History of the Scotch Presbyterian Church St. Gabriel Street, Montreal* (Montreal: W. Drysdale, 1887).

Canny, Nicholas, 'The Permissive Frontier: The Problem of Social Control in English Settlements in Ireland and Virginia, 1550–1650', in K. R. Andrews, N. P. Canny and P. E. H. Hair (eds), *The Westward Enterprise: English Activities in Ireland, the Atlantic, and America 1480–1650* (Liverpool: University of Liverpool Press, 1978), pp. 17–44.

Carroll, Clare, 'Introduction: The Nation and Postcolonial Theory', in Carroll and King (eds), *Ireland and Postcolonial Theory*, pp. 1–15.

Carroll, Clare, and Patricia King (eds), *Ireland and Postcolonial Theory* (Notre Dame: University of Notre Dame Press, 2003).

Chartier, Roger, 'General Introduction: Print Culture', in Alain Boureau, Roger Chartier, Marie-Elisabeth Ducreux, Christian Jouhaud, Paul Saenger and Catherine Velay-Vallantin (eds), *The Culture of Print: Power and the Uses of Print in Early Modern Europe*, trans. Lydia G. Cochrane (Cambridge: Polity, 1989), pp. 1–10.

Chase, Frederick, *A History of Dartmouth College and the Town of Hanover New Hampshire*, vol. 1 (Cambridge: Cambridge University Press, 1891).

Clark, J. C. D., *The Language of Liberty, 1660–1832: Political Discourse and Social Dynamics in the Anglo-American World* (Cambridge: Cambridge University Press, 1994).

Clark, Peter, *The English Alehouse: A Social History, 1200–1830* (London: Longman, 1983).

Clarke, Desmond, *Arthur Dobbs, Esquire, 1689–1765: Surveyor-General of Ireland, Prospector and Governor of North Carolina* (London: Bodley Head, 1957).

Claydon, Tony, *Europe and the Making of England, 1660–1760* (Cambridge: Cambridge University Press, 2007).

Claydon, Tony, and Ian Mcbride (eds), *Protestantism and National Identity: Britain and Ireland, c.1650–c.1850* (Cambridge: Cambridge University Press, 1998).

Claydon, Tony, and Ian McBride, 'The Trials of the Chosen Peoples: Recent Interpretations of Protestantism and National Identity in Britain and Ireland', in Claydon and McBride (eds), *Protestantism and National Identity*, pp. 1–29.

Cleary, Joe, '"Misplaced Ideas" Colonialism, Location, and Dislocation in Irish Studies', in Carroll and King (eds), *Ireland and Postcolonial Theory*, pp. 16–45.

Colley, Linda, *Captives: Britain, Empire and the World, 1600–1850* (London: Jonathan Cape, 2002).

Connolly, S. J., *Divided Kingdom: Ireland 1630–1800* (Oxford: Oxford University Press, 2008).

Connolly, S. J., *Religion, Law, and Power: The Making of Protestant Ireland* (Oxford: Clarendon Press, 1992).

Connolly, S. J., 'Violence and Order in the Eighteenth-Century', in Patrick O'Flanagan, Paul Ferguson and Kevin Whelan (eds), *Rural Ireland 1600–1900: Modernisation and Change* (Cork: Cork University Press, 1987), pp. 42–61.

Conway, Stephen, *The British Isles and the War of American Independence* (Oxford: Oxford University Press, 2000).

Conway, Stephen, *War, State, and Society in Mid-Eighteenth-Century Britain and Ireland* (Oxford: Oxford University Press, 2006).

Coulter, Milton J., *Gilbert Tennent, Son of Thunder: A Case Study of Continental Pietism's Impact on the First Great Awakening in the Middle Colonies* (New York: Greenwood Press, 1986).

Cowan, Brian, *The Social Life of Coffee: The Emergence of the British Coffeehouse* (New Haven: Yale University Press, 2005).

Crawford, W. H., *The Handloom Weavers and the Ulster Linen Industry*, 2nd edn (Belfast: Ulster Historical Foundation, 1994).

Crawford, W. H., *The Impact of the Domestic Linen Industry in Ulster* (Belfast: Ulster Historical Foundation, 2005).

Crawford, W. H., 'Landlord–Tenant Relations in Ulster, 1609–1820', *Irish Economic and Social History* 2 (1975), pp. 5–21.

Cressy, David, *Bonfires and Bells: National Memory and the Protestant Calendar in Elizabethan and Stuart England* (London, Weidenfeld and Nicolson, 1989).

Cross, Arthur Lyon, *The Anglican Episcopate and the American Colonies* (New York: Longmans, Green & Co., 1902).

Croxson, Bronwyn, 'The Public and Private Faces of Eighteenth-Century London Dispensary Charity', *Medical History* 41.2 (April 1997), pp. 127–49.

Cullen, L. M., 'Economic Development, 1691–1750', in Moody and Vaughan (eds), *New History of Ireland, Vol. IV*, pp. 123–58.

Cullen, L. M., *An Economic History of Ireland since 1660*, 2nd edn (London: Batsford, 1987).

Cullen, L. M. (ed.), *The Formation of the Irish Economy* (Cork: Mercier Press, 1969).

Cullen, L. M., 'The Irish Diaspora of the Seventeenth and Eighteenth Centuries', in Nicholas Canny (ed.), *Europeans on the Move: Studies on European Migration, 1500–1800* (Oxford: Oxford University Press, 1994), pp. 113–49.

Cullen, L. M., 'The Irish Economy in the Eighteenth Century', in Cullen (ed.), *Formation of the Irish Economy*, pp. 9–21.

Cummings, Hubertis M., 'The Paxton Killings', *Journal of Presbyterian History* 44.4 (1966), pp. 219–43.

Curtin, Nancy J., *The United Irishmen: Popular Politics in Ulster and Dublin, 1791–1798* (Oxford: Oxford University Press, 1994),

Darnton, Robert, *The Great Cat Massacre and Other Episodes in French Cultural History* (London: Allen Lane, 1984).

Dean, Carolyn J., *The Fragility of Empathy after the Holocaust* (Ithaca, NY: Cornell University Press, 2004).

Denham, Terence, '"Hibernia officinal militum"': Irish Recruitment to the British Regular Army, 1660–1815', *Irish Sword: The Journal of the Military History Society of Ireland* 20.80 (Winter 1996), pp. 148–66.

Devine, T. M., *Scotland's Empire, 1600–1815* (London: Allen Lane, 2003).

Dickson, David, *Arctic Ireland: The Extraordinary Story of the Great Frost and Forgotten Famine of 1740–41* (Belfast: White Row Press, 1997).

Dickson, David, *New Foundations: Ireland 1660–1800*, 2nd edn (Dublin: Irish Academic Press, 2000).

Dickson, David, *Old World Colony: Cork and South Munster, 1630–1830* (Cork: Cork University Press, 2005).

Dickson, R. J., *Ulster Emigration to Colonial America, 1718–1775* (London: Routledge & Kegan Paul, 1966).

Donnelly, James S., 'The Whiteboy Movement, 1761–5', *Irish Historical Studies* 21.81 (March 1978), pp. 20–54.

Dow, J. B. 'Early Actuarial Work in Eighteenth-Century Scotland', *Transactions of the Faculty of Actuaries* 33 (1971–3), pp. 193–229

Doyle, David Noel, *Ireland, Irishmen, and Revolutionary America, 1760–1820* (Dublin: Mercier Press, 1981).

Doyle, David Noel, 'Scots Irish or Scotch-Irish', in Lee and Casey (eds), *Making the Irish American*, pp. 151–70.

Dunaway, Wayland F., *The Scotch-Irish of Colonial Pennsylvania* (London: Archon Books, 1944).

Feather, John, 'The Power of Print: Word and Image in Eighteenth-Century England', in Jeremy Black (ed.), *Culture and Society in Britain, 1660–1800* (Manchester: Manchester University Press, 1997), pp. 51–68.

Fishburn, Janet F., 'Gilbert Tennent, Established "Dissenter"', *Church History* 63.1 (March 1994), pp. 31–49.

Fitzgerald, Patrick, '"Black '97": Reconsidering Scottish Migration to Ireland in the Seventeenth Century and the Scotch Irish in America', in William Kelly and John Young (eds), *Ulster and Scotland, 1600–2000: History, Language and Identity* (Dublin: Four Courts Press, 2004), pp. 71–84.

Flavell, Julie, *When London was Capital of America* (New Haven and London: Yale University Press, 2010).

Foster, Roy, *Modern Ireland, 1600–1972* (London: Allen Lane, 1988).

Franz, George W., *Paxton: A Study of Community Structure and Mobility in the Colonial Pennsylvania Backcountry* (New York: Garland, 1989).

Garnham, Neal, 'How Violent Was Eighteenth-Century Ireland?' *Irish Historical Studies* 30 (1996–7), pp. 377–92.

Garnham, Neal, 'Ireland's Protestant Militia 1715–76: A Military Assessment', *Irish Sword: The Journal of the Military History Society of Ireland* 20.80 (Winter 1996), pp. 131–6.

Gibbons, Luke, '"The Return of the Native": The United Irishmen, Culture and Colonialism', in Bartlett, Dickson, Keogh and Whelan (eds), *1798*, pp. 52–74.

Gilborn, Craig, 'The Reverend Samuel Davies in Great Britain', *Winterthur Portfolio* 8 (1973), pp. 45–62.

Gill, Conrad, *The Rise of the Irish Linen Industry* (Oxford: Oxford University Press, 1925).

Gillespie, Raymond, *Early Belfast: The Origins and Growth of an Ulster Town to 1750* (Belfast: Ulster Historical Foundation, 2007).

Gillespie, Raymond, *Reading Ireland: Print, Reading and Social Change in Early Modern Ireland* (Manchester: Manchester University Press, 2005).

Gould, Eliga H., *The Persistence of Empire: British Political Culture in the Age of the American Revolution* (Chapel Hill: University of North Carolina Press, 2000).

Green, E. R. R. (ed.), *Essays in Scotch-Irish History* (London: Routledge & Kegan Paul, 1969).

Green, E. R. R., 'Ulster Emigrants' Letters', in E. R. R. Green (ed.), *Essays in Scotch-Irish History* (London: Routledge & Kegan Paul, 1969), pp. 87–103.

Greene, John, and Elizabeth McCrum, '"Small Clothers": The Evolution of Men's Nether Garments as Evidenced in *The Belfast Newsletter* Index 1737–1800', *Eighteenth-Century Ireland: Iris an dá chultúr* 5 (1990), pp. 153–71.

Griffin, Patrick, *The People with No Name: Ireland's Ulster Scots, America's Scots Irish, and the Creation of a British Atlantic World, 1689–1764* (Princeton: Princeton University Press, 2001).

Guild, Reuben Aldridge, *Early History of Brown University, including the Life, Times, and Correspondence of President Manning. 1756–1791* (Providence: Snow & Farnham, 1896).

Guy, Alan J., 'The Irish Military Establishment, 1660–1776', in Thomas Bartlett and Keith Jeffery (eds), *A Military History of Ireland* (Cambridge: Cambridge University Press, 1996), pp. 211–30.

Halttunen, Karen, 'Humanitarianism and the Pornography of Pain in Anglo-American Culture', *American History Review* 100.2 (April 1995), pp. 303–34.

Harley, J. Brian, 'Deconstructing the Map', in Trevor Barnes and James Duncan (eds), *Writing Worlds: Discourse, Text and Metaphor in the Representation of Landscape* (London: Routledge, 1992), pp. 231–47.

Harley, J. Brian, 'Maps, Knowledge and Power', in Denis Cosgrove and Stephen Daniels (eds), *The Iconography of Landscape* (Cambridge: Cambridge University Press, 1988), pp. 277–312.

Harper, Steven C., 'Delaware and Pennsylvanians after the Walking Purchase', in Pencak and Richter (eds), *Friends and Enemies in Penn's Woods*, pp. 167–79.

Harris, Bob, *Politics and the Rise of the Press: Britain and France, 1620–1800* (London: Routledge, 1996).

Hatch, Nathan O., *The Democratization of American Christianity* (New Haven: Yale University Press, 1988).

Hayton, D. W., 'Review: *People with No Name: Ireland's Ulster Scots, America's Scots Irish, and the Creation of a British Atlantic World* by Patrick Griffin', *Eighteenth Century Ireland: Iris an dá chultúr* 19 (2004), pp. 232–5.

Henry, Brian, *Dublin Hanged: Crime, Law Enforcement and Punishment in Late Eighteenth-Century Dublin* (Dublin: Irish Academic Press, 1994).

Hick, Vivien, '"As nearly related as possible": Solidarity amongst the Irish Palatines', in Kevin Herlihy (ed.), *The Irish Dissenting Tradition, 1650–1750* (Dublin: Four Courts Press, 1995), pp. 11–125.

Higgins, Padhraig, *A Nation of Politicians: Gender, Patriotism, and Political Culture in Late Eighteenth-Century Ireland* (Madison: University of Wisconsin Press, 2010).

Hill, Jacqueline, 'National Festivals, the State and "Protestant Ascendancy" in Ireland, 1790–1829', *Irish Historical Studies* 24.93 (May 1984), pp. 30–51.

Hindle, Brooke, 'The March of the Paxton Boys', *WMQ*, 3rd series, 3.4 (October 1946), pp. 461–86.

Hixson, William F., *Triumph of the Bankers: Money and Banking in the Eighteenth and Nineteenth Centuries* (Westport, CT: Praeger, 1993).

Hofstra, Warren R., 'Introduction: From the North of Ireland to North America: The Scots-Irish and the Migration Experience', in Hofstra (ed.), *Ulster to America*, pp. xi–xxvii.

Hofstra, Warren R. (ed.), *Ulster to America: The Scots-Irish Migration Experience, 1680–1830* (Knoxville: University of Tennessee Press, 2012).

Holmes, Andrew R., *The Shaping of Ulster Presbyterian Belief and Practice 1770–1840* (Oxford: Oxford University Press, 2006).

Hulme, Peter, *Colonial Encounters: Europe and the Native Caribbean, 1492–1797* (London and New York: Routledge, 1986).

Hulme, Peter, 'Introduction: The Cannibal Scene', in Barker, Hulme and Iversen (eds), *Cannibalism and the Colonial World*, pp. 1–38.

Humphrey, David C., *From King's College to Columbia, 1746–1800* (New York: Columbia University Press, 1976).

Hylton, Raymond Pierre, 'The Less-favoured Refuge: Ireland's Nonconformist Huguenots at the Turn of the Eighteenth Century', in Kevin Herlihy (ed.), *The Religion of Irish Dissent, 1650–1800* (Dublin: Four Courts Press, 1996), pp. 83–99.

Ingram, Robert G., '"The Trembling Earth Is God's Herald": Earthquakes, Religion and Public Life in Britain during the 1750s', in Braun and Radner (eds), *Lisbon Earthquake*, pp. 97–115.

Jardine, Lisa, and Anthony Grafton, 'How Gabriel Harvey Read His Livy', *Past & Present* 129 (November 1990), pp. 30–78.

Jolly, David C., *Maps in British Periodicals: Part I, Major Monthlies before 1800* (Brookline, MA: David C. Jolly, 1990).

Jones, Colin, 'Some Recent Trends in the History of Charity', in Martin Daunton (ed.), *Charity, Self-interest and Welfare in the English Past* (London: University College London Press, 1996), pp. 51–63.

Kelly, James, *Gallows Speeches from Eighteenth-Century Ireland* (Dublin: Four Courts Press, 2001).

Kelly, James, '"The Glorious and Immortal Memory": Commemoration and Protestant Identity in Ireland, 1660–1800', *Proceedings of the Royal Irish Academy* 94 C.2 (1994), pp. 25–52.

Kelly, James, 'Harvests and Hardship: Famine and Scarcity in Ireland in the Late 1720s', *Studia Hibernica* 26 (1991–2), pp. 65–105.

Kelly, James, '"We were all to have been massacred": Irish Protestants and the Experience of Rebellion', in Bartlett, Dickson, Keogh and Whelan (eds), *1798*, pp. 313–16.

Kennedy, David, 'Thurot's Landing at Carrickfergus', *Irish Sword: The Journal of the Military History Society of Ireland* 6.24 (Summer 1964), pp. 149–53.

Kennedy, Máire, 'The Distribution of a Locally-Produced French Periodical in Provincial Ireland: The *Magazin à la mode*, 1777–1778', *Eighteenth-Century Ireland* 9 (1994), pp. 83–98.

Kennedy, Máire, 'Eighteenth-Century Newspaper Publishing in Munster and South Leinster', *Journal of the Cork Historical and Archaeological Society* 103 (1998), pp. 67–88.

Kenny, Kevin, *Peaceable Kingdom Lost: The Paxton Boys and the Destruction of William Penn's Holy Experiment* (Oxford: Oxford University Press, 2009).

Kirkham, G. E., '"To Pay the Rent and Lay up Riches": Economic Opportunity in Eighteenth-Century North-West Ulster', in Rosalind Mitchison and Peter Roebuck (eds), *Economy and Society in Scotland and Ireland, 1500–1939* (Edinburgh: John Donald Publishers, 1988), pp. 95–104.

Kirkham, Graeme, 'Economic Diversification in a Marginal Economy: A Case Study', in Roebuck (ed.), *Plantation to Partition*, pp. 64–81.

Kirkham, Graeme, 'Ulster Emigration to North America, 1680–1720', in Blethen and Wood, Jr. (eds), *Ulster and North America*, pp. 76–97.

Klein, Berhard, *Maps and the Writing of Space in Early Modern England and Ireland* (London: Palgrave, now Basingstoke: Palgrave Macmillan, 2000).

Koehn, Nancy F., *The Power of Commerce: Economy and Governance in the First British Empire* (Ithaca, NY: Cornell, University Press, 1994).

Kopperman, Paul E., *Braddock at the Monongahela* (Pittsburgh: University of Pittsburgh Press, 1977).

Kopperman, Paul E., 'The British High Command and Soldiers' Wives in America, 1755–1783', *Journal of the Society for Army Historical Research* 60.241 (Spring 1982), pp. 14–34.

Landsman, Ned C. (ed.), *Nation and Province in the First British Empire: Scotland and the Americas, 1600–1800* (Lewisburg, PA: Bucknell University Press, 2001).

Landsman, Ned C., 'Roots, Routes, and Rootedness: Diversity, Migration, and Toleration in Mid-Atlantic Pluralism', *Early American Studies* 2.2 (Fall 2004), pp. 267–309.

Landsman, Ned C., *Scotland and Its First American Colony, 1683–1765* (Princeton: Princeton University Press, 1985).

Lee, Grace Lawless, *The Huguenot Settlements in Ireland* (London: Longmans, 1936).

Lee, J. J., and Marion R. Casey (eds), *Making the Irish American: History and Heritage of the Irish in the United States* (New York: New York University Press, 2006).

Leersen, Joep Th., 'Anglo-Irish Patriotism and Its European Context: Notes towards a Reassessment', *Eighteenth-Century Ireland: Iris an dá chultúr* 3 (1988), pp. 7–24.

Legg, Marie-Louise, 'Money and Reputations: The Effects of the Banking Crises of 1755 and 1760', *Eighteenth-Century Ireland: Iris an dá chultúr* 11 (1996), pp. 74–87.

Lepore, Jill, *New York Burning: Liberty, Slavery, and Conspiracy in Eighteenth-Century Manhattan* (New York: Alfred A. Knopf, 2005).

Leyburn, James, *The Scotch-Irish: A Social History* (Chapel Hill: University of North Carolina Press, 1962).

Lockhart, Audrey, *Some Aspects of Emigration from Ireland to the North American Colonies between 1660 and 1775* (New York: Arno Press, 1976).

Loveland, Jeff, 'Guéneau de Montbeillard, the *Collection académique* and the Great Lisbon Earthquake', in Braun and Radner (eds), *Lisbon Earthquake*, pp. 191–207.

McAnear, Beverly, 'College Founding in the American Colonies, 1745–1775', *Mississippi Valley Historical Review* 42.1 (June 1955), pp. 24–44.

McAnear, Beverly, 'The Raising of Funds by the Colonial Colleges', *Mississippi Valley Historical Review* 38.4 (March 1952), pp. 591–612.

McBride, Ian, *Eighteenth-Century Ireland: The Isle of Slaves* (Dublin: Gil and Macmillan, 2009).

McBride, Ian, 'Introduction: Memory and National Identity in Modern Ireland', in McBride (ed.), *History and Memory in Modern Ireland* (Cambridge: Cambridge University Press, 2001), pp. 1–42.

McBride, Ian, 'Presbyterians in the Penal Era', *Bullán: A Journal of Irish Studies* 1.2 (Autumn 1994), pp. 73–86.

McBride, Ian, 'The School of Virtue: Francis Hutcheson, Irish Presbyterians and the Scottish Enlightenment', in D. G. Boyce, R. Eccleshall and V. Geoghegan (eds), *Political Thought in Ireland since the Seventeenth Century* (London: Routledge, 1993), pp. 73–99.

McBride, Ian, *Scripture Politics: Ulster Presbyterianism and Irish Radicalism in the Late Eighteenth Century* (Oxford: Oxford University Press, 1998).

McDowell, R. B., *Ireland in the Age of Imperialism and Revolution, 1760–1801* (Oxford: Oxford University Press, 1979).

Mackie, Alexander, *Facile Princeps: The Story of the Beginning of Life Insurance in America* (Lancaster, Pennsylvania: Lancaster Press, 1956).

MacSuibhne, Beandán, 'Politicization and Paramilitarism: North-West and South-West Ulster, *c.* 1772–98', in Bartlett, Dickson, Keogh and Whelan (eds), *1798*, pp. 243–78.

Magennis, Eoin, 'In Search of the "Moral Economy": Food Scarcity in 1756–57 and the Crowd', in Peter Jupp and Eoin Magennis (eds), *Crowds in Ireland, c.1720–1920* (Basingstoke: Macmillan, now Palgrave Macmillan, 2000), pp. 189–211.

Magennis, Eoin, 'Politics and Government in Ireland during the Seven Years War, 1756–63', PhD thesis (Queen's University Belfast, 1996).

Majewicz, Carey, *Collection 3101: Presbyterian Ministers' Fund Records*, Historical Society of Pennsylvania collection finding aid (2009),

Marshall, P. J., *The Making and Unmaking of Empires: Britain, India, and America c. 1750–1783* (Oxford: Oxford University Press, 2005).

Marshall, P. J., 'A Nation Defined by Empire, 1755–1776', in Alexander Grant and Keith J. Stringer (eds), *Uniting the Kingdom? The Making of British History* (London: Routledge, 1995), pp. 208–22.

Marshall, P. J., 'Who Cared about the Thirteen Colonies? Some Evidence from Philanthropy', *Journal of Imperial and Commonwealth History* 27.2 (May 1999), pp. 53–67.

Martin, James Kirby, 'The Return of the Paxton Boys and the Historical State of the Pennsylvania Frontier, 1764–1774', *Pennsylvania History* 38.2 (April 1971), pp. 117–33.

Medick, Hans, 'The Proto-Industrial Family Economy', in Peter Kriedte, Hans Medick and Jürgen Schlumbohm (eds), *Industrialization before Industrialization: Rural Industry in the Genesis of Capitalism*, trans. Beate Schempp (Cambridge: Cambridge University Press, 1981), pp. 38–93.

Merrell, James H., *Into the American Woods: Negotiators on the Pennsylvania Frontier* (New York: W. W. Norton, 1999).

Miller, David, W., 'Religious Commotions in the Scottish Diaspora: A Transatlantic Perspective on "Evangelicalism" in a Mainline Denomination', in Wilson and Spencer (eds), *Ulster Presbyterians in the Atlantic World*, pp. 22–38.

Miller, David W, 'Searching for a New World: The Background and Baggage of Scots-Irish Immigrants', in Hofstra (ed.), *Ulster to America*, pp. 1–24.

Miller, Kerby A., *Emigrants and Exiles: Ireland and the Irish Exodus to North America* (Oxford: Oxford University Press, 1985).

Miller, Kerby A., 'James MacSparran's *America Dissected* (1753): Eighteenth-Century Emigration and Constructions of "Irishness"', *History Ireland* 11.4 (Winter 2003), pp. 17–22.

Miller, Kerby A., 'Ulster Presbyterians and the "Two Traditions" in Ireland and America', in Lee and Casey (eds), *Making the Irish American*, pp. 258–70

Miller, Kerby A., and Líam Kennedy, 'Appendix 2: Irish Migration and Demography, 1659–1831', in Kerby A. Miller, Arnold Schrier, Bruce D. Boling and David N. Doyle (eds), *Irish Immigrants in the Land of Canaan: Letters and Memoirs from Colonial and Revolutionary America, 1675–1815* (Oxford: Oxford University Press, 2003), pp. 656–78.

Mitchison, Rosalind, and Peter Roebuck (eds), *Economy and Society in Scotland and Ireland, 1500–1939* (Edinburgh: John Donald Publishers, 1988).

Moody, T. W., and W. E. Vaughan (eds), *A New History of Ireland, Vol. IV, Eighteenth-Century Ireland, 1691–1800* (Oxford: Clarendon Press, 1986).

Morgan, Hiram, 'An Unwelcome Heritage: Ireland's Role in British Empire-Building', *History of European Ideas* 19.4–6 (July 1994), pp. 619–25.

Morley, Vincent, *Irish Opinion and the American Revolution, 1760–1783* (Cambridge: Cambridge University Press, 2002).

Muldoon, James, *Identity on the Medieval Irish Frontier: Degenerate Englishmen, Wild Irishmen, Middle Nations* (Gainsville: University of Florida Press, 2003).

Muldoon, James, 'The Indian as Irishman', *Essex Institute Historical Collections* 3 (1975), pp. 267–89.

Munter, Robert, 'A Hand-list of Irish Newspapers, 1685–1750', *Cambridge Bibliographical Monograph* 4 (London: Bowes & Bowes, 1960).

Munter, Robert, *The History of the Irish Newspaper, 1685–1760* (Cambridge: Cambridge University Press, 1967).

Murnane, James H., and Peadar Murnane, *At the Ford of the Birches: The History of Ballybay, It's People and Vicinity* (Monaghan: R & S Printers, 1999).

Murphy, Sean, 'The Dublin Anti-Union Riot of 3 December 1759', in Gerard O'Brien (ed.), *Parliament, Politics and People: Essays in Eighteenth-Century Irish History* (Dublin: Irish Academic Press, 1989), pp. 49–68.

Nash, R. C., 'Irish Atlantic Trade in the Seventeenth and Eighteenth Centuries', *WMQ*, 3rd series, 42.3 (July 1985), pp. 329–56.

Nash, Roderick Frazier, *Wilderness and the American Mind*, 4th edn. (New Haven: Yale University Press, 2001).

Neal, Larry, 'Interpreting Power and Profit in Economic History: A Case Study of the Seven Years' War', *Journal of Economic History* 37 (1977), pp. 20–35.

Newman, Gerald, *The Rise of English Nationalism: A Cultural History, 1740–1830*, 2nd edn (Basingstoke: MacMillan, now Palgrave Macmillan, 1997).

Nicholson, Eirwen, 'Eighteenth-Century Foxe: Evidence for the Impact of the *Acts and Monuments* in the "Long" Eighteenth Century', in David Loades (ed.), *John Foxe and the English Reformation* (Aldershot, UK: Scolar Press, 1997), pp. 143–57.

Nybakken, Elizabeth, 'New Light on the Old Side: Irish Influences on Colonial Presbyterianism', *Journal of American History* 68 (1982), pp. 813–32.

O'Brien, Michael Joseph, *A Hidden Phase of American History: Ireland's Part in America's Struggle for Liberty* (New York: Dodd, Mead & Co., 1919).

Ó Ciosáin, Niall, *Print and Popular Culture in Ireland, 1750–1850* (Basingstoke: Macmillan, now Palgrave Macmillan, 1997).

Oram, Hugh, *The Newspaper Book: A History of Newspapers in Ireland, 1649–1983* (Dublin: MO Press, 1983).

Parkhill, Trevor, 'Philadelphia Here I Come: A Study of the Letters of Ulster Immigrants in Pennsylvania, 1750–1875', in Blethen and Wood, Jr. (eds), *Ulster and North America*, pp. 118–33.

Pencak, William A., and Daniel K. Richter (eds), *Friends and Enemies in Penn's Woods: Indians, Colonists, and the Racial Construction of Pennsylvania* (University Park, PA: Pennsylvania State University Press, 2004).

Plummer, Wilbur C., 'Consumer Credit in Colonial Pennsylvania', *PMHB* 66.4 (October 1942), pp. 385–409.

Pocock, J. G. A., 'British History: A Plea for a New Subject', *Journal of Modern History* 47.4 (December 1975), pp. 601–21.

Powell, Martyn J., 'Political Toasting in Eighteenth-Century Ireland', *History: The Journal of the Historical Association* 91.304 (October 2006), pp. 508–29.

Powell, Martyn J., *The Politics of Consumption in Eighteenth-Century Ireland* (Basingstoke: Palgrave Macmillan, 2005).

Power, Thomas P., *Land, Politics and Society in Eighteenth-Century Tipperary* (Oxford: Oxford University Press, 1993).

Power, Thomas P., 'Publishing and Sectarian Tension in South Munster in the 1760s', *Eighteenth Century Ireland: Iris an dá chultúr* 19 (2004), pp. 75–110.

[Presbyterian Historical Society of Ireland], *A History of Congregations in the Presbyterian Church in Ireland, 1610–1982* (Belfast: Presbyterian Historical Society of Ireland, 1982).

Price, Jacob M., 'Who Cared about the Colonies: The Impact of the Thirteen Colonies on British Society and Politics, circa 1714–1775', in Bernard Bailyn and Philip D. Morgan (eds), *Strangers within the Realm: Cultural Margins of the First British Empire* (Chapel Hill: University of North Carolina Press, 1991), pp. 395–436.

Reid, James Seaton, *History of the Presbyterian Church in Ireland: Comprising the Civil History of the Province of Ulster, from the Accession of James the First*, vol. 3 (London: Whittaker, 1853).

Richardson, A. J. H., 'Busby, Thomas', in *The Dictionary of Canadian Biography* IV, pp. 115–16.

Richardson, Leon Burr, *History of Dartmouth College*, Vol. 1 (Hanover, New Hampshire: Dartmouth College Publications, 1932).

Richter, Daniel K., *Looking East from Indian Country: A Native History of Early America* (Cambridge, MA: Harvard University Press, 2001).

Rodgers, Nini, *Ireland, Slavery and Anti-Slavery: 1612–1865* (Basingstoke: Palgrave MacMillan, 2007).

Roebuck, Peter, 'The Lives Lease System and Emigration from Ulster: An Example from Montgomery County, Pennsylvania', *Directory of Irish Family Research* 18 (1995), pp. 75–7.

Roebuck, Peter (ed.), *Plantation to Partition: Essays in Ulster History in Honour of J. L. McCracken* (Belfast: Blackstaff, 1981).

Roebuck, Peter, 'Rent Movement, Proprietorial Incomes, and Agricultural Development, 1730–1830', in Roebuck (ed.), *Plantation to Partition*, pp. 82–101.

Ryan, Simon, 'Inscribing the Emptiness: Cartography, Exploration and the Construction of Australia', in Chris Tifflin and Alan Lawson (eds), *De-Scribing Empire: Post-colonialism and Textuality* (New York: Routledge, 1994), pp. 115–30.

Ryder, Michael, 'The Bank of Ireland, 1721: Land, Credit and Dependency', *Historical Journal* 25.3 (September 1982), pp. 557–82.

Schlesinger Jr., Arthur, *Violence: America in the Sixties* (New York: Signet Books, 1968).

Schweitzer, Mary M., *Custom and Contract: Household, Government, and the Economy in Colonial Pennsylvania* (New York: Columbia University Press, 1987).

Severns, Kenneth, 'Emigration and Provincialism: Samuel Cardy's Architectural Career in the Atlantic World', *Eighteenth-Century Ireland: Iris an dá chulúr* 5 (1990), pp. 21–36.

Sher, Richard B., 'Witherspoon's *Dominion of Providence* and the Scottish Jeremiad Tradition', in Richard B. Sher and Jeffrey R. Smitten (eds), *Scotland and America in the Age of the Enlightenment* (Edinburgh: Edinburgh University Press, 1990), pp. 46–64.

Sheridan, Geraldine, 'Irish Literary Review Magazines and Enlightenment France, 1730–1790', in Graham Gargett and Geraldine Sheridan (eds), *Ireland and the French Enlightenment, 1700–1800* (Basingstoke: Macmillan, now Palgrave Macmillan, 1999), pp. 21–46.

Sheridan, Geraldine, 'Irish Periodicals and the Dissemination of French Enlightenment Writings in the Eighteenth Century', in Bartlett, Dickson, Keogh and Whelan (eds), *1798*, pp. 28–51.

Shute, John Raymond, 'The Irish in North Carolina', *Journal of the Royal Society of Antiquaries of Ireland* 2, Series 7 (1932), pp. 116–19.

Silver, Peter, *Our Savage Neighbors: How Indian War Transformed Early America* (New York: W. W. Norton, 2008).

Simmons, Richard, A., 'Americana in British Books, 1621–1760', in Karen Ordahl Kupperman (ed.), *America in European Consciousness 1493–1750* (Chapel Hill: University of North Carolina Press, 1995), pp. 361–87.

Simms, J. G., 'The Irish on the Continent, 1691–1800', in Moody and Vaughan (eds), *New History of Ireland, Vol. IV*, pp. 629–53.

Smith, Woodruff D., 'From Coffeehouse to Parlour: The Consumption of Coffee, Tea and Sugar in North-Western Europe in the Seventeenth and Eighteenth Centuries', in Jordan Goodman, Paul E. Lovejoy and Andrew Sherratt (eds), *Consuming Habits: Drugs in History and Anthropology* (London: Routledge, 1995), pp. 148–64.

Smyth, William J., *Map-making, Landscapes and Memory: A Geography of Colonial and Early Modern Ireland c.1530–1750* (Notre Dame: Field Day, 2006).

Spencer, Mark G., '"Stupid Irish teagues" and the Encouragement of Enlightenment: Ulster Presbyterian Students of Moral Philosophy in Glasgow University, 1730–1795', in Wilson and Spencer (eds), *Ulster Presbyterians in the Atlantic World*, pp. 50–61.

Strain, R. W. M., *Belfast and Its Charitable Society: A Story of Urban Social Development* (Oxford: Oxford University Press, 1961).

Szasz, Margaret Connell, *Scottish Highlanders and Native Americans: Indigenous Education in the Eighteenth-Century Atlantic World* (Norman: University of Oklahoma Press, 2007).

Tosh, R. S., 'An Examination of the Origin and Development of Irish Presbyterian Worship', PhD thesis (Queen's University Belfast, 1983).

Truxes, Thomas M., *Irish-American Trade, 1660–1783* (Cambridge: Cambridge University Press, 1988).

Tully, Alan, *Forming American Politics: Ideals, Interests, and Institutions in Colonial New York and Pennsylvania* (Baltimore: The Johns Hopkins University Press, 1994).

Updike, Wilkins, *History of the Episcopal Church in Narragansett, Rhode Island* (New York: Henry M. Onderdonk, 1847).

van Leeuwen, Marco H. D., 'Logic of Charity: Poor Relief in Preindustrial Europe', *Journal of Interdisciplinary History* 24.4 (Spring 1994), pp. 589–613.

Vaughan, Alden T., 'Frontier Banditti and the Indians: The Paxton Boy's Legacy, 1763–1775', *Pennsylvania History* 51.1 (1984), pp. 1–29.

Vries, Jan de, 'Between Purchasing Power and the World of Goods: Understanding the Household Economy in Early Modern Europe', in John Brewer and Roy Porter (eds), *Consumption and the World of Goods* (London: Routledge, 1993), pp. 85–132.

Waldstriecher, David, *In the Midst of Perpetual Fetes: The Making of American Nationalism* (Chapel Hill: University of North Carolina Press, 1997).

Walford, Cornelius, *Kings' Briefs; Their Purposes and History. Being a Paper read before the Royal Historical Society, and reprinted from its Transactions*, 10 (London, 1882).

Walsh, Patrick, 'The Differing Motivations for Preventing Transatlantic Emigration: A Case Study from West Ulster, 1718–1729', in Shane Alcobia-Murphy, Joanna Archibold, John Gibney and Carole Jones (eds), *Beyond the Anchoring Grounds: More Cross-currents in Irish and Scottish Studies* (Belfast: Cló Ollscoil na Banríona, 2005), pp. 324–30.

Webster, Richard, *A History of the Presbyterian Church in America, From its Origin to the Year 1760* (Philadelphia: Joseph M. Wilson, 1857).

Webster, Robert, 'The Lisbon Earthquake: John and Charles Wesley Reconsidered', in Braun and Radner (eds), *Lisbon Earthquake*, pp. 116–26.

Wilson, David A., and Mark G. Spencer (eds), *Ulster Presbyterians in the Atlantic World: Religion, Politics and Identity* (Dublin: Four Courts Press, 2006).

Wilson, Kathleen, *The Island Race: Englishness, Empire and Gender in the Eighteenth Century* (London: Routledge, 2003).

Wilson, Kathleen, *Sense of the People: Politics, Culture and Imperialism in England, 1715–1785* (Cambridge: Cambridge University Press, 1995).

Witherow, Thomas, *Historical and Literary Memorials of Presbyterianism in Ireland (1731–1800)* (London and Belfast: William Mullan and Sons, 1880).

Wokeck, Marianne S., 'Searching for Land: The Role of New Castle, Delaware, 1720s–1770s', in Hofstra (ed.), *Ulster to America*, pp. 51–76.

Wokeck, Marriane S., *Trade in Strangers: The Beginnings of Mass Migration to North America* (University Park, PA: Pennsylvania State University Press, 1999).

Wood, Gordon S., 'Conspiracy and the Paranoid Style: Causality and Deceit in the Eighteenth Century', *WMQ*, 3rd series, 39.3 (July 1982), pp. 401–41.

Woolverton, John Frederick, *Colonial Anglicanism in North America* (Detroit: Wayne State Press, 1984).

Index